Born of Need

"*Born of Need* represents the heart and soul of John Schuit's fruitful teaching ministry at Emmanuel Bible College, through which he has inspired countless students, myself included, to faithfully preach the gospel of Jesus Christ. Schuit's own Spirit-inspired conviction is contagious, and I am delighted to see this book in print, knowing that the impact he has had on so many in the classroom can now be extended across North America and beyond."

—**Josh Wilhelm**, pastor, Freshwater Community Church, Mindemoya, Ontario

"As one of the author's former students, I can confidently say that this is the fruition of his scholarly labors. He has drunk deep from the well of Scripture and has carefully listened to those who 'being dead yet they speaketh.' This study calls for our attention to likewise hear the voices from our rich Evangelical heritage and rediscover the vital necessity of Spirit-led conviction in life and ministry."

—**Andrew Cheeseman**, evangelical pastor, Breadalbane Baptist Church, Dalkeith, Ontario

"A right view of sin is essential for a right view of the Gospel. This book will help you understand both sin and Jesus Christ more deeply and inspire you to preach Him more faithfully to the world. Well-written, historical, and biblical, it is a much-needed call to contemporary Christianity and a must-read for every Christian."

—**Aaron Safley**, Redeemer Baptist Church, Gulfport, Mississippi

"I have always admired authors who can tackle difficult subjects with both truth and grace. *Born of Need* exemplifies such pastoral handling of a complex yet necessary topic for today's world. Readers will find their understanding of the gospel deepened, their faith strengthened, and their lives and relationships transformed. In essence, readers will discover hope and love in unexpected places."

—**David Robinson**, evangelical pastor

Born of Need

Restoring a Sense of Sin in Christian Conversion

JOHN SCHUIT

FOREWORD BY
Brendan DePhillippeaux

WIPF & STOCK · Eugene, Oregon

BORN OF NEED
Restoring a Sense of Sin in Christian Conversion

Copyright © 2024 John Schuit. All rights reserved. Except for brief quotations in critical publications or reviews, no part of this book may be reproduced in any manner without prior written permission from the publisher. Write: Permissions, Wipf and Stock Publishers, 199 W. 8th Ave., Suite 3, Eugene, OR 97401.

Wipf & Stock
An Imprint of Wipf and Stock Publishers
199 W. 8th Ave., Suite 3
Eugene, OR 97401

www.wipfandstock.com

PAPERBACK ISBN: 979-8-3852-2874-4
HARDCOVER ISBN: 979-8-3852-2875-1
EBOOK ISBN: 979-8-3852-2876-8

VERSION NUMBER 10/15/24

To the memory of my dad
George Schuit (1927–2005)

If you think you're alright, you aren't alright
> Dr. Lois Fuller Dow (2023)

Your first task is to be dissatisfied with yourself
> St. Augustine (354–430)

Contents

Foreword by Brendan DePhillippeaux | ix
Preface | xiii
Acknowledgements | xvii
Introduction | xix

1. Stony Hearts: The Rebellion of Humanity | 1
2. The Nature and Necessity of Conviction of Sin | 15
3. A Preacher's Heart: Jonathan Edwards's Self Awareness | 31
4. Darkening Skies | 43
5. Hearts Stricken and Hearts Ablaze | 62
6. A Cloud of Witnesses: The Great Itinerants | 91
7. Calling for Conviction | 112
8. Preaching Today, Part A | 126
9. Preaching Today, Part B | 137

Conclusion | 157
Bibliography | 161
Subject Index | 171
Name Index | 175
Scripture Index | 181

Foreword

During my doctoral studies, I regularly found myself lost in other worlds. That is, I often had the experience of suddenly becoming aware—as though waking up from some sort of mystical trance in the middle of a bustling café—that while my nose was buried in a volume or two on a single subject, all the available daylight had disappeared. The PhD is meant to push the rational mind to its limit; this is widely understood. But such experiences have helped me see that rigorous reflection is more deeply driven by a cultivated imagination, whether theological, historical, scientific, etc. It's only by envisioning another world that we can truly take hold of its riches.

From the very first undergraduate class I took from Professor Schuit over a decade ago, it was abundantly clear to me (and anyone else who took classes from him) that this was a man whose soul imaginatively *lives* in the theological and historical worlds about which he taught. Even to the young, developing mind of an undergraduate, it was also evident to me in those days that the Protestant Reformation, and more specifically the Great Awakening in Britain and America, was one of Schuit's most lived-in worlds. This volume is the fruit of his many pilgrimages to this historical and theological landscape and a testament to how deeply he has drunk of its richness.

In the pages that follow, the author offers us a penetrating diagnosis of the state of modern evangelicalism by imaginatively drawing us back to its earliest roots. By setting the Great Awakening in the broader context of church history since the first century, he challenges evangelicals to remember and embrace the deep significance and importance of their own tradition—and this at a time when historical self-critique to the point of self-loathing is considered trendy. Having laid this foundation, Schuit then delves deep into the details of this period's most prominent preachers in order to drive home an even deeper challenge, one which forms the primary substance of this book: the preaching that animated this young movement and yielded thousands of conversions was *necessarily* aimed at fostering the *conviction of sin* in individual hearts.

Let the reader be warned; intuitive and simple as this proposal may seem on the surface, the abundant quotations and biographical details provided in this volume—interwoven with Schuit's skillful prose—may begin to paint in the mind of each reader a consistent and vibrant picture of a world that seems dreadfully unfamiliar to those brought up in the morally thin and therapeutic world of much contemporary evangelicalism, and yet nevertheless bears the same name! In other words, those who read this book out of detached interest in the *subject* of conviction may well find themselves inadvertently encountering it as an *experience*. In this Schuit accomplishes what all worthwhile projects of retrieval should aim for: a compelling portrayal of a bygone world aimed at reclaiming its lost riches for use in our own.

This volume is both timely and valuable for a number of reasons. Firstly, though it comes at a time when evangelicalism is under intense public scrutiny, the author's proposal is remarkably fair and constructive. In this he moves past a simple critique of modern evangelicalism toward a *renewal* of its core tenets. Critiques are common nowadays, but constructive proposals are rare, and even rarer are proposals with such specificity, lucidity, and practical applicability as the one Schuit offers in this volume. The stress on conviction or "law preaching" as a necessary stage prior to "gospel invitation" does not reject or reduce the evangelical emphasis on *feelings*, but rather elevates this category to a fuller vision by expanding it to include the "sense of sin" as a necessary precursor to genuine saving faith. In this, he calls not for the abandonment of evangelical theology, but a *retrieval* of its true essence.

Secondly, while generalizations about evangelicalism are all too easy to make at present, Schuit's diagnosis is penetrating and focused. From the analysis presented in this volume, it is not hard to see how the semi-Pelagian separation of "law preaching" from "gospel invitation" has led to the showy, results-based ministry models of the present day, making this book a valuable resource for pastors and lay leaders alike to gain perspective on their own tradition. It should also be noted that, while this is not a volume directed at academics, the footnotes and abundant citations of both primary and secondary sources reveal a substantial backbone of academic research lurking underneath its smooth and accessible writing style.

Finally, in the midst of a highly ideological and often pessimistic cultural moment, this book is refreshingly practical and hopeful. Schuit not only draws attention to the implicit theology of leaders in the Great Awakening, but also their *methods*. The final two chapters are devoted to applying this classic evangelical homiletic to contemporary preaching, featuring specific examples of biblical exposition aimed at producing convicting sermons. With such a practical prognosis—presented with seasoned pastoral nuance and sensitivity—this volume offers the hopeful prospect of *renewal* to a movement that so often struggles to disentangle itself from the unbiblical assumptions of the world it so deeply desires to reach with the life-giving Gospel of Jesus Christ. By reemphasizing the individual's dire need for salvation in contemporary preaching, evangelicalism has the prospect of purifying its witness and anticipating the kind of *cultural renewal* that, as Schuit demonstrates, so often accompanies the conviction of sin.

In short, the title says it all. Just as genuine faith is "born of need" through convicting preaching, I believe this volume is likewise "born of need" in another sense, that of filling an important gap in modern evangelical preaching with the aim of producing both ecclesial and cultural renewal in the power of the Spirit, who was sent to "convict the world concerning sin" (John 16:8 ESV).

Brendan DePhillippeaux
McMaster Divinity College.

Preface

CHRISTIAN CONVERSION IS AN important doctrine. It is vital that we get it right. Are we getting it right? Our theological vision in regard to the trajectory the church is taking on conversion needs to be anchored in the word of God, not on current societal norms. This book is an invitation to pay a visit to an aspect that lies at the foundation of Christian conversion.

During many years of involvement in Christian ministry, mostly as an instructor at the bible college level, I became increasingly alarmed that a critical piece is missing from how many view salvation. In some quarters there seems to be little awareness that it was sinners that Jesus came to save. This fact is being ignored from the front of the church. The loss of a felt sense of need for the blessing of forgiveness that Jesus offers can lead to pseudo conversions and spiritual malaise.

The observable tendency to soft pedal sin doctrine has prompted me to write this book. Conviction of sin and recognizing the need for the grace of God due to our brokenness are in danger of losing relevance on wide swaths of the evangelical front. This is not something new. It has happened before in history. Will we learn the lessons history offers?

A few anecdotes from my involvement in ministry will illustrate:

At the peak of enrollment numbers prior to the great Pandemic, the student body represented some twenty-five different Christian denominations. This diversity provided the institution and its faculty with a general picture of the evangelical community at large. At the beginning of each semester, we would introduce ourselves to each other in the classroom. One question each student addressed was what it really means for them to be a Christian. The answers varied widely: "Now that I go to church, I don't feel as lonely as before," or "Some of my friends were church-goers and I wanted to hang with them," or "It's just fun," and many more. Alarmingly the frequency of such responses increased over the years. Few students identified with any personal need for God or even a basic sense of sin. The whole idea of what it means to be forgiven seemed alien to many. Only a few gave testimony of saving grace and the healing by the power of the Gospel. On a positive note, our task as instructors was clear. We were grateful that the Spirit of God was at work and as students grew in knowledge and understanding changes did take place. But the point is that first year students, fresh out of high school, mostly from Christian families who attended church regularly, had little understanding of the basic truths of Christianity.

On a much different plain another example: even those more deeply rooted in the Christian faith, demonstrated a denial of the unpleasant realities of our innate natures once that reality came too close to home. Earlier in my career in education a young teen was engaged in some really awful activity, harmful and sinister enough that the parents were called in. The mother protested vehemently that such behavior was impossible for him to carry out. He was a good boy, moral and upright. She would not let go of that. I asked whether she believed that by nature we all have a tendency to bad conduct and are afflicted with the crippling contamination we call original sin. She was astonished that my question seemed to challenge her orthodoxy. She believed in the truths of the Bible! And then it dawned that I was referring to her son, the wrongdoer. She is not alone. Many believe the doctrines. Many are ok with the theory and defend it, as long as it remains theory.

These two anecdotes, one from a broad variety of backgrounds and the other from an established church tell much of the story. The former reveals ignorance of basic truth. The latter reveals a strong reticence when the doctrine of sin becomes personal.

Jesus did miracles. They are real and true. They reveal his love, his compassion for sufferers, and his authority over the consequences of the fall. But they reveal more. In a sense they are parables. Invariably, when Jesus healed, he informed the patients that their sins were forgiven: *their sins!* He said, "Those who are well have no need of a physician, but those who are sick."

It is the work of the Holy Spirit to convict us of our lost condition as a means to bring us to the Savior. Paul the Apostle said that the whole world stands guilty before God but that is not realized personally until the Holy Spirit reaches us with his convicting touch. People were not browbeaten for

Preface

being sinners, like the Pharisees were wont to do. Instead, Jesus was and is still attracted to them. And, once the need for healing and forgiveness is felt, the reverse happens. We are attracted to him. For those who need the new birth, conviction is a necessity. For believers, it is a blessing. A desire to see a change in the trajectory first mentioned encouraged me to write this book.

Acknowledgements

SEVERAL KIND FOLKS HAVE been meaningful to the completion of this book. Words don't approximate the gratitude I feel. This project has taken a few years to complete and I'm afraid of missing one or two. Still, a few do need special mention. Many thanks to David Doherty whose professional skill in editing and organizing the manuscript made my job so much easier. Others, like former students, Pastors Andrew Cheeseman, and Josh Wilhelm for their endorsements and; Stu Philips, Zack Thornton, Tony Her, and David Robinson, all in pastoral ministry for affirmation; Brendan DePhillippeaux for his willingness to write the Foreword. Thanks for the kindness of Brian Roe, David Yoon, and Charlie McCordick. Many thanks to a distant friend, Pastor Jon Hartman of Wisconsin, whose several telephone conversations were encouraging and kept me focused. I want to mention two pastors in Gulfport, MS where we spend time each winter, Aaron Safley and Chase Owen, whose conversations and interests were stimulating.

My kids and their spouses: Michelle and Don; Melissa and Yasin; and Mark were instrumental and by their presence gave purpose to the writing. This book is dedicated to the memory of my dad whose nurture and example in what the Puritans called "vital piety," is not forgotten.

And to Jennifer, my wife and dear companion, whose unfailing encouragement and prompting were indispensable. Often, Jennifer noticed idiosyncrasies of style or substance that challenged me to think twice before submitting the finished product.

It is a great honor for me to have friends and family whose care and interest are without limits.

May the Lord bless all of you and your ministries.

Gulfport, MS and Kitchener, ON, April 2024

Introduction

THE RATIONALE FOR WRITING this book is a desire for revival and growth in the appropriation of biblical truth throughout the broader evangelical church. Thankfully, evangelicals have witnessed a resurgence of interest in the salvific work of God in recent years. Since the latter part of the twentieth century, this resurgence has grown by God's grace to appreciable proportions. One of the generative means for this development has been the republication of the works of the Reformers, the Puritans, and their evangelical successors.

But there remains a remarkable number of churches scattered throughout the evangelical landscape that are still content to see membership of sufficient numbers to support operational budgets and to whom theological positioning and the quality of preaching is not of vital concern. The hollow blandness that attended the seeker-sensitive movement of the last few decades spoke for itself. Typically, for those churches, the thought was to avoid strong, penetrating statements from the front of the church, especially with regard to prevailing sin and conviction and other pertinent topics. But a quick look at history will confirm that even the early church, after the Edict of Milan (312 AD), drifted similarly, when the establishment of churches was allowed and attendance soared and church membership was without cost and added to one's prestige. The spiritual quality of churches dropped accordingly. What was needed was preaching that reminded people of a lost condition and the need for redemption. The Protestant Reformers effected that required change, and the evangelicals of the eighteenth and nineteenth centuries preached from the biblical text and brought the claims of God from Scripture to bear upon the needs of the hearers.

Introduction

It is my belief that the church needs to reclaim the sense of one's need of redemption as a key element in the conversion process. Both Scripture and the history of the church confirm conviction as the ordinary first step of coming to faith in the Savior. But there is a reluctance among some clergy to engage in preaching that is a bit pointed and that divides, successful examples of history notwithstanding. I and others have observed, over the last few decades, a lethargy with respect to the sharper, two-edged character of the Word of God. We have heard comments such as "It might engender hypocrisy" or "The average church-goer is a good person and is incapable of handling sermons that are too convicting" or "It would drive our young people out of the church" (as if that is not happening now, without such preaching) or "It is brutish to try to create a sense of need when the average attendee is content already." Instead, it is suggested, a preacher should encourage the happiness of people and help them feel good about themselves and about a good-doing God who loves them and is not looking for very much spiritual transformation.

These well-meaning pastors unwittingly and unintentionally keep their congregants away from the cross and from the biblical Christ, who "came to seek and to save the lost" (Luke 19:10). C. S. Lewis laid his finger on this malady decades ago:

> Now why do we men need so much alteration? The Christian answer—that we have used our free will to become very bad—is so well known that it hardly needs to be stated. But to bring this doctrine into real life in the minds of modern men, and even of modern Christians, is *very hard*. When the apostles preached, they could assume even in their Pagan hearers a real consciousness of deserving the Divine anger. The Pagan mysteries existed to allay this consciousness, and the Epicurean philosophy claimed to deliver men from the fear of eternal punishment. It was against this background that the Gospel appeared as good news. It brought news of possible healing to men who knew that they were mortally ill. But all this has changed. *Christianity now has to preach the diagnosis—in itself very bad news—before it can win a hearing for the cure.*[1]

Broadly speaking, we have exchanged the good news of the gospel for good advice for living in this world. Reducing the gospel of God's grace in salvation to good advice for daily life is consistent with the widest norms of

---

1. Lewis, *The Problem of Pain*, 43, emphasis added.

Introduction

materialist culture, where life coaching is in demand. Reductionist Christianity that tries to sell itself as the best of all therapies has simply lost credibility in a world of self-help, and self-improvement therapies. The Christ of the Scriptures is not needed there. We can better ourselves with a bit of counseling, nicotine patches, healthier eating habits, and so on, all without the gospel. But Christianity is not merely good advice. It is the good news of redemption in the cross and resurrection of Jesus Christ. And it is for all who feel their need of it.[2]

Knowledge of the bad news of our sin and our corruption leads to a felt need for the gospel. Take the example of Augustine of Hippo. As a young man he was promiscuous and a thief. When he was much older, he reflected on his stealing pears from an orchard. The young Augustine had taken great enjoyment in so doing, not because he loved pears but because he loved the act of stealing, the sin. He and his friends laughed as they stole them. He wrote, "What profit did I, a wretched one, receive. . . from that theft, which *I loved only for the theft's sake*?" Augustine took delight not in the pears but in the sin of theft; it just felt good! As part of his conversion, he was convicted of his delight in sin. This conviction turned into a godly sorrow, and in the end it led to happiness and joy: "'What shall I render unto the Lord' for the fact that while my memory recalls these things my soul no longer fears them? I will love thee, O Lord, and thank thee, and confess to thy name, because thou hast put away from me such wicked and evil deeds. . . To thy grace I attribute it and to thy mercy, that thou hast melted away my sin as if it were ice."[3] The goal of conviction is the blessedness of the forgiveness that can follow under the tutelage of the Spirit of God. It is important to remind ourselves that God is not in the business of making people miserable. They are already in a state of misery by nature, whether they realized it or not. He is in the business of making us happy through the means of faith and repentance. Saving faith is born of need.

The Puritan Richard Baxter asked, "Can men take Christ for their Savior before they 'heartily perceive that they want [need or lack] a Savior'?" He also observed that "the heart that is truly broken will yield readily to Christ."[4] This is the psychological necessity that was carried forward in

---

2. See also Horton, *Christless Christianity: The Alternative Gospel of the American Church*, 101–57.

3. Augustine, *Confessions* 2.7.15, ed. and trans. Albert C. Outler, emphasis added.

4. Baxter, *Catholik Theologie 1675 II*, 221 cited in Beougher, *Richard Baxter and Conversion: A Study of the Puritan Concept of Becoming a Christian*, 86.

Introduction

preaching from the Puritan era into what is called the Evangelical Revival or Great Awakening of the eighteenth century.[5]

In many instances in history, the riper sort of preaching was the means for the awakening of sinners into a desire to be in God's favor. The Evangelical Revival was driven to a significant degree by preaching that fostered this spiritual conviction. That is why this little book will take the reader through short biographical studies of a few leaders of the revival, their religious experience, the subsequent content and style of their preaching, and the effect that such preaching had on the audiences. The lessons that can be learned, it will be argued, should be considered for the way preaching is done in our day.

The first chapter introduces the biblical underpinning. The Old Testament is replete with the idea that the loss of a sense of sin gave way to rank disobedience on the part of the children of Israel. In the New Testament, Jesus is seen contrasting starkly the self-righteous with self-aware sinners, befriending not the righteous but those who know sin and suffering. He ministers in a way that shocks the established religious leaders of his time. The chapters that follow will track the loss of a sense of sin in the English-speaking world of the eighteenth century prior to the great revivals. Next, selections from the history of the Evangelical Revival will be surveyed. Then the personal experience of conviction on the part of leaders such as Jonathan Edwards will be considered, and after some practical reflection on sin doctrine the book will finally close with suggestions for homiletical method and the content of sermons today.

There is no attempt here to write for the academy. This book is a straightforward attempt at helping the church at large, the intention being that whoever reads it might consider the lessons of our evangelical heritage.

There is one academic question that needs to be addressed, however. In recent decades a debate has emerged among historians and theologians about how to write history as a Christian. The issue came into sharp relief when Harry Stout's book on George Whitefield entered the market.[6] Admirers of George Whitefield were offended that the premise of the book suggested Whitefield's success as a leader in the Great Awakening depended on his theatrics, in essence denying the involvement of the Holy Spirit. Stout

---

5. The movement is generally referred to, in the UK, as the Great Evangelical Revival. In North America it is referred to as the Great Awakening.

6. Stout, *The Divine Dramatist: George Whitefield and the Rise of Modern Evangelicalism*. See the further discussion in chap. 6.

wrote in unsympathetic detachment from his subject. This choice represented a significant departure from the traditional approach to theological and historical writing taken by Christian writers. Baptist historian Robert W. Oliver represents the traditional evangelical standpoint when he writes, "Ultimately . . . the secular historian misses the one factor without which the Reformation [he would presumably include the Evangelical Revival in Britain too] cannot be understood, the activity of the Holy Spirit. Unless the Reformation is seen as a mighty intervention by God in the affairs of Europe it will never be understood."[7] Without the presence of this ingredient, historical writing on Christianity will be hedged in by secularist reasoning.

These two approaches can be labeled as the confessional approach, traditionally taken by evangelicals, and the secular approach, taken by Stout and by secular writers. In the world of academia, the confessional approach is seen as tending toward hagiography, the writing of history that is uncritical and too sympathetic with the subject. This is not considered objectively sound. Yet I have chosen to write from a confessional or providentialist perspective because as stated above, it is my hope that this work will help the church. I have little interest in seeing it sit on the shelf of an academic library, occasionally to be picked over by students who need to write a term paper. I expect that the overtly confessional approach here is moderate and not captive to the myth-making tendencies of some writers. I will take seriously observations and comments by historical figures contemporary with the era of the Great Awakening, and I will assume references to divine involvement and initiative are relevant and even necessary to an understanding of the revival period. In everything I will try to be self-critical and fair. It is my fervent hope that this balanced approach will produce something of use to the kingdom of our Lord. It is his church. It is his cause. With all its bruises and wrinkles, faults and blemishes, the church remains the main instrument in this world for eternal good.

> O Lord, I have heard thy speech,
> and was afraid:
> O Lord, revive thy work in the midst of the years,
> in the midst of the years make known;
> in wrath remember mercy (Hab 3:2 KJV)

---

7. Oliver, "Review of Euan Cameron *The European Reformation*" in *Banner of Truth Magazine* 474 (March 2003), 27, cited in Clary, *Reformed Evangelicalism*, 38.

1.

Stony Hearts

The Rebellion of Humanity

> Cain said to his brother Abel, "Let us go out to the field." And while they were in the field, Cain rose up against his brother Abel and killed him.
>
> Genesis 4:8

THE BIBLICAL STORY

To see the importance of a sense of one's need for salvation, we turn to the biblical text, beginning where everything went wrong. In Genesis our first parents enjoy an idyllic, comfortable life characterized by intimate relation with their Creator. They walk with him in the afternoon breezes in the midst of a wonderful environment the likes of which humanity has not seen since. But Adam and Eve are not immune to temptation. It is possible for them to sin. They betray God's trust in them, falling for the tempter's lies. God responds with righteous disapproval (Gen 3). The fall of humanity in the garden of Eden produces a profound curse on all creation. There is no exception. Paraphrasing James Carse, a crippling frost has fallen on the garden God created as a reflection of his glory and for his own pleasure and that of every person.[1] The intention was that humans would know God

---

1. Carse, *Jonathan Edwards and the Visibility of God,* 69.

and enjoy him forever and, conversely, that God would relish the relation with the amazing creatures he had made. Instead, Adam and Eve involved the entire human race in their guilt and passed on their corrupt natures. There is no human person who does not sin. Humankind is alienated from God and henceforth suffers loneliness and estrangement and forfeits the blessedness of life in harmony with God.

The only remedy is typified by the animal skins that help cover their nakedness, which suddenly become a problem. This remedy involves the substitutionary shedding of the blood of an innocent. It is accompanied by the great mother promise of Genesis 3:15,

> I will put enmity between you and the woman,
> and between your offspring and her offspring;
> he shall bruise your head,
> and you shall bruise his heel

In Genesis 4, Cain murders his brother Abel, and Lamech kills someone who has wounded him: two murders. It is significant that immediately after the account of the fall into sin, we read of extreme consequences. Humanity, in its natural state, will not hesitate to reveal the furthermost extent of its waywardness. Nothing but the restraining hand of God will deter fallen humanity from committing murder, genocide, infanticide, and all manner of lawlessness that directly impinges on the image of God in humanity. The human will is predisposed to divest itself of that image. The maleness and femaleness of that image is actively being challenged. The revolt does not need to be conscious to be wilful. It is simply the natural way. Human nature will resent a personal God who is in charge. There is, at bottom, ultimate disrespect for the claims of God as moral governor of the universe. Murder can be and sometimes is the eventual outcome, and throwing one's fist high-handedly in the face of God is the logical end of contempt. Therefore, it is the deep misery of humanity that it lives with a will that impedes the sweet contentment of a well-ordered relation with God and instead suffers maximum alienation.

Throughout the Old Testament it is substitutionary sacrifice that secures forgiveness for the wrongful acts that Adam and Eve's offspring participate in. The deadly virus of original sin affects them and all succeeding generations. At first, families engage in familial sacrifice ceremonies. When Israel, God's chosen, is established, it is through an intricate series of rites that the nation is relieved of God's displeasure on a yearly basis. The Israelite calendar is replete with holy days serving to uphold the system of sacrifice and forgiveness, in which the sacrificial blood of animals suffices to demonstrate God covenant faithfulness. His promises to send a Redeemer who will heal the nation is the goal of faith. Redemption from the fall is typified by the shedding of blood and accomplished through the second Adam, Jesus Christ (Rom 5:12–21; 1 Cor 15:21–22).

In the case of the Israelites, however, the path of promise proves not to be an easy road. God's people are stubborn and "stiff-necked"[2] (Ps 81:11; see Exod 32–33). Through the prophet Ezekiel, God promises to provide healing, replacing their hearts of stone with hearts of flesh (Ezek 36:26). Most, or at least a large portion of them, are unaware that they are laboring under the malady of having a stony heart. The sinful condition has an intrinsic quality that empowers it to hide itself, and unmitigated self-deception is the result (Isa 42:20). In Israel this insensitivity reigns. Consequently, Israel needs to be pulled up short and become aware of its failing. The nation needs to hear the diagnosis of their faithlessness and of God's righteous displeasure. The business of living daily without faith and trust in their God anesthetizes them into a dullness of heart. The Lord has warned them, "Do not harden your hearts, as at Meribah as on the day at Massah in the wilderness, when your fathers put me to the test. For forty years I loathed that generation. . . . They shall not enter my rest," and, "I have called and you refused to listen. . . . You have ignored my counsel. . . . You will call upon me, but I will not answer," and, "He who is often reproved, yet stiffens his neck, will suddenly be broken beyond healing" (Ps 95:8–11; Prov 1:24–30; 29:1). Circumstances need to become exhaustingly critical before a cry of need is heard in Israel. But even in the extreme, Israel is recalcitrant. Especially when the economy is rolling along smoothly, the nation has no felt needs, and the worship of their jealous covenant God suffers.

God has told the nation who he was with unmistakable clarity:

> I am the God of your father, the God of Abraham
> the God of Isaac, and the God of Jacob. (Exod 3:6)

> God said to Moses, "I am who I am." And he said, "Say this to the people of Israel: 'I am has sent me to you.'" (Exod 3:14)

> To whom then will you compare me that I should be like him?
> Says the Holy God. Lift up your eyes on high and see
> Who created all these stars?
> He calls them all by name. (Isa 40:25)

---

2. Unless otherwise noted, all Scripture quotations are from the ESV.

> The heavens are telling of the glory of God;
> And their expanse is declaring the work of God's hands.
> Day to day pours forth speech,
> And night to night reveals knowledge. (Ps 19:1–2)

> And I will make of you a great nation
> and I will bless you and make your name great,
> So that you will be a blessing
> I will bless those who bless you
> and him who dishonors you I will curse
> and in you all the families of the earth shall be blessed. (Gen 12:2–3)

Incredibly, in spite of God's clear self-disclosure, many Israelites find alternative gods to worship, especially the Baal gods. Often, with the royal family leading the way, the descent into pagan worship ended in disaster. In Jesus' time the account of the rich man and Lazarus (Luke 16:19–31) speaks to this. The rich man cries to Father Abraham that if someone could step out from the realm of torment, his five brothers would be all ears and repent. Abraham answers, "If they do not hear Moses and the Prophets, neither will they be convinced if someone should rise from the dead" (Luke 16:31). The children of Israel, formally God's chosen people, often live in a state of disobedience and care little. Whole generations come and go with little personal conviction, albeit countered by a few revivals of worship of the one true God.

Yet, there are people who are aware and are grieved. About one-third of the Psalms are lament psalms, wherein the poet, usually King David, is being smitten by his enemies or by his own spectacular gross sins or by the trials of his family or by the sinful propensity of his own heart. Often, his lament is in behalf of the nation, which is in deep trouble. These laments, written for the musicians in David's court, reflect what it is like to live without the experience of the presence of God.

Paradoxically, the lament psalms demonstrate something even more difficult to bear than a bad conscience. It is trying to deal with life as a believer when one's conscience is asleep. It is trying to deal with a stony heart, hardness of heart, deadness, dullness, or however one labels it. This is one of the chief encumbrances in a believer's experience, then and now. To have experienced repentance and faith in conversion and then to run into periods, long or brief, of cold lifelessness is a crushing affliction. So many of the psalms bewail this state of being. God is not near, and the comfort of his presence is missed. Loneliness and homesickness for communion set in: "O

Lord, do not forsake me; be not far from me, O my God. Come quickly to help me, O Lord my Savior" (Ps 38:21–22). It was the case in ancient times, and it is still the case. Believers recognize the hollowness and the longing.

On the one hand, it has been the burden of many prophets, pastors, and preachers to foster, through biblical teaching, an awareness of need. On the other, obedient servants of the Lord God have often labored through periods of spiritual drought when God has seemed to be absent. What is so necessary in the one case is paradoxically vexing to the other. For unbelievers and nominal Christians, a conviction of being lost creates a healthy unrest, a sense of need for reconciliation to their Creator God. But for believers, having tasted gospel grace, to experience the deadness and hardness of heart is distressing indeed.

Pigheadedness does not plague the entire population. Even during the life and times of Elijah, appallingly wayward as Israel is, there are still seven thousand who have not engaged in Baal worship. A remnant always prevails. For them life is hard. Living under conviction for the sin of the nation, trying to preserve loyalty to the claims of God in the midst of an unyielding society, places a heavy spiritual burden upon them. Moreover, conviction directed inward for personal culpability plagues every believer. The Psalmist confesses, "But I am like a deaf man; I do not hear, like a mute man who does not open his mouth. I have become like a man who does not hear, and in whose mouth are no rebukes. But for you, O Lord, do I wait; it is you, O Lord my God, who will answer. . . . I confess my iniquity; I am sorry for my sin" (Ps 38:13–18). The account of King David's conviction after the Uriah and Bathsheba incident, and his affecting confessions, are well known (2 Sam 9:12–13; Psalms 32, 51). And Daniel, convicted of the sins of his nation, prays in exile, "O Lord, the great and awesome God, who keeps covenant and steadfast love with those who love him and keep his commandments, we have sinned and done wrong and acted wickedly and rebelled, turning aside from your commandments and rules. We have not listened to your servants the prophets, who spoke in your name to our kings, our princes, and our fathers, and to all the people of the land" (Dan 9:5–6).

Still, the usual fare is blank unawareness. The Lord God exercises patience and forbearance for decades, but finally judgment comes. Cruel Assyrians overrun Jerusalem. The author of Lamentations expresses the horror experienced by the panicked population: "The Lord is in the right, for I have rebelled against his word. . . . Look, O Lord, for I am in distress; my stomach churns; my heart is wrung within me, because I have been very rebellious. In the street the sword bereaves; in the house it is like death" (Lam 1:8, 20). God had not been silent. He was transparent. Judah could have minded the persuasive claims of the Lord, but instead remained in dogged unbelief. Earlier admonitions apply to the whole nation: "Then I will walk contrary to you in fury, and I myself will discipline you sevenfold for your sins" (Lev 26:28).

It is the stony heart that the prophets have to contend with most of the time. Ezekiel is called to minister to the exiles: "The descendants also are impudent and stubborn. . . . Say to them, 'Thus says the Lord God.' And whether they hear or refuse to hear (for they are a rebellious house) they will know that a prophet has been among them" (Ezek 2:4–5). Isaiah leaves a frightful picture of the level of spirituality in his day:

> Ah, sinful nation,
> a people laden with iniquity,
> of children who deal corruptly!
> They have forsaken the Lord,
> they have despised the Holy One of Israel,
> they are utterly estranged. . . .
> The whole head is sick,
> and the whole heart faint.
> From the sole of the foot even to the head,
> there is no soundness in it. (Isa 1:4–6)

"And you, Capernaum," says Jesus later, "will you be exalted to heaven? You will be brought down to Hades. For if the mighty works done in you had been done in Sodom, it would have remained until this day" (Matt 11:23). Such was the level of the Jews' stubborn unbelief at that time.

The prophet Hosea outlines the method God uses to bring his people to heel. The book provides ample reason for God's anger with them, and the content within the book is placed in tension with his covenant loyalty. Israel has lapsed into worshiping other gods, celebrating the feast days of Baal, as the analogy Hosea and Gomer's failed marriage illustrates. But the Lord God will provide a way of transforming the nation. He will "allure her, and bring her into the wilderness." There, bereft of comfort, without resources, the Israelites will come to a sensible realization of what they have done and they will turn in remorse and repentance. Once that is achieved, God will, in mercy, "speak tenderly to her" and bring restoration (Hos 2:14).

That the gospel is for sinners is, of course, a truth well established and is easily demonstrated by multiple incidents in the ministry of Jesus. But it must be said at the outset that the good news is available to all who sense their need of it. No one is excluded, and the unfettered, unconditional offer of the gospel to all who call upon the name of the Lord is sincere. However, it is emphatically the case that in the ministry of our Lord, it is those who know pain—the marginalized, the sick and the ailing, the guilty, and others, all of whom represent the ragged edges of the fall into sin—who are included. The so-called righteous are not. In today's church this biblical principle is not given its proper place and does not function as it should. Jesus invariably declares that people who come to him in need of healing are not only relieved of their affliction but also have their sins forgiven.

In Jesus' time, divine reproach is aimed at the church leaders, usually the Pharisees. When Jesus begins his earthly ministry, the needy flock to him. They come from all over Judea for personal healing, or they bring dear ones who are unable to travel.[3] But they come by the hundreds to hear his authoritative preaching and to be healed. On a particular Sabbath, Jesus enters the synagogue and encounters a man with a withered hand. The Pharisees wait to see whether Jesus will desecrate the holy day by performing a miracle of healing. Jesus "looked around at them in anger and, deeply distressed at their stubborn hearts, said to the man, 'Stretch out your hand.' He stretched it out, and his hand was completely restored." (Mark 3:5)

Who are these sinners and sufferers who come to Jesus? Mark 5 presents a wonderfully tender example. The woman with twelve years of incurable hemorrhaging finally comes to Jesus for healing. She has been ostracized by the rules of a religious society, has been banned from the temple worship, and has stumbled through life with no resources. She has no recourse but to apply at the source of all mercy for relief and touches the edge of Jesus' coat in the hope that mere contact will be a blessing to her. Jesus is aware of her touch and, commending her faith, declares her whole. Here is an incident typifying the transactional character of the atonement. The great transfer took place. Jesus took her disease onto himself and gave her his righteousness.

In Luke's account, several groupings of people can be identified as those who willingly attend to the preaching of the Word and on the other hand, those who hear and are rankled by it. The one is comprised of the needy, the sinners, and the broken. The other is made up of the smug and

---

3. Mark 1:5 says, "And all the country of Judea and all Jerusalem were going out to him and were being baptized by him in the river Jordan, confessing their sins."

self-righteous, usually Pharisees or doctors of the law,[4] also known as scribes. Luke has made obvious the stark difference between the two, and he has seemingly pitted the one against the other deliberately. In most instances where Jesus is performing miraculous healing and declaring forgiveness of sins, the cocky religious leaders are present, proverbial clipboard and pencil in hand. The issue will slowly intensify and then come to a murderous head when the Pharisees appeal to Pontius Pilate to have Jesus crucified.

Earlier, folk came to hear John the Baptist and submitted to his baptism. Many people accepted the baptism of repentance, even the universally despised tax collectors. Luke, seemingly by design, does not mention the fact, as Matthew 3:7 does, that the Pharisees refused his ministry, thereby opposing the work of preparation for the Messiah's coming. But that tax collectors are mentioned is significant (Luke 3:12). They represent, in the vision of that society, the immoral worst, often grouped *with sinners*. Here the self-righteous leaders are not deserving of mention, while scoundrels coming to repent receive recognition. For Jesus' ministry, this incident is a foretoken of things to come.[5]

The same groups appear in Luke 5:17–26, where friends of a man with palsy[6] bring him to Jesus. The crowd is thick, so they climb onto the roof, remove a few tiles, and lower the man down in front of Jesus. The man's friends have exceptionally strong faith to go through the troubling difficulty of lowering him through the roof. Jesus sees their faith and has insight into the life of the paralytic. He declares his sins forgiven and says, "Pick up your bed and go home" (Luke 5:24). Immediately, the Pharisees and scribes who have gathered denounce him, not for the miracle of healing, which they avoided mentioning, but for forgiving the man's sin. To them it is an act of blasphemy.

On another occasion Jesus is teaching in the synagogue on the Sabbath. A man is present who has a withered hand. The Pharisees and the

---

4. The Pharisee party originated during the time of Ezra, after the Babylonian captivity, when the educated taught the law of God and guarded against foreign influence. Eventually these men formed a strong leadership class and led the nation's religious life. The group known as doctors of the law, or simply scribes, were researchers of the Mosaic law who interpreted Old Testament teaching as handed down to them by previous generations of priests and scribes. Most of these men belonged to the Pharisee party and wielded tremendous power among the Jews.

5. Neale, *None but the Sinners*, 100–194.

6. "Palsy" is a term for various types of paralysis or weakness, often with shaking or loss of sensation. It can have different causes, such as nerve damage, brain injury, stroke, infection, or genetic disorders. Most recent translations use the word "paralytic."

scribes are ready to pounce on Jesus again. The text says the "scribes and the Pharisees watched him, to see whether he would heal on the Sabbath, so that they might find a reason to accuse him" (Luke 6:7). Jesus, in his omniscience, knows their thoughts and turns them upside down. "But they were filled with fury and discussed with one another what they might do to Jesus" (Luke 6:11). In this case it is the Pharisees and scribes who are guilty. They are watching Jesus with murder in their hearts on the Sabbath.

The same groups reappear in Luke 7:29. "All the people, even the tax collectors, when they heard Jesus' words, acknowledged that God's way was right [or "just"] because they had been baptized by John. But the Pharisees, experts in the law, rejected God's purpose for themselves, because they had not been baptized by John." (NIV)[7] Again, note the contrast: tax collectors believe, but the religious leaders are aggrieved and offended at the call to repent. In Luke 7:36–50 we read the account of the sinful woman who anoints Jesus' feet in the house of Simon, a Pharisee who invited Jesus as a lunch guest. She is a known sinner, and the Pharisees think, "If this man were a prophet, he would have known who and what sort of woman this is who is touching him, for she is a sinner." (Luke 7:39) Little do they understand that it is exactly such that Jesus has come to save.

The parable of the prodigal son (Luke 15:11–32) provides the finest example of the two groupings. The element of a sense of sin, too, is made explicit. The prodigal son makes a misbegotten and disrespectful demand for his inheritance and leaves home loaded with money to experience the fleshly pleasures of the world. He burns through all of his resources and ends up alone and lonely, at which point he *comes to himself* (Luke 15:17). Coming to himself means repenting and receiving clarity about what he has done and what that says about his actual condition. Consequently, he determines to return to his father to confess his great sin.

The older brother, when he learns about the homecoming of his brother and is invited to join in happy celebration, refuses, even when pleaded with. The lost son is found. He has come to an end of riotous living and has been received by his father, who still loves him. The dead has been made alive. But the older, righteous brother reacts with indignation. The sinner has been saved, but the self-righteous man remains utterly senseless of his natural condition. Luke begins the chapter by highlighting the great dichotomy between the strutting Pharisees and needy sinners, thus setting the stage for

---

7. In this instance, the NIV is used because it captures the sense of the text: "*even* the tax collectors."

the contrast in the parable. The truth of the matter is that the gospel comes to all but is understood only by those for whom it is good news.

Another example, provided by Luke, is the parable of the two men who pray in the temple (Luke 18:9–14). Here, too, a sense of sin is made explicit. One, a Pharisee, religious ruler, exemplar of moral excellence in the church of that time, has no self-knowledge and is puffed up with pride about his perceived goodness. Clearly, he simply cannot help praying with long-faced earnestness, expressing gratitude that he is not like the other man. That other man, a tax collector, has a deep sense of his own depravity and prays, "God be merciful to me, a sinner"—literally "I am the one that is the sinner"—agreeing with the prayer of the deluded Pharisee. It is the tax collector, the one who sees his need of wholesale renewal, that Jesus declares justified. The Pharisee, by contrast, remains intractably blind and lost.

Also from the Lukan corpus, is the case of Paul the apostle, a man of great attainments, by his own account (Phil 3:5–6). However, Paul is living a lie, substituting goodness for evil and misconstruing evil as good, until he is arrested by the divine voice of the ascended Christ on the Damascus Road. Confronted with omnipotent power and penetrating omniscience, he is changed in an instant and pleads, "Who are you, Lord?" (Acts 9:5). Paul then discovers he is a sinner, a blasphemer and a persecutor of Christians. His new sense of heart prompts his oft-repeated confession "I am the chief of sinners."[8]

The Lukan theme of contrasting the puffed-up self-righteous with the needy in their respective encounters with Jesus has pastoral significance. Luke's insistence on highlighting this distinction between two types of people throughout Jesus' ministry is instructive for the church today. When preaching on the ministry of Christ, this should not be missed. Moreover, it could be considered as one of the many important ingredients of pastoral ministry. The contrasting reactions to Jesus' ministry are a reflection of the momentous statement in the Epistle to the Hebrews that "the word of God is living and active, sharper than any two-edged sword, piercing to the division of soul and of spirit, of joints and of marrow, and discerning the thoughts and intentions of the heart" (Luke 4:12; see also Rev 1:16; 2:12). Jesus' unfavorable response to self-righteousness in the Gospels and his tender empathy toward the sinners and the sufferers can serve paradigmatically for how these two groupings are seen from a pastoral point of view.

---

8. For example, 1 Tim 1:15 (KJV); or "sinners. . .of whom I am the foremost" (ESV).

Stony Hearts

What gives this Lukan theme divine affirmation is Jesus' eloquent testimony to his Father in Luke 10:21–24:[9] "In that same hour he rejoiced in the Holy Spirit and said, 'I thank you, Father, Lord of heaven and earth, that you have hidden these things from the wise and understanding and revealed them to little children; yes, Father, for such was your gracious will.'" The Gospels record three times when Jesus weeps; only once do they record him rejoicing. His joyous prayer is for God's revelation of salvation to the least in terms of earthly importance.[10] Who, then, were the "wise and understanding?" They were the Pharisees, the scribes and doctors of the law, and elders of the Jews, who were, in their own eyes, wise and understanding, superior in knowledge and learning, morally pure and not at all like the *hoi polloi*. Jesus rejoices in his Father's sovereign act in hiding salvation truth from some and revealing it to others. Who are the others, the "children?" These are the fishermen, the carpenters, the tax collectors, the poor and uneducated, and all who come with their conviction of need.[11] The contrast is one of attitude, not education. It is between the self-sufficient and those with an attitude of childlikeness.

The "wise and understanding" are the victims of sheer self-deception. Their greatest delusion is the idea that their superior knowledge gives them spiritual pre-eminence. The Pharisees have convinced the people at large of their superiority, causing some to dismiss Jesus as a result. They ask at one point, "Have any of the authorities or the Pharisees believed in him?" (John 7:48), inferring that if Jesus is authentic as he claims, the knowledgeable folk will endorse him and his ministry.

Jesus' rejoicing is wondrous in its beauty. He is virtually euphoric with joy over the sovereignty of his Father in his hiddenness on the one hand and his revelation on the other. He rejoices, too, in that he is the revealer not only of his Father's will but also, even more profoundly, his Father's character (Luke 10:22). Luke's use of ἠγαλλιασατο ("rejoiced") is a strong word

---

9. See also Matt 11:25–30.

10. It is important to include J. C. Ryle's reminder about this passage: "We must not infer that any persons on earth are naturally more deserving of God's grace and salvation than others.... Let us remember that God's offers of salvation are free, wide, broad, and unlimited." J. C. Ryle, *Luke*, 365–66.

11. Note the apostle's statement in 1 Cor 1:26–29: "For consider your calling, brothers: not many of you were wise according to worldly standards, not many were powerful, not many were of noble birth. But God chose what is foolish in the world to shame the wise; God chose what is weak in the world to shame the strong; God chose what is low and despised in the world, even things that are not, to bring to nothing things that are, so that no human being might boast in the presence of God."

with superlative overtones. It is the same word used by Mary the mother of Jesus when she rejoices over her pregnancy: "And my spirit *rejoices* in God my Savior" (Luke 1:47). Jesus is thrilled that the truth of his message goes not to the cocky and presumptuous but, rather, to "little children" (Luke 10:21), those like his disciples, who are humble and open to his teaching.

The Gospel writers, Luke especially, pit the self-righteous who lack nothing against the needy. It is the broken who receive the gospel. Others, even though the gospel is available to them, invariably are repelled by it. To them it is ridiculous foolishness. Confidence in their own righteousness is the overriding hindrance to an open heart. The religious folk in Jesus' time want affirmation of their moral excellence, their strictness in law keeping, and their status as paragons of social virtue. They are exasperated that Jesus is unable to discern their principled rectitude and disgusted that Jesus welcomes sinners and tax collectors.

This theme running through Luke's writings, the Gospel and the book of Acts, is consistent with the rest of Scripture. On the one hand, sinful and hurting people, despised by their peers, with no delusions about moral uprightness, come to knowledge of and faith in the Lord. On the other hand, self-righteous religious leaders, intransigent in conceit, fail to understand the awful reality and remain lost. This theme plays out in the history of the Christian church, especially in times of revival.

The kingdom of God that Jesus ushers into our world (Luke 4:18–19) is characterized by this reversal. This characteristic of Jesus' ministry is not what is expected. He turns to the marginalized of society: the poor, the lame, and those living in open sin. They are attracted to him. The amazing thing is that Jesus is attracted to them! In fact, Jesus is notorious for accepting the company of the unacceptable. He touches lepers and heals demoniacs, welcomes prostitutes and eats with tax collectors, approaches women with respect and treats the poor with dignity. This insults the religious leaders. An obvious question is, would this Jesus be accepted by every churchgoer today?

Jesus was open to outsiders. In our multicultural societies in the West, Jesus is the paragon of tolerance and inclusiveness: *Come to me, all who labor and are heavy laden!* So, the tables will be turned; those who are self-righteous now will be on the outside then. The first will be last, and last first (Mark 10:31; Luke 13:30).

That the record in the Synoptics shows Jesus preferring the company of sinners and sufferers is, from our perspective, remarkable. The self-righteous do not like him. They do their utmost to bring him down. But each time that it appears they have caught him in some inconsistency, he proves to have the upper hand. The Pharisees come to watch, and in watching they are hoping to catch him in some fault and plot to destroy him. They do not come for instruction or for healing or for the sake of the gospel. They see the huge crowds that cluster around Jesus to partake of his goodness and his grace, and they are appalled and confounded. Luke appears to set up this contrast deliberately and in so doing reveals an aspect of Christ's ministry that is truly breathtaking.

For the self-righteous it implies judgment. Their rejection of the Savior of sinners results in them being bypassed by the opportunity offered in the gospel. There is relevance here for today. Judgment is not everyone's favorite topic. It brings bad memories out of the closet. Kind-hearted and well-meaning pastors who eliminate the doctrine of God's judgment from their preaching are understandable, if dead wrong. Grace is easier to sell. Love is always welcome. We like to emphasize those Scriptures that speak of God's extraordinary forgiveness and mercy, his companionship in times of loneliness, his readiness to heal, his love for little children, his great heart that attracted the crowds. The parable of the prodigal son plays well. We hear sermons about Jesus' uncondemning attitude toward the woman caught committing adultery. But rare is the time we sit in church and hear sermons about the condemnation that Jesus pronounced on the self-righteous.

It is all very understandable but tragically dishonest. One needs to come face to face with the fact that a substantial portion of Jesus' teaching concerns his interaction with those who feel morally superior, of whom he is critical. One group of parables speaks of the eschatological division of the human race; we are sheep or goats (Matt 25:31–46), good fish or bad fish (Matt 13:47–52), wheat or weeds (Matt 13:24–30). Other parables speak of different outcomes based on different responses—for example, the Sower (Matt 13; Mark 4; Luke 8), the ten bridesmaids (Matt 25:1–13), and the talents (Matt 25:14–30). Add to the mix the many instances in which Jesus, in his daily walk, shows his propensity to be a friend of sinners and sufferers and his aversion to the arrogant and presumptuous, and the portrait begins to take shape.

Jesus speaks of condemnation and judgment. The big picture is fairly clear. He speaks of the destruction of Jerusalem. He talks of hellfire, of outer darkness, of gnashing of teeth. He relegates whole groups of people to categories such as "white-washed tombs" (Matt 23:27). He talks about the coming of the Son of Man and the reign of God, at which time a final judgment will take place. The Jesus of the Gospels is not so comfortable a figure as we might imagine or like him to be.

We turn next to the history of the church, from the post-Reformation period in the English-speaking world to the times of the Evangelical Revival and the Great Awakening. The leaders of Protestantism were keenly aware of the aforementioned aspect of conversion. Conviction of sin became a key element in preaching and in theological writing, regardless of geography or language.

2.

The Nature and Necessity of Conviction of Sin

> All the world is under sin, and knows it not.
>
> JOHN DONNE (1572–1631)

PURITANS AND THE 'CIVIL MAN'

EDMUND MORGAN, IN HIS book on Puritan domestic affairs, begins his first chapter with an intriguing paragraph.[1] "There was a type of man," he says, "whom the Puritans never tired of denouncing. He was a good citizen, a man who obeyed laws, carried out his social obligations, never injured others." This "civil" man, this model of social virtue, "was on his way to hell and preachers continually reminded him of it."[2]

However perfunctory that may appear to be, there is a profound aspect to it. Morgan highlights one of the salient elements of Puritan preaching. The Puritans were concerned to repeat to their congregations that true religion was not only being "civil" or moral. Good behavior in society did not

---

1. In a few areas I have adapted material from my unpublished thesis *Jonathan Edwards and Conviction of Sin*.
2. Morgan, *The Puritan Family*, 1, 2.

mean righteousness before God. Respectable conduct was not synonymous with religious piety. What this civil man lacked was the realization that in his heart he was full of "rottenness."[3] The influential Thomas Shepard (1605–1649) of New England asserted that "God looks to the heart" and sees there "heart whoredom, heart sodomy, heart blasphemy, heart drunkenness, . . . heart idolatry."[4]

Humans are not only sinners by their very nature, an inherited disorder; sin nature is also characterized by a fiendish propensity to hide itself. A person in an unregenerate state can, for all appearances, be known as a genuine Christian, a civil man. Innate sin includes an element of deceit whereby one could easily slide into a semi-comfortable condition, thinking all is well with the soul, on his or her way to heaven, when in fact the person is languishing in an unconverted state. The Puritan preacher therefore believed it his pastoral and homiletical duty to uncover to his people the subtle vagaries of their reprehensible disposition by nature, always contrasting it with the righteous perfection of the Lord. Human sin could not be dealt with unless a genuine rebirth took place, and this involved, in the first-place, self-awareness, conviction, and the humbling that would come as a result.

Hence, the Puritans were concerned to instill a sense of sin in others. Richard Sibbes (1577–1665) of Cambridge was of a spiritually sensitive mind and gracious temperament. In Sibbes's writings the work of the Holy Spirit in conviction was presented with a minimum of the rigidity found in the dogma that characterized some of his colleagues. Yet Sibbes was emphatic that it was through granting a sense of sin that the Spirit encouraged an eager reception of the biblical gospel. In his famous book *The Bruised Reed and Smoking Flax*, he represented a considerable portion of early Puritanism when he made clear that by bruising a person's heart before conversion, "the Spirit may make way for Himself into the heart by levelling all proud, high thoughts, and that we may understand ourselves to be what indeed we are by nature." Thereupon the heart would take on a posture of surrender to God and to the salvation that was wrought by grace through faith. Sibbes itemized several other advantages of a sense of sin. For one thing, the gospel was appreciated for the first time, and the discovery was made that the "fig-leaves of morality will do us no good." This bruising "maketh us set a high price upon Christ" as the only refuge from God's just

3. Morgan, *The Puritan Family*, 2.
4. Shepard, *Works*, 1:2, quoted in Morgan, *Puritan Family*, 2.

wrath. Moreover, it produced thankfulness, and thankfulness engendered fruits of grace. The lack of conviction of sin at the outset of conversion was, for Sibbes, often the reason for "relapses and apostasies" later on. Therefore, this part of the Spirit's work was "necessary before conversion."[5]

Not every Puritan preacher supposed a stage of conviction of sin to be chronologically prior to conversion, however. John Howe, a second generation Puritan (1630–1705), sometime chaplain to Oliver Cromwell and leader of the Dissenter movement after the so-called Glorious Revolution of 1688, acknowledged, "God's method may vary, or not in every respect be the same, with everyone he savingly works upon." Nevertheless, the absence of a sense of sin signified for Howe a heart unchanged. The process of reconciliation between God and humanity had to be seen as including "a thorough conviction, with deep and inward sense, wrought into your hearts, of your former enmity." This was, in fact, one of the great hindrances to conversion. By nature, said Howe, sinners "feel not an enmity boiling in their hearts against God, therefore they will not yield there is any such thing."[6] For Howe, then, chronology was not the issue as long as a sense of sin played a significant role in the conversion process.

Thomas Shepard (1605–1649) affirmed the great advantage of a thorough persuasion of depravity. Sinners would never "come to be affected or awakened . . . because men consider not of God's wrath daily, nor the horrible nature of sin." Conviction was a means to gaining the happiness that accompanies salvation. "Awaken therefore," he exclaimed, "all you secure creatures; feel your misery, that so you may get out of it." For then "the Lord may pity thee." Shepard believed conviction preceded regeneration. Saving faith grew only in the soil of felt transgression. Without it a sinner would go lost: "Thou must mourn here or in hell."[7]

Richard Baxter, the famous pastor of Kidderminster (1615–1691), believed that the first thing a sinner who was being saved received was a clear knowledge of the facts of their situation by nature. This knowledge usually led to humiliation, a surrendering posture that was open to the transforming work of the Holy Spirit. He taught that humiliation was preparatory to the great change of the new birth. It was an aid to the sinner, bringing them nearer to God, "though it be not a full closure with Him." This period of

---

5. Sibbes, *The Bruised Reed and Smoking Flax*, in *Works* 1:43–44.

6. Howe, "Of Reconciliation between God and Man," in *Works of English Puritans: Howe*, 244–45.

7. Shepard, "The Sincere Convert," in *Works*, 1:93

humiliation was characterized by a fear of being lost; a recognition of the heinousness of one's sin and the wrath of God; the foolishness of sinning against a good-doing, holy God; a deep sense of sin that was, at times, expressed in groaning and tears; and confessions of sin to the Lord. To Baxter what ensued was a heart prepared to be a temple of the Holy Spirit.[8]

The foregoing is representative of the Puritan theological landscape in England. It must also be said that for Puritan pastors, it was not mere theory. For many, it was first-person experience. A healthy personal spiritual sense characterized the Puritan pastor, and it was this acquaintance with the divine life that they wished to engender in their hearers.

Ironically, perhaps, and bewildering to an outside observer, believers sometimes faced periods during which there was a debilitating absence of conviction. Spiritual life ought to be known and felt as experience. Vital piety, or true Christianity, was synonymous with experimental divinity. If knowledge of saving grace remained purely head knowledge, it was questionable whether the great change had taken place. Paradoxically, however, the complaint of Puritan pastors often was the dullness, hardness, dryness, or coldness of the heart regarding anything spiritual. Hardness of heart in the Old Testament sense was a frightful thing to undergo, especially in view of the promise that God would remove His people's hearts of stone and give them hearts of flesh (Ezek 11:19, 36:21). The sense of being stony hearted, "blankly indifferent to God, was one which many . . . shared and which . . . they deplored in themselves."[9] Baxter recalled that he "wondered at the senseless hardness of my heart, that could think and talk of Sin and Hell, and Christ and Grace, of God and Heaven, with no more feeling: I cried out from day to day to God for Grace against this senseless Deadness."[10]

William Gouge (1575–1653), a member of the Westminster Assembly,[11] confessed that as surely as weight was drawn to the earth, so

8. Beougher, *Richard Baxter and Conversion*, 86.

9. Ryrie, *Being Protestant in Reformation Britain*, 20.

10. Baxter, "Reiquiae Baxterianae, Vol. 1, Introduction and Part 1:217.

11. The Westminster Assembly was a council of theologians and members of the English Parliament and several Scots appointed from 1643 to 1653 to restructure the Church of England. Many other ministers were called to participate. The Assembly produced a new *Form of Church Government*, two catechisms, the *Shorter* and the *Larger* and a liturgical manual, the *Directory for Public Worship*, for the Churches of England and Scotland. The Confession and catechisms were adopted as doctrinal standards in the Church of Scotland and other Presbyterian churches, where they remain in use. The *Confession* became influential throughout the English-speaking world and is considered by historians to be the most mature creedal document of Protestant Christianity.

the Christian's natural tendency was to ever greater coldness, formality, and faintness: "Wherefore as fire must constantly be put under water to keepe it hot . . . so must we by constant praier quicken yp our soules."[12]

William Perkins (1558–1602) had warned that the "best Christians were beset by their doubting and distrust, their dulnesse and deadnesse of heart."[13] Here, too, the foregoing fairly represents the experience of the Puritan. The stony, lifeless heart was a condition always near, and constant spiritual vigilance was needed to guard the heart against it. Fervent prayer and watchfulness, along with the renewed visitation of the Spirit of God, was the only remedy.

Puritanism had analyzed the condition of humanity before God as fallen, guilty, and corrupt, in fact in bondage to a state of sin, self-assessments to the contrary notwithstanding. The civil man needed new birth as much as one who sinned in the open. To meet that need and provide a remedy, the Puritans sought to bring into view the state of soul that underlay sins. They wanted to convict their listeners of their inability for self-improvement, to convince them to rely solely on the grace of God revealed at the cross of Christ. This, they believed, was part of the main role of the preacher. In order for saving faith to be true and sound, it had to spring from a conviction of need. J. I. Packer says, "Their constant aim was to make men feel that to be in a wrong relationship with God was intolerable here and now."[14]

During the reign of King Charles II of England, when thousands of evangelical preachers were relieved of their pastoral positions in the Church of England, there was a subsequent decline in church attendance and piety.[15]

THE EIGHTEENTH-CENTURY EVANGELICAL REVIVAL

The children of the Puritans, leaders of the Evangelical Revival in England and in the colonies, where it was called the Great Awakening, by and large remained loyal to the themes of their forebears. Samuel Davies

---

12. Gouge, "The Whole Armour of God, 1616", quoted in Ryrie, *Being Protestant*, 22.

13. Perkins, "A Godly and learned exposition of Christ's Sermon on the Mount," quoted in Ryrie, *Being Protestant*, 22.

14. Packer, "The Puritan View of Preaching the Gospel, iii: #2" Monergism, accessed March 11, 2023

15. See chap. 4 for more information on the loss of a sense of sin in Britain.

(1724–1761), a contemporary of Jonathan Edwards and a fellow leader in the Great Awakening, exemplifies the continuity. Challenging his congregation on one occasion regarding human ingratitude and indifference toward the crucified and risen Christ, he lamented,

> Try to persuade men to give over their sins, which grieve Him, dishonor Him, and were the cause of His death; try to engage them to devote themselves entirely to Him, and live to His glory, alas! You try in vain; their hearts still continue cold and hard as a stone; try to persuade them to murder or robbery and you are more likely to prevail.[16]

Jonathan Dickinson (1688–1747) of Elizabethtown, NJ, and leader of the Presbyterian Synod, wrote "if we consider the first Change wrought in a Sinner by the Spirit of God, it will appear to be no more than his bringing him to *realize his own miserable Condition, and see it as it is.*"[17]

To men such as Shepherd, Davies, Dickinson and a host of others, humanity by nature was corrupt and vile, regardless how proper and how virtuous a person might be in society. Salvation was not attainable through the exercise of respectable behavior. Of this truth a person must become aware.

Another evangelical, James Hervey (1714–1758), fellow member of the Holy Club with George Whitefield and John and Charles Wesley while at Oxford, believed that conviction was the "preparative" for the gift of faith. The penitent had to cultivate within himself a sense of his great depravity, his extreme guilt, and this utterly undone condition.[18]

Jonathan Edwards

As in other areas pertaining to conviction, the writings of Jonathan Edwards (1703–1758) demonstrate penetration and clarity. To him, too, this civil man's heart was still hard and incorrigible. He was "dumb and stupid," full of self-love, glorifying the creature rather than God, thinking himself to have arrived morally and spiritually.[19] Not only was this man still in an unregenerate state, but his sorry predicament was compounded by the fact

---

16. Davies, "The Nature and Universality of Spiritual Death," in *Sermons on Important Subjects*, 1:90–91.

17. Dickenson "The Theology of the New Birth: True Scripture-Doctrine, 1741" cited in Richard L. Bushman, ed. *The Great Awakening*, 78.

18. Hervey, *The Whole Works of the Rev. James Hervey A.M.*, 3:14.

19. Edwards, "The Hypocrite Deficient in the Duty of Prayer," in *Works* 2:73.

that he was blind to it. He was aware only of the natural realm. His heart was dead to the spiritual. If there was any apprehension of divine things, it was only with the intellect, not with the heart. This was true of all the unregenerate. The great challenge, then, was to confront them with their fallen state.

This was the crux of the problem. Humanity, in its natural state, as blind to spiritual realities. People could not see. Their understanding was darkened through the great fall in Adam so that his only hope of gaining spiritual perception was by a divine work of grace. Men were "blind," Edwards said elsewhere, "ignorant of God, and ignorant of Christ, ignorant of the way of salvation, ignorant of their own happiness, blind in the midst of the brightest and clearest light, ignorant under all manner of instruction."[20] Men show themselves "senseless" enough in temporal things but in "spiritual things far more so."[21] Edwards, on the contrary, was very much cognizant of the sinful inclinations of his heart and life, having undergone that great change from spiritual blindness to light, so that when he observed the callousness and torpor of the civil man in his congregation, the contrast was remarkable.

People were in such an unseeing condition that they were heedless to the danger it posed then and careless as to how they lived. Indeed, Edwards discerned that though the civil man was in "such a dreadful condition" that he still went about "easy and quiet," with no apparent concern, as if he had already secured his salvation. In his "senselessness" he believed it was not "worth his while to make any considerable effort to escape."[22] If he was "in the exercise of his reason," we might expect to see him trembling and quaking on account of his misery, . . . regardless of all else, spending his days and nights in tears, and groans, and lamentations, crying for help and pity, crying with an exceedingly loud and bitter cry, crying to everyone to pity him, and pray for him."[23] But this was not happening. It was not happening, because of blindness to the reality of sin and blindness to the resultant estrangement from God.

But not only humanity's faculties of perception are affected. To Edwards there was a corroborating effect on the will. Nothing would move a person away from the inclination toward sin apart from supernatural help

---

20. Edwards, "Sermon I," 2:817.
21. Edwards, "Sermon I," 2:818.
22. Edwards, "Sermon I," 2:825.
23. Edwards, "Sermon I," 2:825.

by the Spirit of God. The person would "cleave to sin, and go on in sin, let what will be done with him."[24] This condition reached such climactic proportions that humans would never come to Christ in a trusting and surrendering frame of mind. They had no felt need of the Christ presented in the gospel. Edwards said, "They would fain divide him."[25] There were some things in Christ that appealed to them and others that did not. For instance, they would be very willing to have Christ keep them from everlasting punishment, yet they would not receive him as Lord, for in so doing "they must of necessity part with their sins." They had to "sell the world, and part with their own." But, they would, rather than leave their darling sins, "run the venture of going to hell."[26]

This blindness of the mind and this obstinacy of the will came about not through any deficiency in the faculties. Man was given faculties that were "truly noble and excellent."[27] Nor was there a lack of opportunity to know, for the preaching of the Word, when done faithfully, brought the natural condition of humanity to light. The cause lay, rather, in the presence in humanity of a crippling virus that successfully resisted the light: "There is a principle in his heart, of such a blinding and besotting nature, that it hinders the exercises of his faculties about the things of religion; exercises for which God has made him quite capable, and for which he gives him abundant opportunity." Thus, Edwards paints the gloomy picture of humanity's natural condition of blindness to the spiritual realm.

That being the case, what must be done? Must humanity continue in blindness until such time as the Spirit of God chooses to convert him? This, was the opinion of the few hyper-Calvinists among New England clergy, to be sure. Since salvation was entirely of the Lord, there was no need for people to begin a hopeless attempt to procure grace. Ministers advised they remain passive and wait the Lord's time. But this was not the inclination of Edwards. It was his conviction that the people of New England, including the civil man, needed Christ desperately and immediately and could have him. From the perspective of God, nothing stood in the way of the salvation of sinners. The great, debilitating dilemma was, however, that there was no native attraction to Christ in their minds and will.[28] They were blind

24. Edwards, "Sermon I," 2:819.
25. Edwards, "Men Naturally Are God's Enemies," 2:138.
26. Edwards, "Men Naturally Are God's Enemies," 2:138.
27. Edwards, "Man's Natural Blindness in the Things of Religion," 2:247.
28. Edwards, "Men Are Naturally God's Enemies," 1:38.

and stubborn. Hence, there was an urgent necessity of awakening people to this desperate impasse. They had to be stirred up to a sense of sin. Until sinners were convinced of their sin and misery, they were not prepared to receive the redeeming mercy and grace of God as through a Mediator, because they did not see their need of a Mediator.[29] Edwards recorded a time of many conversions in 1734 in Northampton, relating that "persons are first awakened with a sense of their miserable condition by nature, the danger they are in of perishing eternally, and that it is of great importance to them that they speedily escape, and get into a better state."[30]

In his wisdom God had deigned to be compassionate. He determined to come to the aid of blind sinners and had a prescribed way of bringing them from a state of darkness into the light of his mercy. He first brought a man to reflect upon himself and to consider and be "sensible" of his sin. It was "God's manner to make men sensible of their misery and unworthiness, before he appears in his mercy and love to them."[31]

The question was not only about the spiritual-psychological method whereby God drew a sinner to Christ. Edwards also saw that it was a question of simple logic. He argues, "They who are not sensible of their misery cannot truly look to God for mercy, for it is the very notion of divine mercy, that it is the goodness and grace of God to the miserable. Without misery in the object, there can be no exercise of mercy. To suppose mercy without supposing misery, or pity without calamity is a contradiction: therefore, men cannot look upon themselves as proper objects of mercy unless they first know themselves to be miserable."[32]

We must remember that, to Edwards, misery was not only an objective reality. On that level he would say that all men were truly miserable. But when the term was applied to the issue of coming to Christ for mercy, the word referred primarily to the affective domain. It was necessary to *feel* miserable without Christ. It was highly desirable to possess a sense of sin. Edwards was speaking of what he referred to as the "sense of the heart." Whenever Edwards dealt with subjects related to experiential religion, he used language derived from the root word "sense." He wrote of a sense of

---

29. Edwards, "Sermon II," 2:836.

30. Edwards, "A Faithful Narrative of the Surprising Work of God in the Conversion of Many Hundred Souls in Northampton," 4:160 (Yale University Press). Please note that further references to the Yale edition will be identified in order to distinguish from the Banner edition.

31. Edwards, "Sermon II," 1:830.

32. Edwards, "Sermon II," 2:111.

sin, of love, of misery, of sweetness. In one paragraph, in which he outlined the various elements of misery, he used the word "sensible" five times.

John Locke's Empiricism and Edwards

For Edwards, there was a distinction to be made between what was purely cognitive and what affected the feelings, the heart. It could not be otherwise for one for whom religion had become personal. Proponents of experiential divinity made reference to "vital piety" to highlight the distinction between nominal belief and a full and personal embrace of the gospel. Edwards's analyses of conversion are contained in such monuments as *The Religious Affections* and *Distinguishing Marks of a Work of the Spirit of God*. In his interpretation of religious experience, he received a significant degree of help from reading British empiricist John Locke's *Essay of Human Understanding*. Edwards had read the work at the age of fourteen with a greater pleasure, he wrote, "than the most greedy miser finds, when gathering up handfuls of silver and gold, from newly discovered treasure."[33]

John Locke's quest had been to discover where the "materials" of reason and knowledge came from. He had found the solution: "To this I answer in one word, from *experience*." So, knowledge was derived primarily from the senses, according to Locke. Edwards exulted in the reading. Ideas in the mind were inseparable from feeling or sensing. Locke asserted that the channel whereby knowledge entered people's understanding was sensory perception. It depended "wholly upon our senses," and this "derived by them [meaning, our senses] to our understanding, I call *sensation*."[34]

While Locke's essay went a long way toward crystallizing epistemological principles in Edwards's mind, a word of caution is in order. It is on this point that the great Perry Miller (1905–1963) has been criticized. Edwards did not follow Locke's sensational psychology in every respect. He taught, for example, that there was a kind of knowing that did not affect the senses. This was "mere cogitation without any proper apprehension of the things thought of."[35]

In distinction from Locke, Edwards believed there were two kinds of knowing. Only one of them could be termed, as did Locke, "sensation." The

---

33. Dwight, *Memoirs of Jonathan Edwards*, in *The Works of Jonathan Edwards*, 1:xvii.

34. Locke, *An Essay Concerning Human Understanding*, 2.1.2; 2.1.4.

35. Edwards, "Ideas, Sense of the Heart, Spiritual Knowledge or Conviction, Faith" ed. Perry Miller, *Harvard Theological Review*, #41:135.

first source of knowledge was a mere "mental reading," by which people saw only the signs of things. Therefore, the "things themselves are before our eyes only indirectly." But there was also a more direct, more intimate way of knowing, "wherein the mind has a direct, ideal view, or contemplation of the thing thought of." The one was just cognition; the other as Edwards coined it, was "the sense of the heart."

Nevertheless, it was in this area that he found Locke's ideas so helpful. Locke's psychological sensationalism, when applied to religious knowledge, signified that a person could not really know the glory and the love of God unless experiencing it as a power acting upon his mind. And the person could know the misery of the human condition after the great fall in Adam, including the loneliness of estrangement from his Creator, only when convicted of it in the heart. Heart knowledge was derived from experience and from sensation. It was for this reason that Edwards and other leaders of the Great Awakening were as concerned with leaving an impression as they were with actual and cognitive teaching. Conviction was of more value than having a proper understanding of the facts.

It is this knowledge alone that has an effect on the will. Mere cognition involves discerning, judging, or speculation. But the "sense of the heart" includes "all agreeableness, disagreeableness, all beauty and deformity, all pleasure and pain, and all those sensations, exercises and passions of the mind which arise from either of those."[36]

Edwards had found, in Locke's epistemology, a method of interpretation and categorization and the ability to expound upon Christian experience. It was the Spirit of God who impacts the heart with a new sense. He gave "sensible apprehension of the heinousness of sin, and His wrath against it, and the guilt of it, and the terribleness of the sufferings denounced against it and so they have a sense of the importance of the things of religion in general. And herein consists what we commonly call *conviction*."[37]

Finding Rest in Christ

Conviction of sin, however, did not result from the Holy Spirit infusing special grace. Rather, it consisted "only in assisting natural principles" in order that the sinner could clearly see what was his state by nature. In a key statement on this point, Edwards said that "common grace differs from

---

36. Edwards, "Ideas," 136.
37. Edwards, "Ideas," 142. Emphasis added.

special in that it influences only by assisting of nature, and not by imparting grace, or bestowing anything above nature."[38] More was needed, therefore, than conviction of sin. It was not the end of the matter of salvation. In a sermon in which he distinguished between convictions that issued in saving faith and conviction that devils may also have, he said that a sense of sin "is no certain sign that persons have true faith," even though it was a necessary element of Christian experience.[39]

Why, then, was a sense of sin so crucial? Simply, it played the role of preparing "the mind for a sense of spiritual excellency." Thus, a sense of "the excellency of God's mercy in forgiving sin depends on a sense of the great guilt of sin." Edwards summarized his argument as follows:

> Men, by being made sensible of the great guilt of sin or the connection or natural agreeableness there is between that and a dreadful punishment and how that the greatness of the majesty of God seems to require and demand such a punishment, are brought to see the great need of a satisfaction, or something to intervene to make it honorable to that majesty to show them favor, and being for a while blind to the suitableness of Christ's satisfaction in order to this, and then afterwards have a sense given them of Christ's divine excellency, and what He did and suffered for sinners, hereby their eyes are as it were opened to see the perfect fitness there is in this to satisfy for sin, or to render their being received into favor consistent with the honor of God's offended majesty.[40]

The convicted sinner, thus transformed in the inner being, began to "sense" the ineffable excellence of Christ, who would intervene on his behalf. And to be impacted in wonderment by a sense of God's mercy and by a realization that Christ's work made salvation consistent with the "honor of God's offended majesty" was to awaken to a whole new reality. The person thus enlightened had been told these truths countless times before but was left unimpressed. However, when the Spirit of God impacted the heart, the senses were enlivened. When "at last it is seen," said Edwards, "man is convinced that it was beyond the invention of men to discover it; for by experience they found themselves all their lifetime wholly blind to it."[41] What had

---

38. Edwards, "A Divine and Supernatural Light Immediately Imparted to the Soul by the Spirit of God Shown to be Both a Scriptural and Rational Doctrine," *Works*, 1:13.

39. Edwards, "True Grace Distinguished from the Experience of Devils," *Works* vol. 25, *Sermons and Discourses 1743–1758*, Yale, 618–20.

40. Edwards, "Ideas," 144.; see also Edwards, "A Divine and Supernatural Light," 1:14.

41. Edwards, "Ideas," 144.

been restricted to the purely cognitive had penetrated the affective domain. It was then fully apprehended with the shock of new discovery, and with all joy and relief, the sinner experienced the application of the healing balm of the gospel.

A spiritual being, thus awakened, could find rest in Christ. When one was smitten with a sense of sin and became aware of estrangement from God, there was "no peace of mind"; "his mind is tossed with tempest, and not comforted, and courage is ready to fail, for how can a poor worm bear the wrath of the great God?" When such fears existed in the human heart, they would "greatly enfeeble" it and bring it into a "trembling posture."[42]

But for such persons there was a "fountain abundant for peace and safety in Jesus Christ." One who had a sense of sin could find "abundant satisfaction" that he was safe and that God would be at peace with him "in Christ."[43] The marvelous consolation was that when the sinner came to Christ, the guilt was "at once taken away, the soul is left free, it is lighted of its burden, it is delivered of its bondage, and it is like the bird escaped from the fowler."[44]

Edwards's belief in the necessity of a sense of sin was rooted in careful study of the Scriptures. He was adept at biblical interpretation. But he was convinced of its necessity also by a review of the history of his own spiritual pilgrimage. Saving faith, he knew, would grow only on the soil of felt need, and it will be seen that Edwards would find this belief confirmed by what he could observe during the revival of 1734.

It must be pointed out that there was no reluctance in Christ to receive whoever would come to him. On the contrary, Edwards often exhorted his congregation to flee to the throne of grace. He portrayed the Redeemer standing with arms stretched wide, calling to whoever would to come. The problem was, rather, that sinners were unwilling to come, felt no need to come, the gospel offer notwithstanding. Invariably, they had been duped, either by unfaithful preaching or by the incredible innate propensity to self-deception, into reliance on their own righteousness. And until such time as the sinner was emptied of delusion, there would be no motivation to saving faith. For this reason there was a great need for preaching that was convicting.

---

42. Edwards, "Sermon XII," 1:930.
43. Edwards, "Sermon XII," 1:931.
44. Edwards, "Sermon XII," 1:934.

Edwards had more to say on this matter. In a sermon on Hosea 2:14, he discussed the purpose of the convicting work of the Holy Spirit. Initially, a person being placed on the road to saving faith was in need of humbling. "God, by His Spirit, leads them into the wilderness before He speaks comfortably to them, for the same cause that He led the Children of Israel into the wilderness before He brought them into Canaan, which we are told was to humble them."[45] Israel forsook the worship of Yahweh to serve other gods such as Baal. They achieved a degree of material wealth and the accompanying sense of self-sufficiency. Their successes were ascribed to Baal as much as to the true God of Abraham, Isaac, and Jacob. Before they would return to obedient faith, they needed to be stripped of self-sufficiency and pride. In this way God intended to bring sinners to realize the "insufficiency of their wisdom" and to a discovery that all human effort fell with "respect to their relief."[46]

The purpose of a sense of sin was also to "have the heart turned from, and turned against it [sin], in hatred," so that what was loved was then hated and what was despised was then the great desire of the "renovated nature." Humans could pretend what they would, but their hearts were not turned from sin "if they do not forsake it," and the person was not really and truly "converted, who is not really come to a disposition utterly to forsake all ways of sin."[47] The humbling of the soul and the turning away from sin implied a disposition of heart that "embraces Christ and trusts in Him as the Savior from sin, and said Edwards, "when sin is thus slain then God is wont to open a door of hope, a door through which there flashes a sweet light out of heaven upon the soul. Then comfort arises, and then is there a new song in the mouth, even praise unto God."[48] The same sermon offers a helpful comment on the psychological component employed in this process: "We see in temporal things, that the worth and value of any enjoyment is learned by the want of it. He who is sick values health the more. People at war value peace. He who is a captive or in a state of forced subjection learns to prize freedom." Similarly, "a sense of pardon of sin, and the favor of God, and a hope of eternal life, do not afford comfort and joy to the soul any farther than they are valued and prized." Hence, the "darkness which

---

45. Edwards, "Sermon III," 1:840.
46. Edwards, "Sermon III," 840.
47. Edwards, "Sermon III," 841.
48. Edwards, "Sermon III," 841.

go before comfort serve to render the joy and comfort the greater when obtained, and so are in mercy to those for whom God intends comfort."[49]

The mature Christian benefitted from this process too. Edwards's wish was to "humble himself before God, to "annihilate" himself, to be "abased," and to "lie low in the dust." For the Christian, however, the sense of sin was not only a painful prerequisite for communion with God. Humble acknowledgement of one's remaining fleshly inclinations in daily life was, for Edwards, one of the fruits of grace. Humility was therefore a pleasing temper of mind. For times of greatest humility often came together with times of greatest joy. Humility emptied one of self-confident triumphalism and brought the soul to a posture of renewed dependence upon grace. To Edwards, the "pleasures of humility are really the most refined, inward and exquisite delights in the world." He was "exceedingly sensible" of discovering "how much more lovely is a humble than a proud disposition." He wished to be "emptied and annihilated" and "full of Christ alone."[50]

A sense of sin had the power to humble the saint as well as the sinner so that a place was made in the heart for the love of Christ. And for Edwards, it was primarily this strand of the conversion experience that certified the veracity of the doctrines of his religious heritage. The doctrines of grace tended to strip humanity of false optimism with respect to personal spiritual life.

For the unregenerate, then, a sense of sin was a necessity. For the mature believer, it was a great blessing. Edwards wrote a series of guidelines for the "Judging of Persons' Experiences" in which two things were prominent. First, when anyone asked for an opinion on his or her spiritual life, Edwards tried to discern whether the inquirer was "convinced of sins of heart and life. And in both, that what troubles them be those things wherein their wretchedness chiefly consists." Second, they were to be examined as to "whether their joy be truly and properly in God and in Christ or whether it be not wholly joy on themselves, joy in their excellencies or privileges or experiences."[51]

When Edwards and the other leaders of the Great Awakening aroused inert consciences, the necessity of a sense of sin was given wide exposure. They preached on the themes of humanity's natural blindness, people's indifference to the claims of the gospel, and a host of similar themes in

---

49. Edwards, "Sermon III," 845.
50. Edwards, "His Diary," 1:xxvii.
51. Edwards, "Directions for Judging of Person's Experiences," *Works*, Yale, 21:522–24.

order to shake loose the shackles of arrogant independence and self-righteousness. They preached with a conviction seldom seen by sleepy New Englanders, because the import of the subject had been impressed upon their own hearts, because the Bible gave divine sanction to it, and because it proved to be of salvific value.

3.

A Preacher's Heart
Jonathan Edwards's Self Awareness

"I cannot help feeling that the final explanation of the state of the church today is a defective sense of sin and a defective doctrine of sin."

Dr. Martyn Lloyd-Jones (1899–1981)

INTRODUCTION AND EARLY YEARS

As an example of religious experience by an acclaimed leader of the great revival, that of Jonathan Edwards presents us with the most clarity. It is for this reason that we turn in this chapter to his writings for a clear exposition of personal experience with respect to conviction. And in considering the role the doctrine of sin played in the preaching and the revival theology of the leading evangelists, it is necessary to look at the early years of one whose analytical ability surpassed that of his peers. Here we can discover what they reveal about Edwards's spiritual awakening. It is here that we find sufficient information to explain the passion with which he and other preachers of the period exhorted their audiences on the biblical doctrines of sin and grace. To Edwards, just like the others, grace was not merely a presumed reality for all who were churchgoing. Rather, it was a glorious visitation from the Spirit of God, known and felt. Sin was not merely a part of the creed one needed to be aware of in order to explain the disappointments and trials of life. Rather, it was a condition of heart to which humanity was naturally blind.

He wrote in careful prose about his apprehension of the depth of human depravity on the one hand and the height of the experience of divine grace on the other. In the preface to his *Treatise Concerning Religious Affections*, he noted that a consideration of the exact nature of religious experience had "long engaged" his mind, for he knew he must "attend to this matter with the utmost diligence and care and all the exactness of search and inquiry of which I have been capable."[1] Moreover, he was resolved at an early age, as soon as he became conscious of divine things, to record his findings: "It is a subject on which my mind has been peculiarly intent, ever since I first entered on the study of divinity."

Edwards (b. 1703) was a third-generation colonist in New England, born of a village minister, the only brother of ten sisters. He spent his childhood years in East Windsor, Connecticut, a frontier settlement, his exposure to the world restricted to his immediate environs. Little is known of his habits or playful activities during these early years, but it can be safely surmised that the deeply religious spirit of his parents governed the way they raised him. The need to search the Word of God for life direction and to call upon the name of the Lord were things pressed upon him from his youth. Edwards recalls in his *Personal Narrative*, written much later, that he had a variety of "concerns and exercises about my soul, from my childhood." There were particular periods in his young life when he was uncommonly moved in mind, "very much affected . . . about the things of religion, and my soul's salvation; and was abundant in religious duties." He used to pray five times a day "in secret" and spent "much time in religious conversation with other boys."[2] Edwards's life entered, very early, on a course from which it never deviated.

The schooling Edwards received until his thirteenth year was from his father, to whom he was exceptionally close, in the parsonage where all the children of East Windsor received their education. Even as a young boy he found intellectual and spiritual stimulus in his father's library. His mother was the daughter of Solomon Stoddard, for decades a towering figure in the New England churches along the frontier. At the age of thirteen Edwards went off to Yale College in New Haven to receive formal education. Edwards, highly disciplined and studious, read John Locke and Isaac Newton

---

1. Edwards, "Religious Affections," *Works*, Yale, 2:84.
2. Edwards, *Personal Narrative*, 1:xii.

and started on a career characterized in part by philosophical inquiry related to the things of the heart and mind.

Upon completion of his schooling at Yale, in the year 1722, Edwards was licensed to preach. He accepted a call to a small Presbyterian congregation in New York City, where he began his ministry in the same year. Wishing to place himself in a position of wider influence, however, he left New York despite his attachment to his charge. While revisiting his alma mater in 1723 to receive a Master of Arts degree, he was elected tutor in the college. Edwards spent two years at Yale as tutor and used the opportunity to prepare himself further for the work of the ministry. In 1727 Edwards received and accepted an invitation to join his aging grandfather Solomon Stoddard as junior pastor and successor in Northampton. In the same year, he married Sarah Pierrepont, daughter of one of Yale's founders and granddaughter of the well-known Puritan scholar Thomas Hooker, leader of the 1630 emigration to Connecticut. Thus socially connected, Edwards could have become a ministerial autocrat like his grandfather. But he was content to remain a frontier preacher of the Calvinistic[3] sort of piety he himself had learned, and he spent his life's strength disseminating the doctrines of the Reformation.

In 1731 he was invited to be the main speaker at the "Great and Thursday Lecture" in Boston's First Church. Edwards faced an audience here that was intimidating. The representatives from western Massachusetts and Connecticut were still amenable to the Puritan heritage. But the seaboard clergy had immersed themselves in a more liberal consensus imported from England. Edwards took the opportunity to pitch into the teeth of Boston's clergy a sermon entitled "God Glorified in the Work of Redemption, by the Greatness of Man's Dependence upon Him in the Whole of It."[4] This can be seen as his first attack on the malleable and the unorthodox. The sermon called them back to an older doctrine of sovereign grace than the Bostonians were comfortable with. He reminded them that their immediate fathers had steadfastly believed and preached the "absolute and universal dependence of the redeemed on God . . . in everything, directly, immediately and entirely."

---

3. It is barely enough to say Edwards was a Calvinist. He was that, like his Puritan forebears, but his personal piety was sprinkled throughout with an intensity reminiscent of continental Pietism.

4. Edwards, "God Glorified in the Work of Redemption," Yale, 17:196–99.

This sermon gave notice that Edwards would not be joining the liberal crowd. It was a milestone, not only for Edwards but also in the history of New England theology. An earlier biographer has said that "this sermon appears to mark the beginning of both the new emphasis in doctrine and the new fervor in preaching which ten years later were to bring about the Great Awakening."[5] In the sermon, Edwards expounded on the proper approach to theology, saying that humble acknowledgment of God's sovereignty in redemption was a prerequisite for a faithful view of all doctrine. This was the principle a preacher took along with him when interpreting Scripture. Several ministers arranged to have the lecture published and prefaced the first edition with an expression of "joy and thankfulness that the great Head of the Church is pleased still to raise up, from among the children of His people, for the supply of His churches, those who assert and maintain these evangelical principles."[6]

The Northampton Awakening of 1734

Edwards preached with growing confidence, reinterpreting Puritan theology in terms relevant to his own generation. Confirmation of his efforts came a few years later when about three hundred souls professed saving faith. Apparently, the whole town of Northampton came under the influence, for "a great and earnest concern about the great things of religion, and the eternal world, became universal in all parts of the town. It was then a dreadful thing to lie out of Christ, in danger every day of dropping into hell; and what person's minds were intent upon, was to escape for their lives, and to fly from the wrath to come."[7]

This surprising work was but a precursor to the Great Awakening of the early and middle 1740s, when George Whitefield visited the colonies. The revival had its detractors. Edwards rose to its defense, writing detailed arguments for the place of emotion in religion, which detractors were deriding as "enthusiasm."[8] He welcomed the appearance of precisely what

---

5. Winslow, *Jonathan Edwards*, 145.
6. Dwight, *Memoirs of Jonathan Edwards*, in *Works*, 1:xii.
7. Edwards, "A Faithful Narrative of a Surprising Work of God in the Conversion of Many Hundred Souls in Northampton," Yale 4: 149–50.
8. For the first few centuries that it was used in English, the word "enthusiasm" was primarily employed to refer to beliefs or passions that related to religion. The noun comes from the Greek word *enthousiasmos*, meaning "possessed by a god, or inspired." It was originally used to convey negative opinion of excessive religious zeal.

had been missing of late in the religious life of the English-speaking world, namely, heart-knowledge. In achievements such as *A Treatise Concerning the Religious Affections* and *Distinguishing Marks of a Work of the Spirit of God*, he set forth what he considered genuine, heartfelt religious experience. Though he was still to write his major theological works, Edwards in 1750 passed the summit of his influence as a preacher, and after a collision with church leaders over attendance at the Lord's Supper, he was released from his charge. For a time he pastored, after declining calls to Scotland and to Virginia, a very small congregation at Stockbridge, Massachusetts, with an outreach to native Americans and then was called to the presidency of the College of New Jersey, later named Princeton University. Shortly after accepting the invitation to the college, he was inoculated against smallpox and died. It was 1758.

PERSONAL PIETY

The leaders of the Great Awakening were inclined to self-examination. Their piety was of the heart. Accordingly, a considerable part of their attention was drawn to scrutinizing their inner consciousness in search of hidden sins, unchristian motives, and evidence of pride. But this was not something that required conscious planning, for it was a thing learned in the process of conversion, when they had become personally acquainted with innate depravity. George Whitefield would say, for example, in later life, "If I trace myself from cradle to my manhood, I can see nothing in me but a fitness to be damned; and if the Almighty had not prevented me by His grace, I had now either been sitting in darkness and in the shadow of death, or condemned, as the due reward of my crimes, to be forever lifting up my eyes to torments."[9]

Jonathan Edwards was of the same mind. He gave the religious world an absorbing account of inner piety, and it ranks with the best in terms of penetration and originality. Edwards was in the habit of reflecting in order to understand the level of his own vital piety. And while it is true that a variety of his works and sermons contain the fruit of introspection, it is his personal writings that reveal the degree of attention he gave to the inner life, both as an individual and in his ministry to others.

---

9. Whitefield, "The Method of Grace," in MacFarlan *The Revivals of the Eighteenth Century*, 18.

On July 30, 1723, when he was nineteen, he wrote in his diary, "... have concluded to endeavor to work myself into duties by searching and tracing back all the real reasons why I do them not, and narrowly searching out all the subtle subterfuges of my thoughts." He wished to discern with the utmost of his power "what are the very first originals of my defect, as with respect to want of repentance, love to God, loathing of myself." He resolved to construct some sermons around themes related to indwelling sin such as pride, malice, speaking evil of others, and he would use those occasions to bewail his own sins.[10] Sereno Dwight, one of his first biographers, states that Edwards received much of his uncanny insight into the psychology of religious experience from "his thorough acquaintance with his own heart."[11] As with other leaders of the period, there was an intelligent and profound connection between what Edwards experienced himself and what he preached. This accounts for his repeated return to the basics of salvation doctrine.

During the initial stages of his religious experience, Edwards was still relatively unacquainted with the sin of the world and with the tendency existing within his own heart. Doctrinally, too, considering the nurture his parents had given him, Edwards had not matured. He was full of objections, for instance, against the doctrine of God's sovereignty. He rebelled as a youth against God's absolute supremacy "in choosing whom He would to eternal life; and rejecting whom He pleased." He remembered when that changed and the doctrine became "exceedingly pleasant, bright and sweet.... But my first conviction was not so," he wrote.[12] Edwards, in his youth, was often absorbed in contemplation of "the glory of the Divine Being,"[13] immersed in a "sort of inward, sweet delight in God and divine things ... a new sense, quite different from anything I had ever experienced before."

During this time of youthful piety, he could perceive little in the world but beauty and, in that beauty, the presence of God. "God's excellency," he would write, "his wisdom, his purity and love, seemed to appear in everything; in the sun, moon and stars; in the clouds and blue sky; in the grass, flowers and trees; in the water and all nature." He often used to sit and view the moon for long periods of time at night and the clouds by day, "to behold the sweet glory of God in these things; in the meantime, singing forth with

10. Edwards, "His Diary," 1:xxx.
11. Dwight, "Memoirs of Jonathan Edwards" Works, 1:clxxxix.
12. Edwards, "His Diary," 1:xiii.
13. Edwards, "His Diary," 1:xii.

a low voice, my contemplations of the Creator and Redeemer."[14] Nothing was so "sweet" to him as the rumble and boom of a storm. He could say, "It rejoiced me!" He "felt God . . . at the first appearance of the thunderstorm; and used to . . . fix myself in order to view the clouds, and see the lightnings play, and hear the majestic and awful voice of God's thunders." Always, when thus engaged, he used to sing or chant his meditations upon the character of God.

Edwards's mind appropriated an unmistakable sense of the majesty and grace of God in such full measure that he admitted to an inability to express it. But, he says, "I seemed to see them both in a sweet conjunction; majesty and meekness joined together; it was a sweet, and gentle, and holy majesty; and also a majestic meekness; an awful sweetness; a high and great and holy gentleness." He was frequently "meditating on Christ, on the excellency of His being, and the lovely way of salvation by free grace in him." These times of musing were accompanied by "a calm, sweet abstraction of soul from all the concerns of this world; and sometimes a kind of vision, or fixed ideas and imaginations, of being alone in the mountains, or some solitary wilderness, far from all mankind, sweetly conversing with Christ, and wrapt and swallowed up in God." This new sense of divine things would kindle in his heart a burning love and "ardour of soul" that he could not express.[15]

Edwards felt grieved that he had not turned to God sooner in life so that his religious consciousness would have had more time to grow and mature. As it was, he spent most of his free time during his late teens and early twenties thinking of divine things, year after year, "often walking alone in the woods, and solitary places, for meditation, soliloquy, and prayer, and converse with God; and it was always my manner, at such times, to sing forth my contemplations. . . . Prayer seemed to be natural to me, as the breath by which the inward burnings of my heart had vent."[16]

To the secularist, rationalistic mind of our century, it can appear that such eruptions of inner affection are a little overdone, a result of an exaggerated sensibility, and therefore unbefitting a man of this caliber. They might convey the impression of an earlier mysticism with little or nothing to say to our age. However, one must not forget that while Edwards was capable of deep, demonstrable emotion, he was also capable of keen observation.

---

14. Edwards, "His Diary," 1:xii.
15. Edwards, "His Diary," 1:xii.
16. Edwards, "His Diary," 1:xii.

Indeed, he had set out with the purpose of analyzing religious experience "with utmost diligence and care, and exactness of search and inquiry."[17]

The fact that Edwards was a man of towering intellect is not a hard sell. He usually dominated the intellectual turf of his choice in his day. A cursory reading of his early scientific essays such as "Notes on the Mind," "Of Insects," and "Of the Rainbow"[18] will satisfy the skeptic. These essays were written while he was yet in his teens. Perry Miller, in his study of Edwards, goes to great length to show that he is the first of American empiricists, far ahead of his time.[19] But the point is that Edwards's keenness of mind enabled him to interpret and then to reconstruct the religion of his heart with striking lucidity. Those sublime and lofty meditations on the Divine Being became a part of his life. Indeed, his "sense of divine things" gradually increased after his graduation from Yale in 1719, "till I went to preach at New York; which was about a year and a half after they began."[20]

As Edwards matured, his experiences of God became more intense, and at times he longed for spiritual consummation. Writing of an occasion in Northampton, Massachusetts, in 1737, when he was thirty-four, he spoke of going for a walk in the woods to contemplate and pray: "I had a view that for me was extraordinary, of the glory of the Son of God, as Mediator between God and man, and his wonderful, great, full, pure and sweet grace and love. . . . I felt an ardency of soul to be, what I know not otherwise how to express, emptied and annihilated; to lie in the dust, and to be full of Christ alone . . . and to be perfectly sanctified and made pure, with a divine and heavenly purity.[21]

Edwards's *Personal Narrative* was written much later in life. He tended to accentuate the periods of joy in his spiritual pilgrimage. Those who study the entries of his diary, written as a young man, discover that valleys of gloom and despondency often followed these peaks of spiritual rejoicing. The diary begins in December of 1722, during the New York period of his ministry, and reveals a heart frequently plagued with a sense of sin.

17. Edwards, Yale 2:84.

18. Edwards, *Representative Selections*, ed. Clarence H. Faust and Thomas H. Johnson, 3–27.

19. Miller, *Jonathan Edwards*, 265–66. Miller overstates his case to the point of inaccuracy and has been surpassed, as will be shown later. Still, the evidence Miller amassed does serve to show that Edwards acquired insights from the fields of philosophy and the sciences.

20. Edwards, *Personal Narrative*, 1:xiv.

21. Edwards, *Personal Narrative*, 1:xlvii.

Gloom and despondency are more easily forgotten than times of delight, and perhaps this accounts for the relative absence of the former in the *Personal Narrative*. In any case, as Edwards's spiritual exercises deepened and matured, he became ruefully aware of his own unworthiness and began to feel the pangs of his own sin and guilt before God. In the diary we find the record of the malevolent tendencies he discovered within himself, and these discoveries brought their own sorrow.

The Sweet and the Vile

All of creation was permeated with sweetness while Edwards continued in that "sense" of the glorious majesty and grace of God. But all was vile when he suffered the sunken condition of darkness in the heart. Those two words, "sweet" and "vile," found repeatedly in his personal writings, capture this contrast.[22] When pummeled by conviction, he felt vile and lonely, exposed and defenseless, without the sheltering presence of Christ. When captivated by the beauty of the Divine Being, he relished the sweetness of harmony with God. It appears, then, that Edwards's appropriation of the consuming love of God did not remain long with him. Quite soon he found himself in a state of decay. And he would always, in such circumstances, examine his own heart and life to find the cause of his heartache. Invariably he found the reason in himself. Even though he resolved to live unerringly in the ways of his Redeemer and give himself wholly to the service of God "so that I am not, in any respect, my own," he lamented, "It seems yesterday, the day before, and Saturday that I should always retain the same resolutions to the same height. But alas! How soon do I decay! O, how weak, how infirm, how unable to do anything of myself! What a poor, inconsistent being! What a miserable wretch, without the assistance of the Spirit of God!"[23]

Subsequent entries in the diary show that he would continue in this disposition for long periods of time, decrying his hateful pride and his blindness. He was "very much convinced of the extraordinary deceitfulness of the heart, and how exceedingly affection or appetite blinds the mind, and brings it into entire subjection."[24] He related, in September of 1726, that for the previous three years he had been for the most part "in a low sunk estate

---

22. See also Bushmen, "Jonathan Edwards and Puritan Consciousness," in *Puritan New England*, Vaughan and Bremer, 350.

23. Edwards, "His Diary," 1:xxv–xxvi.

24. Edwards, "His Diary," 1:xxx.

and condition, miserably senseless, to what I used to be, about spiritual things."[25] The defects he perceived both in "temper" and "conversation" became an acute burden to him, and he would pour out his heart to God in humble confession.

This is not to say that Edwards succumbed to questioning the foundation of his faith. Neither does it mean that he doubted the veracity and faithfulness of the God of his salvation. Rather, he was progressing through a period in which he experienced a chain of deepening convictions, exciting in him a more penetrating sense of human sin on the one hand and divine grace on the other. There were moments in his life when God appeared "as an infinite fountain of divine glory and sweetness; being full, and sufficient to fill and satisfy the soul; pouring forth itself in sweet communications."[26] And yet these moments were matched later or accompanied by ever-widening views of his own unworthiness:

> Often, since I lived in this town (Northampton, Mass.), I have had very affecting views of my own sinfulness and *vileness*. . . . I have had a vastly greater sense of my own wickedness, and the badness of my heart, than ever I had before my conversion. It has often appeared to me, that if God should mark iniquity against me, I should appear the very worst of all mankind. . . . I know not how to express better what my sins appear to me to be, than by heaping infinite upon infinite. Very often, for these many years, these expressions are in my mind, and in my mouth, "infinite upon infinite—infinite upon infinite"!! . . . And, it appears to me, that were it not for free grace, exalted and raised up to the infinite height of all the fullness and glory of the great Jehovah . . . I should appear sunk down in my sins below hell itself. . . . And, it is affecting to think, how ignorant I was, when a young Christian, of the bottomless, infinite depths of wickedness, pride, hypocrisy, and deceit, left in my heart.[27]

This last was written by Edwards when he was thirty-four. Clearly, while he was awakened in heart and conscience as a young man, his own experience of sin and grace was not a phenomenon restricted to the time of his conversion. Whether his heart was uplifted by the "sweetness" or cast down by the "vile," it is plain that this "sense of the heart" was foundational for his religious life. His conversion was not merely an intellectual assent

25. Edwards, "His Diary," 1:xxxvi.
26. Edwards, *Personal Narrative*, 1:xlvii.
27. Edwards, *Personal Narrative*: 1:xlvii.

to a creed or a change in direction ethically, although it was these. Fundamentally, it was a developing and growing recognition of his relationship to his Redeemer and Lord. His preaching and his writing must be seen in this light.

He was preeminently an exponent of experiential divinity because he believed with his whole being that to be a Christian at all was to be one who possessed a holy familiarity with the doctrines of sin and grace. Edwards would stress repeatedly that to be truly religious was to possess the sense of the heart. That is why Edwards intended his written treatises to find their echo in the hearts of his readers. Harold Simonson makes this point when he says that "a distinguishing feature implicit in his whole theology, even when most coldly polemical, is the centrality he gives to man and his condition of the heart—always in relation to God."[28]

One vital aspect of the condition of the heart was, for Edwards, the vileness. It was through lenses colored by this self-awareness that he viewed his relationship to creation and to God. It was due to his conviction of sin that he came to perceive with great clarity that the beauty and innocence he had seen earlier in all creation had been one-sided and untrained. He had found evidence of something wrong in his universe, of a great controversy between the excellencies of God in Christ and what God had created. There was discord between Edwards's experience of the glorious love of the Creator and the distress under which the world groaned. This tension was also the experience of his own heart. There was the sweet; there was the vile. The more he saw of life, the more he was aware that the plague of sin had brought upon mankind a very heavy burden. To repeat the words of Carse, "a crippling frost had fallen on the garden God had fashioned in the full light of his glory."[29] Edwards placed an entry in his diary in the summer of 1724 "I have now abundant reason to be convinced of the troublesomeness and vexation of the world and that it will never be another kind of world."[30]

Edwards therefore did not preach and defend a dry and abstract Calvinism with regard to sin doctrine. Due to his pietistic temperament, he exhorted and wrote with the burden of his own guilt upon him. A biblical precedent can easily be found: Isaiah of old, called to prophesy, was still "undone" (Isa 6:5). Paul the apostle was yet the "foremost of sinners" (1

---

28. Simonson, *Jonathan Edwards: Theologian of the Heart*, 22–23.
29. Carse, *Jonathan Edwards and the Visibility of God*, 69.
30. Edwards, "His Diary," 1:xxxv.

Tim 1:15) worthy only to be relegated to, in Edwards's words, the "lowest places in hell" but for the grace of God.[31]

Only a pastor thus convinced could speak words as convicting as those uttered in a sermon on Romans 3:19 where he described for the congregation that which he himself sensed so profoundly. A small piece deserves quoting:

> If men are sinners, that is enough. . . . But men are full of sin; principles and acts of sin; their guilt is like great mountains, heaped one upon the other, till the pile is grown up to heaven. They are totally corrupt in every part, in all their faculties, in all the Principles of their nature, their understanding, their wills; and in all their dispositions and affections. Their heads, their hearts, are totally depraved, all the members of their bodies are only instruments of sin; and all their senses, seeing, hearing, tasting, etc., are only inlets and outlets of sin, channels of corruption. . . . There is inflexibility in sin, that will not be overcome by threatenings or promises . . . neither by that which is terrifying, nor that which is winning.[32]

A sense of sin, rising from his own Christian experience and from observations of humanity, became a distinct emphasis in his preaching and would form an integral part of Edwards's homiletical purpose. He was keen to express, as clearly as he could, the awful nature of sin from the viewpoint of his own conviction. He found that his contemporary evangelists, fellow leaders in the revivals, held similar views. They were persuaded that their sermons needed to contain application that would engender a felt need for forgiveness and healing.

---

31. Edwards, *Personal Narrative*, 1:xlvii.
32. Edwards, "The Justice of God in the Damnation of Sinners," Yale 19:344.

4.

Darkening Skies

> "A self-righteous prig who goes regularly to church may be far nearer to hell than a prostitute. But, of course, it is better to be neither."
>
> — C. S. Lewis, 1940

THE LOSS OF CONVICTION

Declension in Britain

CHARLES OVERTON, A NINETEENTH-CENTURY historian, lamented that England at the beginning of the eighteenth-century was a moral quagmire and a spiritual cesspool, and he quoted Thomas Carlyle's description: "Stomach well alive, soul extinct." William Blackstone visited the church of every major clergyman in London but "did not hear a single discourse which had more Christianity in it than the writings of Cicero." In most sermons Carlyle heard, it would have been impossible to tell just from listening whether the preacher was a follower of Confucius, Mohammed, or Christ![1]

That the church was in a state of decline during the early eighteenth century is beyond dispute, recent revisionist studies notwithstanding. Various factors helped bring about a declension in the theological

---

1. Overton and Abbey, *The English Church in the Eighteenth Century*, 297.

underpinnings and pastoral concern usually expected of the clergy. One reason was the cold hand of the Enlightenment, celebrating reason and denigrating revelation. The resulting deism and skepticism were largely unopposed by clergy, who lacked the conviction needed to resist.[2] There were but few who could refute Unitarians, deists, and other cynics. With the gospel thus undermined, the appeal of church attendance suffered, and the relevance of the church to society was impaired. In 1738 George Berkeley stated that religion and morality in Britain had degenerated to a point as had "never before been known in any Christian country." Bishop Joseph Butler (1692–1752) was heard to remark concerning the low level of interest in church matters, "In the present turn of the age one may observe a wonderful frugality in everything which has respect to religion, and extravagance in everything else."[3]

In the beginning of the eighteenth century the Reformed doctrines of grace had few strong adherents within the Anglican Church in spite of the Thirty-Nine Articles of Religion's strong position on the divine decrees and on the bondage of the human will. George Whitefield early on, for example, became convinced that a recovery of Reformed doctrine was essential to spiritual renewal and the preaching of the gospel.[4]

Another reason for declension was that the Church of England was far too reliant upon political and economic interests to reform itself. Because it was the state church, the government had the right to appoint clergy as it saw fit. The clerical life attracted the younger sons of the nobility or gentry (the elder sons destined for rank in the military), and to help them collect an income equal to their standing, the government and church allowed them to hold clerical positions in places where they did not even live. The effect of clerical vacancy in the church was the growth of religious indifference among the population. Sin, forgiveness, and themes of healing and transformation through the cross of Christ were quite forgotten or rationalized away in many parishes.

The established church was staid and formal and could not provide the warmth of personal application it had under Puritanism. Neither was the church, generally speaking (for there were many exceptions), able to

---

2. The following are some of the Deist theologians: Matthew Tindal (1653–1733); John Toland; (1670–722); Lord Shaftesbury (1671–1729), with his *Discourse on Free Thinking*; and Lord Bolingbroke (1678–1751). But there were also writers opposing them, one of whom was Bishop George Berkeley (1685–1753).

3. Cragg, *The Church in the Age of Reason, 1648–1789*, 133.

4. The point is made in Kidd, *George Whitefield*, 79.

provide instruction in the gospel. The usual fare did not have much appeal to the men and women living brutal and squalid lives in the disease-ridden slums of the new towns and mining villages of the early Industrial Revolution.

Howell Harris (1714–1773) has been called the greatest Welshman of the eighteenth century. His itinerant preaching[5] all over Wales and England was accompanied with power, and he appears to have been a keen observer of the general level of spirituality in the British Isles. In a letter to a Reverend Ma'Culloch of Scotland, he bemoaned that "great decay prevails among all denominations."[6] The church hierarchy of the time had "threatened to turn these itinerant clergymen out of the Church. . . the great bitterness that is manifest at present against the work, proceeds from the learned men and carnal professors of every sect . . . who cannot rejoice to see the Lord coming in a way so contrary to human expectation."[7]

Titus Knight (b. 1719), a native of Halifax in Yorkshire, gave testimony of the kind of preaching he was accustomed to hearing before his conversion: "I sought and expected the favour of God, and the acceptation of my person, solely on the account of my own righteousness. Nor is this at all to be wondered at, seeing all the sons of Adam naturally seek justification and life, by virtue of that law and covenant which he violated and broke in Paradise. *Nor, was this error in any wise corrected by any of the public sermons I then heard*, all of which were more legal than evangelical, and the preachers rather sent the congregation for life to Moses than to Christ."[8]

Later, Augustus Toplady (1740–778) recalled in one of his sermons, "I believe no denomination of professing Christians were so generally void of the light and life of godliness, so generally destitute of the doctrine and the grace of the Gospel, as was the Church of England, considered as a body about fifty years ago. At that period, a converted minister in the Establishment was as great a wonder as a comet."[9]

---

5. Most accounts credit Harris with being the instigator of George Whitefield's great success as an itinerant open-air preacher.

6. Howell Harris to the Rev. Mr. Ma'Culloch, in *The Life and Times of Howell Harris*, by Edward Morgan, 140.

7. Harris in *The Life and Times of Howell Harris*, by Edward Morgan, 137–38. Harris is referring to the work of itinerant preaching.

8. Knight, in John Gillies, *Memoirs of George Whitefield*, 216, emphasis added.

9. Toplady, in a sermon quoted in Luke Tyerman, *The Life of the Rev. George Whitefield*, 1:65.

Even George Whitefield, who remained a steadfast Anglican during his ministry, had to insist on "understanding the formularies of the Church in their plain grammatical sense." He had no time for the ambiguous doublespeak of Arminian and deistic commentators on the Thirty-Nine Articles. The original authors of the Anglican statement of doctrine, if they could have returned from the dead, would not have thanked men whose "two-fold interpretation" of the Articles "opened a door for the most detestable equivocation."[10]

But what was his opinion of the Church of England? He replied, "My dear brethren, I am a friend to her Articles, I am a friend to her Homilies, I am a friend to her liturgy. And, if they did not thrust me out of their churches, I would read them every day."[11] He lamented that the "wholesome doctrines" of the Church of England were so poorly known because so seldom reprinted, distributed, or read by contrast to the Westminster Standards in Scotland, which were "almost in every hand; and so constantly explained and insisted on."[12]

Thomas Jackson reported that the evidence was "fearfully strong and conclusive" that "it was unquestionably the most unevangelical period that had ever occurred in this country since the Reformation was completed, in the reign of Elizabeth."[13]

Lest these observations exaggerate the issue, it should be noted that the Methodist historian Luke Tyerman listed several Church of England divines who were godly and able men. He wrote, "The episcopal charities, the sermons, and other publications of the period, afford ample proof that, in the pulpits of the Church of England especially, there were a considerable number of not only able and learned, but thoroughly earnest and godly men."[14]

---

10. Whitefield, *George Whitefield's Journals*, 429. He is referring primarily to Bishop Gilbert Burnet, whose 1699 exposition of the Thirty-Nine Articles of Religion alleged that they were open to interpretation from both the Reformed and Arminian sides.

11. Whitefield, "The Folly and Danger of Not Being Righteous Enough" in *The Sermons of George Whitefield*, ed. Lee Gatiss, 1:176.

12. Gatiss, "George Whitefield: The Anglican Evangelist," *Southern Baptist Journal of Theology* 18. 2, 72.

13. Jackson, *The Centenary of Wesleyan Methodism: A Brief Sketch of the Rise, Progress, and Present State of the Wesleyan Methodist Societies Throughout the World*, 10. Jackson (1783–1873) was an English Wesleyan minister and writer who acted as chair of divinity of the Richmond Theological College and president of the Methodist Conference during the mid-nineteenth century.

14. Tyerman, *Life of Whitefield*, 1.65.

Morally, the country was becoming increasingly decadent. Drunkenness was rampant; gambling was so extensive that one historian described England as "one vast casino." Arnold Dallimore cites Lady Mary Wortley Montagu, a member of high society, who said, "To be styled a rake is now as genteel in a woman as in a man," and, "There are now more atheists among genteel women than men." She also joked that Parliament was "preparing a bill to have *not* taken out of the *Commandments* and inserted in the *Creed*."[15] Newspapers advertised such things as the services of gigolos and cures for venereal disease, and one could purchase guidebooks to the numerous brothels in London.[16] It was, as a recent writer has put it well, "an age when atheism was fashionable, sexual morals lax, and drinking and gambling at a pitch of profligacy that have never since been equaled."[17]

Life for the eighteenth-century working class was hard. The poor were abused and left without resources. Newborns were exposed in the streets; 97 percent of the infant poor in the workhouses died as children. Bearbaiting and cockfighting were accepted sports, and tickets were sold to public executions as to a theater. The slave trade brought material gain to many while further degrading their souls.[18] William Hogarth's pictures,[19] far from being caricatures, are realistic glimpses of the country's plight. William Lecky (1838–1903), a writer for the theatre and historian, defined the national gin drinker's drunkenness as the "master curse of English life between 1720–750."[20]

However, several institutions and many concerned individuals, probably thousands, stepped into this moral void. Arnold Dallimore mentions the small groups under the ministry of Anthony Horneck, a London minister, that met for weekly Bible study. These groups proliferated so that by 1730 nearly one hundred of these societies existed in London alone. These societies, along with the Moravian example, formed a basis later for John Wesley's small Bible studies. Hospitals were established; John Oglethorpe

---

15. Dallimore, *George Whitefield*, 1:28.

16. Porter, *English Society in the Eighteenth Century*, 279.

17. Hastings, "A Peeress with a Passion for Piety," *Sunday Telegraph*, December 14, 1997, cited in Haykin, "The Christian Life in the Thought of George Whitefield," *Southern Baptist Journal of Theology*, 18:2, 8.

18. Severance, "Evangelical Revival in England," para. 2. Christianity.com, May 3, 2010

19. Hogarth (1697–1764) was a famous English painter, engraver, pictorial satirist, social critic, editorial cartoonist, and occasional writer on art.

20. Drew, "England before and after Wesley," 3.

studied conditions in England's prisons; legislation was enacted against the gin craze, which threatened to overwhelm the working class;[21] Queen Anne established several charity schools; a Society for the Reformation of Manners, made up of concerned citizens, scouted out cases of immorality and blasphemy and reported in 1735 that they had prosecuted almost one hundred thousand cases of debauchery and profaneness in London and Westminster; the Society for Promoting Christian Knowledge provided Christian literature among the common folk. This organization did much good and contributed toward the Evangelical Revival.[22]

Still, wonderful efforts as they were, England's slide into base mediocrity was so rapid that conditions worsened instead of improved. It was into this moral anarchy that a group of men emerged under the enablement of the Spirit of God to awaken the slumbering nation. These men were fully aware of the current malaise. Moreover, they were given insight into the root cause of it. Their own experience as Christians and their theological understanding gave them the clarity to diagnose what had gone wrong. With these convictions men such as Whitefield and the Wesleys were constrained to do the Lord's work.

Declension in New England

In New England, too, preachers such as Jonathan Edwards realized that the people did not share their perspective nor their self-awareness generally. The prevailing tendency leaned in the opposite direction. Edwards's sermons and papers reveal a growing disregard among New Englanders for the tenets the colonial fathers had lived by. The protracted personal distress experienced by Edwards, according to his diary, was a far cry from the optimism with which much of New England viewed itself. In his polemic on original sin, Edwards made a general statement: "This land was a noble vine, but how is the gold become dim! How greatly have we forsaken the pious example of our fathers!"[23] In an exhortation at Northampton to plead for "that blessed effusion of God's Spirit," he felt need to remind

---

21. Fielding, speaking as a London magistrate, said concerning the Gin Craze, "Should the drinking of this poison be continued at its present height during the next twenty years, there will, by that time, be very few of the common people left to drink it," cited in Dallimore, *George Whitefield*, 1:28.

22. Dallimore, *George Whitefield*, 1:29–31.

23. Edwards, "The Great Christian Doctrine of Original Sin Defended," Yale 3:198.

his congregation of the increasing "decay of vital piety, and the exceeding prevalence of infidelity, heresy, and all manner vice and wickedness" and of the "lamentable moral and religious state of these American colonies! Of New England in particular! How much is that kind of religion which was professed, much experienced, and practiced, in the first and apparently the best times in New England grown and growing out of credit!"[24] Samuel Willard (1640–1707) of Boston's Third Church had bemoaned the situation: "How few thorough Conversions are to be observed? How scarce and seldom.... Yea, were men but pricked at their hearts, they would cry out for help and direction, and we should hear of them.... If men take a great deal of delight in the means of Grace, and yet can be content without settling a saving interest in Christ who is presented and offered to them therein, it saith that they are seeded on a form without the power."[25]

The Puritan minister Increase Mather, recalling the early part of the century, said, "Clear, sound conversions, are not frequent in our congregations; the great bulk of the present generation are ... perishing.... Many are profane, drunkards, lascivious, scoffers at the power of godliness, and disobedient; others are civil outwardly, conformed to good order, but without knowing aught of a real change of heart."[26]

New England was losing its sense of sin and had disowned its religious heritage, both in profession and in practice. To grasp something of the astonishment that was generated when preachers such as Edwards and Whitefield appeared on the scene, and to provide some perspective as to the role of these preachers, it is useful to explore the extent to which New Englanders had become "dull" and "decayed" and were following in the steps of the mother country. We will trace briefly the effects of the Half-Way Covenant, of Stoddardianism, of rumors of Arminianism and deism, of legalism and dead orthodoxy, and of the encroachments of the "world."

---

24. Edwards, 2:293.

25. Willard, "The Peril of the Times Displayed", 88–117, cited in Bushman, ed., *The Great Awakening*. Samuel Willard (1640–1707) was a New England clergyman, Harvard graduate, and minister at Groton and then Third Church, Boston. He opposed the Salem Witch Trials, was acting president of Harvard from 1701, and published many sermons. His *A Compleat Body of Divinity* was published after his death in 1726.

26. Mather, writing toward the end of the 17th century; quoted in MacFarlan, *The Revivals of the Eighteenth Century*, 12. MacFarlan was minister at Renfrew.

An Attempted Solution: The Half-Way Covenant

The ideals of the Puritan fathers of New England soon began to fade. They had aspired to establish a "holy commonwealth" that existed in a national covenantal relation with the Lord. But the children and grandchildren of the settlers, on average, lacked the vision and piety of their forebears. The colonies had become large and prosperous by virtue of dedication, hard work, and the presence of abundant resources. Successive generations felt increasingly complacent and content with the wealth they had carved out of the American wilderness. Simultaneous with this increase in wealth was a marked decline in dependency on the Lord of New England.

Puritan churchgoers were zealous for the Lord and committed to the establishment of the ideals that had been brought to New England. But by the second generation that was beginning to fray. Falling short in this requirement meant denial of the benefits and responsibilities of full membership. Significantly, it meant their children, in turn, would be deprived of becoming members.[27] To counter the downgrade, church leaders dug in their heels. The *Cambridge Platform 1648*, a combined statement of church polity, had insisted that those who wanted to be admitted to the Lord's Supper would need to make a credible and public profession of faith that included a satisfactory account of their conversion. Moreover, only infants of parents who were in full communion were eligible for baptism. Since there were many who could not meet these requirements, a large part of the community was deprived of church membership. Nevertheless, all were required to support the institution of the church financially. Since church membership was inextricably connected to citizenship, those who lacked church privileges also were deprived of civil rights. One had to be a member in good standing of a recognized local church in order to be eligible to vote or hold public office.

A mere thirty years after the original settlers had disembarked from the *Mayflower*, trouble started. A large and vocal minority became understandably grieved with the arrangement, and by the late 1650s controversy raged among the clergy as to the terms of admission. Indeed, church membership had begun to decline after 1650. Kenneth Lockridge, in his study of the congregation in Dedham, Massachusetts, found that between 1654 and 1661, only about 40 percent of infants were baptized. In the eight

---

27. The outline of events leading to the adoption of the Half-Way Covenant is taken largely from Hudson, *Religion in America*, 39–141, and Newman, *A Manual of Church History*, 2:668.

years prior to 1662, when the Half-Way Covenant (explained below) was adopted, only eight persons were admitted to full membership, so that by 1661 only 56 percent of male taxpayers were members of the church. Nonmembers would soon outnumber members.[28]

The clergy found what was hailed as a great solution to the quandary. In 1662 a large council was convened, and it adopted what has been called the Half-Way Covenant. The "solution" read as follows:

> Church members who were admitted in minority, understanding the doctrines of faith, and publickly professing their assent thereto, not scandalous in life, and solemnly owning the covenant before the church, wherein they give up themselves and their children to the Lord and subject themselves to the government of Christ, their children are to be baptized.[29]

Under this scheme the privilege of baptism was extended to the children of parents who were orthodox in outlook, were baptized themselves, and lived moral lives but who were unregenerate and did not qualify for the Lord's Supper. The Half-Way Covenant, while not a sign of declension in itself, did mark the end of an exclusive regenerate membership and was an acknowledgment of the decline of vital piety. The New England churches had mitigated the immediate problem but had compromised the rigorous nature of Puritan ideals.

However, in practice the Half-Way Covenant was controversial and in fact proved counterproductive. Rather than an increase in church membership and a higher degree of concern for personal salvation, what followed was a visible continuation of the decline in matters of the heart. Most "halfway" members were satisfied with merely owning the covenant, and very few made any effort to "achieve the true blessing that would admit them to full communion."[30] A large segment of the clergy bewailed the declension and met in a Reforming Synod in 1679 to plan a strategy for change. The diagnosis was dismal: "imprecations in ordinary discourse, in temperance,

---

28. Lockridge, "History of a Puritan Church: 1637–1736," in *Puritan New England*, Vaughan and Bremer, 97–98.

29. "Propositions concerning the subject of baptism and consociation of churches, collected and confirmed out of the word of God, by a synod of elders and messengers of the churches in Massachusetts-Colony in New England assembled at Boston, 1662," in *Source book and Bibliographical Guide*, Mode, 84.

30. Wright, *The Beginnings of Unitarianism in America*, 13.

want of truth and promise breaking," and so on.[31] To the clergy these were indications of a loss of a sense of sin. The synod had little appreciable effect on the state of affairs, however, and ministers continued in public and private lament until the outbreak of the Great Awakening. Joseph Haroutunian, in a groundbreaking work written in the 1960s, provides a sampling of the unusual earnestness of preachers during this time:

> O Alas! Alas! Are there not many and great impieties to be found in our land? Is not God Himself too much neglected, and our Loyalty to Him forgotten, the guise of many His Professors? Is not His most Dreadful and Sacred Name greatly Dishonored. . . . Is forgetting the Assembling of themselves together, by a Contempt cast upon the plain Ordinances? O then! Let the secure World, drowned in its sensual Pleasures; and such into a deep Sleep of carnal Security; that flatter themselves by saying, The evil Day is afar off; awake out of sleep . . .![32]

Some innovating pastors, keenly aware of the widespread indifference characterizing churchgoers, went far beyond the provisions laid out in the Half-Way Covenant solution.

Solomon Stoddard's "Solution"

One such innovation, however well meant, proved devastating to the New England congregational form of church government. In Northampton, Solomon Stoddard, grandfather to Jonathan Edwards and a pious minister, devised a method whereby respectable and moral but unregenerate folk could partake of the communion table. In a radical departure from the status quo, he invited all those who desired to live a better life and who possessed an interest in the new birth to the Lord's Supper. In 1700 he openly stated and defended this modification: "They may and ought to come though they know themselves to be in a natural condition; this ordinance is instituted for all adult members of the church who are not scandalous." The communion table had to be open to them for the same reason that no man ought to "neglect prayer, or hearing the Word because he cannot do it in faith, so he must not neglect the Lord's Supper."

The sacrament had become a converting ordinance, a means of grace for the unconverted. The venerable Increase Mather, in his *Order of the*

---

31. Mode, *Source Book*, 85–87.
32. Haroutunian, *Piety Versus Moralism*, 3, 5.

Gospel (1700), defended the orthodox position and criticized Stoddard's invention.[33] Refusing to be moved, however, Stoddard rebounded in 1709 with further elaboration of his theory.

> The ordinance has a proper tendency in its own to convert men. Herein men may learn the necessity and sufficiency of the death of Christ in order to Pardon. Here is an affecting offer of Christ crucified; here is a sealing of the Covenant, that if men come to Christ, they shall be saved, which is the great means to convince of safety in coming to Christ. All ordinances are for the saving good of those that they area to be administered unto. This Ordinance is according to the institution to be applied to visible Saints, though Unconverted, therefore it is for their saving good and consequently for their conversion.[34]

In this way Stoddard was trying to obviate the excuse, popular at the time, that since they were unregenerate and unqualified to partake of the Lord's Supper and therefore merely "half-way" members, they were reluctant to support, let alone attend, church services. Large numbers of people remained lax in church attendance in order to pursue worldly concerns, sometimes pretending they were unworthy of the privileges of real saints. By rendering the Lord's Supper a converting ordinance, Stoddard at least invalidated these excuses.[35]

Despite efforts of men like the Mathers, Stoddardeanism spread quickly throughout New England. Especially the Connecticut River Valley was affected, since it was here that Stoddard, the "Pope of the West," as he was known, held sway. The younger clergy in the wealthier churches welcomed an opportunity for change. The Connecticut historian Benjamin Trumbull (1735–1820) wrote, "Spiritual dearth increased, revivals were

---

33. Lest Stoddard be cast in an unfavorable light excessively we note that his concerns were the same concerns as those who opposed his invention. For example, he decried the generally lamentable condition of the clergy in New England and gave straightforward instruction regarding the preaching. In his "Defects of Preaching Reproved, 1723," he rebuked his fellow clergy for intellectualizing the gospel, using the learned Pharisees and Sadducees as examples. He added, "If any be taught that Humiliation is not necessary before Faith, that is not good preaching...Moreover, "When Men don't Preach much about the danger of Damnation, there is want of good Preaching." This was the reason, said Stoddard, why there is "so little conversion," cited in Bushman *Great Awakening,* 11–15.

34. Stoddard, "Inexcusableness of Neglecting the Worship of God," quoted in Schneider *Puritan Mind*, 91.

35. For an account of the antecedents of the Stoddardean controversy, see Hollifield, "The Intellectual Sources of Stoddardeanism," *New England Quarterly* 45, 3:373-93.

uncommon, immorality grew apace, and the state of religion went lower and lower." He reported that a large proportion of the clergy "at that time were of the opinion that unregenerate men, if externally moral, ought to be admitted to all the ordinances."[36] Perry Miller cites a concerned preacher of Westfield, Connecticut, Edward Taylor, who expressed his burden:

> Into ye Realm of Prelates arch, ye place
> Where open Sinners vile unmask indeed
> Are Welcome Guests, if they can say ye Creed
> Unto Christ's Table[37]

What appeared so devastating to the "New England Way" was that the strict dichotomy, maintained up to that period, between the regenerate and the unconverted had been abandoned. Now it was but a small thing to be a member of a church. People could take part in the full range of membership benefits as they pleased and sit contentedly in an unconverted state. By urging the unregenerate to participate in the sacrament, Solomon Stoddard had broken down an important institutional distinction, and when this new practice was widely accepted, the distinction was blurred in the minds of the people as well. The church, instead of calling the broken and the sinful out of the world, was instead becoming increasingly conformed to it.

Several of the clergy of the Connecticut Valley followed Stoddard's lead and accepted this modification if for no other reason than because it somehow compensated for the decline in membership numbers. An increase in communicant numbers soothed and heartened a dejected clergyman who, often without realization, began to adjust his preaching to suit. Sometimes preaching would take on what Calvinist preachers deemed an Arminian quality, which emphasized morality and virtue as a sign of grace rather than insisting on a supernatural change, known as the new birth. Trumbull related that "many of the clergy, instead of clearly preaching the doctrines of original sin, of regeneration, of justification by faith alone, and the other peculiar doctrines of the gospel, contented themselves with preaching cold, unprincipled and lifeless morality . . . for when distinctions were made between the morality of Christians and the morality of heathens, they were offended, and became violent opposers."[38] As they succumbed to the new reality, church leaders allowed members to relax

---

36. Trumbull, *A Complete History of Connecticut*, 2:137, 146.
37. Miller, *Colony to Province*, 240.
38. Trumbull, *Complete History of Connecticut*, 2:137.

into a state of "carnal security." The pressure to seek personal salvation was replaced by lukewarm affirmation of good citizenship and good morals. Calls to repentance and faith were more infrequent, although it must be said that Stoddard himself did not drift in this direction. Joseph Tracy, an early Connecticut historian, commented, "Church discipline was neglected, and the growing laxness of morals was invading the churches. And yet never, perhaps, had the expectation of reaching heaven at last been more general, or more confident.... The hold of the truth on the consciences of men was sadly diminished."[39]

The evidence was clear. It became difficult for any well-meaning clergyman to prevent a slide into mediocrity. Churches gave the nod to a lifeless morality as a way of attaining salvation. The doctrines of grace were compromised. Confirmation of the regenerative work of the Holy Spirit was simply a well-ordered lifestyle. Good citizenship was synonymous with sainthood. It was against these long developments that Whitefield, Edwards, and a host of others set their face.[40]

Encroaching Arminianism, Deism, and Unitarianism

The decline bemoaned by the orthodox clergy was being fueled from another direction. The intellectuals of the East had defected to some form of Arminianism. It should be noted that this was wholly different from the popular optimistic notions regarding human nature that arose from a grassroots American self-reliance. No articulated theology was involved with that. As one writer expresses it, the popular optimism, rather than having any intellectual base, was rather "a native variety of human self-sufficiency which expressed itself still within the forms of covenant theology."[41] Nevertheless, some of the intellectuals in New England were beginning to expound an Arminian outlook.

---

39. Tracy, *The Great Awakening*, 7.

40. Interestingly, in one of Edwards's final efforts to call his people away from their Stoddardean inclinations, he questioned not only the ideas and practices of his grandfather and predecessor at Northampton but also its antecedent, the Half-Way Covenant. After a bitter controversy during 1748 and 1749, Edwards was released from his charge. See Edwards, "Humble Inquiry into the Rules of the Word of God, Concerning the Qualifications Requisite to a Complete Standing and Full Communion in the Visible Church," 1:431.

41. Schaefer, "Jonathan Edwards and Justification by Faith," *Church History* 20, #4, 55.

Since the days of Archbishop of Canterbury William Laud (1573–1645) in England, and especially since the Great Ejection of Charles II in 1662, when thousands of Puritan pastors were released from their ministry, the Church of England had exchanged its Calvinist orientation for a mildly Arminian theology. New England ministers and professors read many books and journals imported from England, so that in 1722 a group of tutors at Yale, including the president, made public their conformity to the new orientation, abandoned the Congregational Way, and joined the Anglican Church. Samuel Johnson (1696-1772), also a defector, had for a long time criticized the Puritan heritage as a "curious cobweb of distributions and definitions."[42]

Jonathan Edwards and several other students left Yale in 1719 to go elsewhere. He wrote to his sister Mary, "I suppose you are fully acquainted with our coming away from New Haven, and the circumstances thereof. Since then we have been in a more prosperous condition.... But the council and trustees, having lately had a meeting at New Haven concerning it, have removed that which was the cause of our coming away, viz. Mr. Johnson from the place of tutor."[43] Although Johnson denied his defection, he did admit that the Church of England had followed Laudian Arminianism on many points.

The orthodox reaction was quick. A minister reported to Cotton Mather, "I hear some in Connecticut complain that Arminian books are cried up at Yale College for eloquence and learning, and Calvinists despised for the contrary!"[44] While several English publications promoting the Reformed doctrines of the grace appeared in New England during the 1720s, Thomas Emlyn, John Taylor,[45] Daniel Whitby, and a host of others with Arminian leanings were widely read. Some of these "discharged a Unitarian leaven." The New England pastor Experience Mayhew claimed to be a Calvinist but admitted reading Arminian books and said he had been led to see that "Calvinism labors under some difficulty."[46]

Orthodox evangelical preaching began to defend the doctrines of the Reformation. However, the drift into a relaxed, optimistic view of human nature continued. Veteran preacher John White complained that even

---

42. Samuel Johnson, quoted in Ahlstrom, *A Religion of the American People*, 1:364.
43. Edwards, "Letter to Miss Mary Edwards at Northampton" in *Memoirs*, 1:xvii.
44. Quoted in Wright, *Beginnings of Unitarianism*, 19.
45. Taylor's writing provided the catalyst for Edwards's great defence of original sin.
46. Boardman, *A History of New England Theology*, 25, 30.

"some of our young men cast a favorable Eye upon, embrace, and as far as they dare, argue for, propagate and preach the Arminian Scheme."[47] Trumbull later related how "every measure appears to have been taken to suppress the zealous, experimental preachers . . . by leaders among the clergy. Numbers of them were Arminian. . . . Experimental religion, and zeal, and engagedness in preaching, and in serving God, were termed enthusiasm."[48]

New England's churches seemed to be sliding into a bland form of piety that, on the one hand, was rooted in the practice of the Half-Way Covenant and Stoddardeanism and, on the other, arose from the attraction of younger pastors to Arminianism, deism and Unitarianism. To the orthodox clergy it seemed that New England was losing something vital. Broadly speaking, it was losing a sense of sin.

Petty Wrangling and Legalism

There were still other problems. The clergy who clung to orthodoxy were not all of one mind. Some overreacted and corrupted their Calvinism by preaching on the inability of humans to contribute toward their own salvation to such extremes that congregations became either terribly discouraged or numb with indifference. This dried-out, scholasticized Calvinism tended toward fatalism rather than the biblical gospel and was so unbalanced toward the doctrine of election that it forgot about the well-meant offer of grace and about human responsibility under the covenant. Dead orthodoxy bred legalism. Having lost sight of the vitality of biblical theology they presented a one-sided gospel and gave up on the spirit of vital piety. Consequently, several of these churches spiraled into dogmatic and petty wrangling.

Take the example of Mendon, Massachusetts where from 1727 to 1731 fifteen congregational meetings argued about the location of the new church building. When the new building was finally started, the losing party chopped it down at night. A battle raged for another ten years before it was finally decided to split the congregation between the two factions.[49] Generally, the colonial churches also clung to the extremely rigid form of discipline inherited from their predecessors. Countless meetings were held for the purpose of deciding what punishment best suited a particularly

---

47. White, quoted in Wright, *Beginnings of Unitarianism*, 21.
48. Trumbull, *History of Connecticut*, 1:176.
49. Parkes, "New England in the Seventeen-Thirties," 409.

minor misdeed. For example, at Columbia, eight pages of the church records and four congregational meetings were devoted to the problem of whether or not a boy named Timothy Hutchinson had laughed during a church service. As it happened, he owned a horse that made odd noises and was therefore nicknamed Old Groan. Timothy had taken his girlfriend for rides on this horse. When the preacher began to speak about horses in the Old Testament that had groaned under the burden of their wicked riders, Timothy exchanged glances with his young lady, whereupon he covered his face with his handkerchief. Many witnesses emerged and put in the claim that "those parts of his face which had remained visible looked as though he were laughing."[50] Incidents such as this were not rare. Spirituality, church attendance and the practice of Christianity had lost their power, while stifling legalism and silliness filled the vacuum.

Society at Large

When we turn to society in general, we find an abundance of evidence that many New Englanders no longer viewed seriously the claims of God on their lives. The New England conscience was blunted by success. They had been so blessed with material resources and wealth that it was assumed the favor of God rested upon them. The slave trade is a case in point. None were more active in bringing captives from Africa as a means of labor than the businesses and homes of New England.[51]

Flagrant intemperance prevailed. By 1731 Boston alone produced 1.25 million gallons of rum for domestic consumption. Other towns did similarly, and what was not consumed at home was sold to slave traders who bartered it off for slaves in West Africa. During the 1730s there were 157 licensed drinking houses, with other, unlicensed saloons staying open for gambling all night. One-eighth of all the buildings in Boston were drinking houses.[52] Even deep in the interior of Massachusetts, in Jonathan Edwards's Northampton, the influence of alcohol was palpable. "It seemed to be a time of extraordinary dullness in religion. Licentiousness for some years greatly prevailed among the youth of the town; they were many of

---

50. Parkes, "New England in the Seventeen-Thirties," 409, 410.
51. Rosenthal, "Puritan Conscience and New England Slavery," *New England Quarterly*, 46. No. 3, 62–81.
52. Rosenthal, "Puritan Conscience," 62–81.

them very much addicted to night-walking, and frequenting the tavern and lewd practices."[53]

Edwards also bemoaned news from England that told of the poor state of religion there:

> Of this a most affecting account has lately been published in a pamphlet ... by which it seems that luxury, and wickedness of almost every kind, is well nigh come to the utmost extremity in the nation, and if vice should continue to prevail and increase for one generation more, as it has the generation past, it looks as though the nation could hardly continue in being, but must sink under the weight of its own corruption and wickedness.[54]

New Englanders did not receive these reports with any dismay, however. In fact, they had become a rather self-righteous people, relishing thoughts about the depravity of others. H. B. Parkes relates how they were "tickled with stories of wicked debauchery, of London noblemen leading country girls astray."[55] They felt especially noble when they read that the inhabitants of Britain "may possibly have reason to think this country no safe abode and may find it necessary to seek a refuge in New England, where justice and industry, seem to have taken up their Residence!"[56]

Moreover, sexual mores in the cities and villages of New England caused some ministers to cringe, while others saw no harm in practices such as "bundling." Conception quite regularly preceded marriage, and many couples joined themselves in wedlock only to legitimize a coming child. This happened so frequently that several churches formally voted to desist from asking embarrassing questions about "seven-months children." Boston's rich merchants, totally immersed in the things of this world during the week, seldom failed to remember their societal obligation on the Sabbath. Invariably, they attended the Brattle Street meetinghouse to hear the sermon in order to set "an example of piety and decorum to the lower classes."[57]

---

53. Edwards, "Faithful Narrative," Yale 4:146.
54. Edwards, "Humble Attempt," 2:293.
55. Parkes, "New England in the Seventeen-Thirties," 399.
56. *Gentleman's Magazine of London*, quoted in Parkes, "New England in the Seventeen-Thirties," 399.
57. Parkes, "New England in the Seventeen-Thirties," 404.

Clergy Reaction

To the orthodox clergy this was painful to behold. The spirit of condescending self-flattery evident in the more prosperous areas of New England stood in diametrical contrast to the spirit of unpretentious humility that characterized genuine Christianity. They were aware that few traces of new vigor and growth existed even though the language, methods, forms, and discipline of an earlier age were retained.

Jonathan Edwards was aware that New Englanders did not share his self-awareness, by and large. Rather than dependence upon God's grace and providential care, New Englanders seemed to him to be ignoring what their colonist parents had lived by. In his polemic on original sin, Edwards makes a general statement: ". . .this land was a noble vine, but how is the gold become dim!"[58]

Independent reports from all over New England seemed to corroborate Edwards's analysis. The impression was conveyed to him that New England was losing true self-awareness and that the world into which the new evangelicals were emerging was beginning to pay increasing attention to the innate moral virtue already present in the industrious, enterprising American intellectual. Religious life was inclined away from the Calvinist consensus of an earlier time and was disposed to welcome encroaching liberalism, which was more positive about humanity's potential for excellence in morality. Moreover, conversions were a rarity and profound religious experience of the kind with which the likes of Edwards were familiar were seen not only as undesirable, but ridiculed as fanaticism. According to Edwards, conversions were a rarity, and genuine religious experience was regarded with distaste: "It seems to be despised, called enthusiasm, and fanaticism. Those who are truly religious are looked upon as beside their right mind; and vice and profaneness dreadfully prevail."[59] The world into which these preachers emerged was beginning to pay more attention to the innate goodness of humanity and to the moral virtue present in industrious, enterprising American life.

Indeed, soon after its founding, the Boston Brattle Street Church, says Edwin Gaustad, stopped the public testimony of religious experience because of recognition that there was little such experience to relate.[60] In

---

58. Edwards, "Humble Attempt," 2:293.
59. Edwards, "Humble Attempt," 2:293.
60. Gaustad, *The Great Awakening in New England*, 14.

many respects, sainthood was becoming synonymous with respectability, true religion with morality. Human sinfulness was seen not as a condition of the heart that required radical transformation but as acts of the social criminal. The great doctrines of Christianity provided little more than a cherished part of the religious heritage of New England and had little impact on the population. The civil man was filling the churches, especially of the Eastern Seaboard, and any adherence to experiential divinity was motivated by a symbolic reference to a cherished tradition. New England had lost its sense of sin.

5.

Hearts Stricken and Hearts Ablaze

> "God has always sent revival in the darkest days.
> Oh, for a mighty, sweeping revival today!"
>
> — ADRIAN ROGERS, (1931–2005)

PREACHING IN THE FIRST GREAT AWAKENING

Background: The Reformation and Puritanism

THE EARLY CHURCH WITNESSED the clarion voice of the biblical gospel. The apostles and the apostolic fathers, while at times immersed in important theological debate, preached with clarity for the edification of the church and the conviction of souls, with great success.[1] After the period known to history as the early church, the preaching of the gospel began to decline. After the Edict of Milan of 312, when Constantine gave official status to the Christian church, it became expedient for ambitious folk whose interest was career enhancement to join a church. The level of spirituality and the conviction of congregations languished. During the medieval age biblical preaching, obscured by the ever-growing primacy of the Mass and a

---

1. Estimates have suggested that by the time of the Edict of Milan (AD 312), there were at least 25 million Christians in the Mediterranean area.

sacramental system of salvation, had become a relic of a misty past. By the time of Martin Luther (1483–1546), but a smattering could expect to hear priestly sermons.[2]

The Reformation laid the axe to a corrupt papacy and to doctrinal positions that, to state it bluntly, did not find biblical support. The Reformers made the sermon the very focal point of the church's regular worship, moving the pulpit from the side to the architectural center. Today, we hail the Reformers as bright theologians who initiated a revolution in theology and a cataclysmic break with Rome. However, their primary task was expository preaching. The commentaries of John Calvin (1509–1564), some twenty-two volumes, are basically his sermons reworked for the printed page and have never lost their freshness.[3] Luther's sermons and lectures are contained in fifty-five volumes. There were many others like these two giants, all like-minded, all lovers of the Word. The young movement changed the heart of Europe. At one point Luther declared, "I have opposed the indulgences and all the papists, but never by force. I simply taught, preached, wrote God's Word; otherwise, I did nothing. And then while I slept, or drank Wittenberg beer with my Philip (Melancthon) . . ., the Word so greatly weakened the papacy that never a prince or emperor inflicted such damage upon it. I did nothing; the Word did it all."[4]

The leaders of the Reformation were primarily preachers of the Word. The Swiss Reformation really began in January of 1519 when Ulrich Zwingli (1484–1531), the first Reformed theologian and a predecessor of Calvin, announced from the pulpit of the Great Minster church in Zurich that rather than preach medieval scholastic subtleties, he would preach expository sermons through the Gospel of Matthew. When that series was completed, Zwingli began to preach through rest of the New Testament. A transformation of large proportions occurred as a result.[5] Folks in Zurich heard the

---

2. See Reeves, "What Role Did Expositional Preaching Play in the Reformation?" paras. 1–3.

3. Calvin's preaching and writing was, at bottom, so true to Scripture that it carried some of the spark of the inspiration of the inscripturated speech of God. This provides a rationale for the continued usefulness and freshness of Calvin's sixteenth-century writings, especially his commentaries. His preaching revolutionized Geneva, and his *Institutes of the Christian Religion* was used as an evangelistic and teaching tool throughout Protestant Europe. See Calvin, *Commentaries in Twenty-Two Volumes*; Calvin, *Institutes of the Christian Religion*.

4. Luther *Works Sermons I*," edited by Pelikan, Oswald, and Lehmann, 51:78.

5. Zwingli had organized an alliance of like-minded neighboring city-states and had enlisted in Zurich's army as a chaplain to encourage the troops in the battle against

unvarnished biblical truth for the first time. In Germany, starting in 1517, Luther preached the Bible expositionally twice on Sundays and usually three times during each week. With few interruptions, he continued until his death in 1546. In Geneva, Switzerland, Calvin spent much of his time preaching expository sermons every day of the week. In an arrangement with the Geneva city council in 1541 Calvin instituted his *Ecclesiastical Ordinances*, which included a listing of the main duties of pastors. Preaching was to take place twice on Sunday and once every other day of the week. The Word became basic to urban life in Geneva. Such was the trust and confidence in the Word that both Luther and Calvin began to teach others in pastoral skills and preaching, Luther at Wittenburg in Germany, Calvin at the Genevan Academy, which he had founded. Luminaries such as the Scottish Reformer John Knox and the English Protestants fleeing the wrath of England's Roman Catholic queen came to Geneva to receive their training there. Once Queen Mary[6] had died, the exiles returned and upended the English world (see also Acts 17:6) with the preached Word, as did Knox in Scotland.

The Reformation saw the start of a permanent division in Western Christendom. No longer was the church a great monolith controlled by a politically powerful papacy and driven by a sacramental system of salvation that did not place the Word front and center. The Protestants placed their trust in the Word of God, preaching became the primary means of grace, and an awakening to scriptural truth emerged as had not been seen since the time of the apostles. Because the Reformers emphasized the priesthood of all believers and denied the efficacy and authority of church-initiated grace, Europeans generally were sensible of an atmosphere of liberation.

In England a refinement of Reformation preaching materialized, and sermons took on a clearer soteriological bent. William Perkins (1558–1602) is by far the most important English Reformer of the sixteenth century. He is known for his lifelong attempt to bring together academic rigor with vital piety. Moreover, he was an eloquent preacher, very effective in the application of doctrines of Scripture. His scholasticism was less pronounced than that of several Continental Reformers that he valued, such as Calvin's successor, Theodor Beza (1519–1605), with whom he shared a high Reformed (i.e., "supralapsarian") approach to theology.

---

the Roman Catholic cantons nearby. He died on the battlefield in 1531.

6. Known by earlier historians as *Bloody Mary*.

Hearts Stricken and Hearts Ablaze

Perkins believed that faith was, first of all, knowledge, not necessarily an experience, which was imparted by the illumination of the Holy Spirit. But this knowledge brought about feelings such as a deep sense of sin and a felt need for the embrace of the gospel. A sense of spiritual poverty, for Perkins, necessarily preceded any degree of assurance of faith, although he admitted that faith could be genuinely present without assurance. Perkins's preaching carried a sharp edge, especially during his early years, as reported by Thomas Fuller (1608–1661).[7] He used to pronounce the word "damn" so ominously that his audience would be left with a "doleful echo" for a long while afterward. As a lecturer at Christ College at Cambridge, he emphasized conviction of sin to his students so powerfully that they nearly fainted from their sense of unworthiness. This, to Perkins, was a necessary stage in the process of conversion.[8] Perkins's works enjoyed wide influence, and his particular concerns regarding salvation doctrine were disseminated far and wide. His writings were translated into many languages on the Continent. In England he was considered the patriarch of a succession of Cambridge teachers whose vision was to inculcate a "visible reformation of the heart" in the hopes of transforming the Church of England.[9] This succession included men such as Richard Sibbes and John Preston. Perkins, along with his famous student William Ames, was read by Dutch theologians such as Gisbertus Voetsius and Willem Teellinck and through them had a great impact on the so-called Second Reformation there.[10]

Even earlier, William Tyndale (1494–1536), known for his translation of the Bible into English from the original text as well as from Erasmus's

---

7. Fuller is known for his *Worthies of England*, published in 1662 after his death.

8. Blacketer, "William Perkins (1558–1602)" in Lindberg, ed. *The Pietist Theologians*, 40–45.

9. It is worthy of note that William Perkins wrote the famous *A Golden Chaine* (1591) which scholasticized the soteriological process at the personal level. Much of subsequent evangelical theology, right up until the late 20th century was held in the grip of Perkins's *ordo salutis* (order of salvation) whereby for centuries the majority of pastors and teachers taught that conversion constitutes a demonstrable series of steps in chronological order. Of late this idea has finally been surpassed. Conversion is now regarded not as a series of chronological steps but as several concurrent strands of the conversion experience. For an account of this change, see Sinclair Ferguson's *The Holy Spirit*. See also Paul Helm's *Beginnings: Word & Spirit in Conversion*.

10. See Lindberg, *Pietist Theologians*, 48. Note that partially as a result of his reading of Voetsius and Teellinck, Great Awakening forerunner Theodor Frelinghuysen became convinced of the necessity of a sense of need before conversion.

Latin translation, was one of the earliest English Reformers.[11] In his prologue to the New Testament in 1525 he stated,

> Christ commanded the gospel to be preached . . . and therewith to give unto all that repent and believe His life wherewith He swallowed and devoured up death; His righteousness, wherewith He banished sin; His salvation, wherewith He overcame eternal damnation. Now can the wretched man that *knoweth himself to be wrapped in sin, and in danger to death and hell hear no more joyous a thing, than such glad and comfortable tidings of Christ.*[12]

It can be said that the earliest English Reformers were more sharply focused on the doctrine of salvation than were the Continental reformers. Tyndale is a good example. He emphasized that the law and the gospel should never be applied separately. People needed the law to make them realize their sin. But at the same time, they needed the promises of the gospel lest they despair. He spoke of those being deceived "which justify themselves with outward deeds" and also of the presumptuous who "without all fear of God give themselves unto all manner of vices with full consent and full delectation, having no respect to the law of God . . . but say, God is merciful, and Christ died for us."[13] Tyndale believed the Holy Spirit could bring about a great change in the hearts of hearers through the means of the preached Word.

This was the time of Thomas Cranmer, Hugh Latimer, Nicholas Ridley and John Hooper, who became martyrs for the faith under Queen Mary Tudor. It was a time when it cost to be a Christian; sometimes it cost people their very lives. Another martyr was John Bradford (d. 1555). Bradford's works reveal a sharpening of focus on soteriology among English preachers of the time. In a sermon on repentance, he defined repentance as "a sorrowing for our sins; a trust of pardon, which otherwise may be called a persuasion of God's mercy by the merits of Christ for the forgiveness of our sins; and, a purpose to amend, or conversion to a new life."[14] The famous Hugh Latimer (1487–1555) said this about the way of salvation: "This Faith

---

11. In 2002 the BBC ranked Tyndale twenty-sixth of the list of the one hundred historically most important Britons. See "100 Greatest Britons (BBC Poll, 2002)," in *Geni*, home of the world's largest family tree, accessed Oct. 26, 23.

12. Tyndale, *Prologue to the New Testament*, quoted in Murray, "The Preaching of the English Reformers," in *Preaching and Revival*, 5, emphasis added.

13. Tyndale, *Prologue to the New Testament*, 6.

14. Bradford, *Writings*, 1:45.

is a great state, a lady, a duchess, a great woman; and she hath ever a great company and train about her as a noble estate ought to have. First, she hath a gentleman usher that goeth before her and where he is not there is not lady Faith. This gentleman usher is called knowledge of sin."[15]

The Reformers and, later, the Puritan pastors operated under one of two assumptions in their application of biblical doctrine. Either conviction of sin was an indispensable first stage in the conversion experience, a stage that must be undergone before the application of God's saving grace, or as John Howe would have it, conviction was one of several strands running concurrently through the conversion process itself. In either case, however, conversion displayed a turning from indifference to sin toward self-knowledge and a surrender to the claims of God. For the Puritan, no such surrender could take place without the person being convinced that he or she was a sinner, hence the emphasis on this theme.

More broadly speaking, the Puritans elevated the sermon to be the most effective means of grace, partly in reaction to the sophistication and eloquence of the English baroque style of preaching employed by such great lights as John Donne and Lancelot Andrewes, both Anglican divines of the late sixteenth century. Preaching that followed the Church of England's 1552 Book of Common Prayer, with its insistence on prioritizing the Bible, raised the level of preaching to a more direct style. Preachers like Nicholas Ridley, the martyr, are typical of this phase. But it was left to the Puritans to concentrate on making the sermon the foremost part of a church service. They moved the pulpit from the architectural side to the center, employed a sounding board for better voice projection, and used a pulpit Bible. The Word of God became central. The Puritans' high view of the scriptures gave preaching a more expository aspect, and they endeavored to "rightly divide the word of truth."[16] John Owen, Richard Baxter, and Stephen Charnock are examples of this tradition as it existed in the seventeenth century.

The Evangelical Revival

In the eighteenth century the Puritan era was a thing of the past. But that century saw a renewed interest in many of the tenets held by the Puritans.

---

15. Latimer, "Sermons and Remains of Hugh Latimer" edited by Corrie for the Parker Society of London, 1845, quoted in Murray, *Preaching of the English Reformers*, 14.

16. Wesley, *The Works of John Wesley: Sermons 1–33*, 18–29. Outler ed.

With respect to the doctrine of sin, the evangelists of the Evangelical Revival and the Great Awakening stood on the heritage passed on from their Puritan forebears, and the preaching of men such as August Francke, John Wesley, George Whitefield, Theodor Frelinghuysen, Gilbert and John Tennent, and Jonathan Edwards are but a few of the hundreds of preachers with similar convictions. It can be argued that this doctrine received even heavier emphasis during the great revival period than it had during the previous century when Puritanism was at its most influential. Indeed, fostering conviction became one of the hallmarks of eighteenth-century revival preaching.

The doctrine of the new birth was central in the theology of the evangelicals, and the congregational pastor or itinerant evangelist stood up to preach assuming some or many—often most—auditors to be in an unregenerate state. And while the seventeenth-century Puritan sermonic diet was periodically sprinkled with references to the need for a sense of sin, the focus of the eighteenth-century evangelist was much sharper. Often used as a homiletic device to foster a spiritual need for salvation, it had a profound effect on slumbering congregations. "Law preaching," as it was called, usually received its due before Christ was offered in the gospel. Itinerant preachers were known to enter an area to hold services for successive days. Two or three of the first sermons preached would invariably contain a weighty emphasis on the guilt and corruption of the audience. Only subsequently did the invitation of the gospel find place in the sermon. This method, by varying degrees, became prevalent in the British Isles as well as in New England.

That the leaders of the revival of the eighteenth-century incorporated conviction of sin into their theology for preaching comes into view with remarkable regularity. Divergent as Pietists,[17] Calvinists, and Wesleyans were on several major points of dogma, the degree to which their minds converged on the doctrine of the new birth and specifically on the need for conviction is noteworthy. Accordingly, the sort of piety learned by congregants in Scotland was similar to the German or New England variety. Soteriology took on a strong experiential character, as it had among Puritans and the Reformers before them. Religion was not considered real unless it was of the personal sort. To the leaders of the movement, grace was not

---

17. Although one must account for the several variations within the Awakening (Lutheran, Reformed, and Wesleyan Methodist), most evangelical leaders of the period were influenced by the Pietist theologians.

a presumed reality for all who were churchgoing. Rather, it was a known, definable work of the Spirit of God, and it was the preacher's great ambition to learn discernment so he could act more ably as a spiritual mentor to individuals who needed encouragement. Sermons focussed on one or two aspects of the new birth and often concluded with urgent exhortations to examine oneself for sensible evidences of grace. The preacher's homiletical purpose usually included an attempt to foster a sense of sin.

In Scotland the Presbyterian Erskine brothers were typical on that point. Ebenezer (1680–1754) maintained, in a sermon entitled "God's Regard to Worthless Man," that the "hammer of the Law must be applied, in order to break the rocky heart in pieces; the fallow ground must be plowed up, to prepare it for the reception of the incorruptible seed of gospel truth." The obstinacy of the will had to be "bended by the almighty power of God, and he persuaded and enabled to embrace Christ and salvation through him, as he is freely offered in the gospel."[18]

German Pietism

The Pietist tradition of the Continent has been seen as originating with Philipp Jakob Spener (1636–1705), although there were precursors to the movement. Spener was a German Lutheran who, early in his life, observed the devotional laxity on the part of Luther's spiritual progeny. He received his doctorate at Strasbourg and by that time had read several of the English Puritans, including Richard Baxter. He accepted a call to be the senior minister at the Lutheran church of Frankfurt am Main and began to preach on the subjective application of the gospel. This was the era known as Lutheran Orthodoxy. While the typical Lutheran pastor of the time emphasized the objective truth, teaching the catechism and preaching the facts of faith with hardly any personal application, Spener's preaching pushed a step further, stressing the personal appropriation of the gospel and the new birth. His ministry included the formation of Bible-study groups or conventicles, a development he probably learned from Martin Bucer, whose Reformed theology was influential at Strasbourg.[19] For Spener, the new birth was essential. The fall into sin affected all humans with guilt and corruption. Seeking betterment was honorable but was futile as a point of merit, and a whole transformation was the only solution. The new birth was achieved

---

18. Erskine, *The Whole Works of the Late Ebenezer Erskine*, 2:137.
19. Brown, *Understanding Pietism*, 16.

by the reception of grace, the effects of which included remorse and godly sorrow for sin. Justification was the outcome, and a life of holiness the fruit. Spener highlighted the priority of a vital relationship with God over against the cold orthodoxy that characterized the Protestant church in Germany and elsewhere and so became the founder of Pietism.

August Francke (1663–1727), a Lutheran pastor and biblical scholar, was one of the early coleaders of that movement. It was one of the Bible-study groups led by Spener that provided the setting for Francke's conversion. Due to his prominence as leader, some of the features of his conversion became a paradigm for a part of the Pietist movement, to some extent due to his own encouragement.

In Francke's teaching, the necessity of a sense of sin received emphasis. Of great importance in his conversion was the *Busskampf*, or penitential struggle, which preceded *Bekehrung*, or conversion. His own testimony reveals the intensity of this struggle: "I now realized earnestly that I found not in myself such faith as I would set forth in the sermon. This weighed on me heavily.... I plunged deeper into unrest and doubt.... This misery caused many tears to come to the eyes. In great anxiety I threw myself on my knees and cried once again to God."[20] During *Busskampf* persons became acutely aware of their innate sinfulness and the need to call upon the Lord for the application of his mercy. Francke's preaching made intentional application of *Busskampf*. In a sermon on David's penitential Psalm 51, he admonished his audience, "But you who have heard this, what is the condition of your hearts? What do you say to this? Have you also experienced such a *Busskampf* in your hearts?"[21] In Francke's order of salvation there were several stages, after which a *Durchbruch*, or breakthrough, occurred, when one received relief and assurance of pardon. The point here, however, is that the penitential struggle became integral to Pietist soteriology.

Not all agreed with this construct and occasionally the stress on conviction as preparatory to conversion created tension in the movement. For example, Count Nikolaus von Zinzendorf (1700–1760), who was a fully committed Christian, loved Jesus, and provided haven for the refugee Moravians,[22] had not experienced *Busskampf* with the same intensity and was therefore considered suspect.

---

20. Francke, quoted in Olson and Winn, *Reclaiming Pietism*, 52.
21. Strom, *German Pietism and the Problem of Conversion*, 44.
22. discussed in chap. 6.

But Zinzendorf responded with criticism of the need for conviction of sin as a prerequisite to conversion. To him *Busskampf* could be brought on by oneself and earned by confession and penance. Hence, he said, the whole process could be turned into legalism and works righteousness. He claimed this was Francke's great mistake. In turn, his detractors defended Francke, charging Zinzendorf with antinomianism, and this became a stress point within the movement. John Wesley (1703–1791) himself became acquainted with this tension later and found it concerning. In the main however, being able to identify penitential struggle in a person, as well as subsequent stages in conversion, became a bulwark against self-deception.[23] In fact, Francke advised preachers to ask of converts "if they have had a lively and affecting Sense of the Corruption of their own Hearts, and of the Misery of the natural State." Philip Spener believed equally that ministers should strive to convince their hearers of moral failure: "A minister not only instructs his Hearers what they must do and how they ought to act, but he labors fully to apprise and to convince them, by the Evidence of Scripture, of their own native Weakness and Impotency for all that is Spiritually good."[24]

Francke's influence was widespread. His writings helped shape the piety of the Dissenters in England. Philip Doddridge and Isaac Watts owed him much. Early Methodism owed a great deal to Francke's influence. Cotton Mather of New England considered him a man of "most shining Piety."[25] Theodor Frelinghuysen[26] owed his Pietistic bent partly to Francke.

During the revival period, although there was continuity between the earlier Puritans and the leaders of the Evangelical Revival with respect to this particular emphasis, there was also change. The direct and determined appeal to the emotions was something new. Under Puritanism, preaching was largely didactic, and pastors generally subordinated the emotions to the intellect, believing the way to the heart was through the mind. People came away from the sermon with a variety of theological constructs settling into their minds. But the preachers leading up to and during the mid-seventeenth century, by contrast, took a different approach.

---

23. Strom, *German Pietism*, 65.
24. Francke and Spener, quoted in Brown, *Understanding Pietism*, 77.
25. Kidd, *The Great Awakening*, 27.
26. discussed in chap. 6.

Awakening in New England

In the period before and during the Great Awakening, preaching was usually a sustained discourse on a single theme, and the homiletical purpose was as much to create an impression on the heart as it was to engage in theological instruction. To a greater or lesser extent, this was true generally of the Great Awakening preachers.

The preaching of Samuel Davies, a contemporary of Edwards and his successor as president of Princeton University after Edwards died, embraced similar themes. Charging his congregation on one occasion to take note of the incomparable nature of Christ in his saving work, he emphasized the point that none would look to Jesus unless they possessed a felt need of him: "When a guilty creature is effectually alarmed with just apprehensions of his danger; when he sees his numberless transgressions in all their horrid aggravations . . ., with what importunate cries will he betake himself to Him for relief!"[27]

Grandson of Jonathan Edwards, Timothy Dwight (1752–1817), president of Yale College for several years, wrote extensively on the new birth and assigned to conviction of sin the place of antecedence to regeneration. In distress the sinner searched for means of deliverance, turned finally to the gospel, and discovered peace in the atoning work of Christ. He "entirely needs thus to understand and feel his condition; his guilt, his danger, his hopelessness, and his absolute necessity of being renewed by the spirit of grace." Conviction, promoted by the preaching of the law, was therefore a "natural and necessary prerequisite to conversion."[28]

Ebenezer Pemberton, a Harvard graduate and a Presbyterian (1705–1777), preaching in a New York Presbyterian church from 1727 to 1753, was the only clergyman there to invite George Whitefield to preach from his pulpit. Their relationship continued, and Whitefield often returned to Pemberton's pulpit, drawing many from various neighboring churches. Pemberton spent the rest of his career in Boston's New Brick Church. He died in 1777. His theology of the usual pattern of salvation was identical to that of Whitefield, as a collection of his sermons reveals. In "The Method of Divine Grace in Conversion," sinners are "convinced of the deplorable misery of an unconverted estate . . . and they have an experimental taste of the bitterness of sin. The first work of the Spirit is to convince men of their

---

27. Davies, "Looking to Christ Opened and Explained," in *Sermons*, 2:259.
28. Dwight, *Theology Explained and Defended*, 3:384–94.

sins." Only then "Christ Jesus is proposed unto them as an almighty and compassionate Savior." Human nature is such that "sinners will never come to Christ if left to follow their own inclinations and desires . . ." and "to fly to the righteousness and atonement of our great Redeemer for justification and life requires a humble acknowledgement of our inability to help ourselves. This is contrary to the pride of man, so disagreeable to the appetites of flesh and blood, that degenerate nature will forever cry out, 'These are hard sayings, and who can hear them?'"[29] In his sermon entitled "The Nature and Necessity of Conviction," the first sentence reads, "Conviction of sin is the first step to conversion."[30]

John Wesley (1703-1791) had learned this idea from the German Pietists.[31] His preaching included sporadic emphases on conviction. His close friend, John Fletcher (1729-1785), himself an able theologian and preacher, incorporated the priority of a sense of sin into his work. In a sermon called "The State of the Natural Man," he began by stating, "The state of a true Christian is a state of peace, joy, love, and holiness; but before a man attains to it, he must go through a course of fear, anxiety, and repentance, whether long or short; for no one was ever cured in soul, by the great Physician, Jesus Christ, till he *felt himself sin sick*; especially that of a hard impenitent heart, which he could not himself break and soften." Later in the same sermon, he appealed to the self-interest of his audience: "O you who are in that condition, if I have showed you in some measure the state of your hearts, let me beseech you not to harden them. . . Rather *give place to conviction*. For Christ's sake, let conscience be heard."[32]

The congruency between the English Puritans, Continental Pietists, British Evangelicals, and New England preachers is remarkable. On the doctrine of salvation and its various stages, their application in preaching

---

29. Pemberton, "The Method of Divine Grace in Conversion" *Ebenezer Pemberton 1704-1777*, 37-46.

30. Pemberton, "The Nature and Necessity of Conviction" *Ebenezer Pemberton 1704-1777*, 131.

31. Dreyer, *The Genesis of Methodism*, 48-49. Dreyer was my thesis supervisor, and I am indebted to him for his insight. Where Methodism comes from is a disputed question in historical scholarship, and this small work makes a significant contribution. Essentially, Dreyer shows that Methodism relies more on Moravian or Lutheran Pietism than it does on Wesley's roots in Anglicanism.

32. Fletcher, "State of the Natural Man," in *Works*, 4:118, 124, emphasis added. John Fletcher (1729-1785) was Swiss born and of French Huguenot stock. He began to work with Wesley, becoming the main early interpreter of Wesleyan theology. He is Methodism's first great theologian.

was, for the most part, uniform, as the examples above have shown. Moreover, there was usually a close connection between the personal conversion experience of the preachers and the eventual outcome in their preaching.

We turn again to the unparalleled example of this in the case of Jonathan Edwards, whose diary and *Personal Narrative*, along with his analysis of the revival, reveal similar patterns.

The Preaching of Jonathan Edwards

It is, of course, most likely that Edwards would have preached just as he did even if there had been no decay in piety during his time. Edwards's own theological conviction and study were enough to undergird his sermon preparation, independent of what he observed in the social milieu. However, the malaise that he did observe gave him an occasion to press the point home with greater vigor.

In his attempt to restore conviction and dependence of the sovereign grace of God, Edwards found that sermons containing an imprecatory element in them were the most useful. Of a series preached, called "The Five Discourses...," the one that had the most effect on his hearers was entitled "The Justice of God in the Damnation of Sinners."[33] Edwards himself attests to the effectiveness of this sermon: "I have never found so much immediate saving fruit, in any measure, of any discourse I have offered to my congregation as some from these words, Rom. 3:19, 'That every mouth may be stopped,' endeavoring to show from thence that it would be just with God forever to reject and cast off mere natural man."[34]

It was partly for this reason that the horror of alienation from the Creator God and the eternal destiny of unrepentant sinners were topics to which he often returned throughout his ministry. Edwards defended his homiletical methods. To those who accused him of using scare tactics, he answered, "Some talk of it as an unreasonable thing to fright persons to heaven; but I think it is a reasonable thing to fright persons away from hell. They stand upon its brink, and are just ready to fall into it." But he rebuked ministers who "preach of hell, and warned sinners to avoid it, in a cold manner.... They contradict themselves."[35]

---

33. Edwards, "The Justice of God in the Damnation of Sinners," *Works*, Yale, 19:339.

34. Edwards, "A Faithful Narrative of the Surprising Work of God in the Conversion of Many Hundred Souls in Northampton," *Works*, Yale, 4:168.

35. Edwards, "The Distinguishing Marks of a Work of the Spirit of God," *Works*,

However, he did not believe there ought to be an undue emphasis on the terror of the state of damnation. To him it was possible that a preacher could concentrate on this aspect of the truth excessively, thereby neglecting the gospel. Rather, imprecatory preaching was but a means to an end. Foundational to his revival theology was the idea that a sense of sin was basic to evangelical conversion. His imprecations were designed, in the first place, as a means of fostering conviction, leading to faith and thoroughgoing repentance under the blessing of the Holy Spirit. The second reason was that a gospel of a full and free salvation by the redeeming blood of Christ Jesus might be received more readily if congregants understood their need of it. Indeed, it was Edwards's belief that the main duty of a minister was to preach the gospel of Jesus Christ: "The law is to be preached only to make way for the Gospel, and in order to an effectual preaching of that. . . . A minister would miss it very much if he should insist so much on the terrors of the law, as to forget his end, and neglect to preach the gospel, but yet the law is very much to be insisted on, and the preaching of the gospel is like to be in vain without it."[36] In a sermon entitled "The True Excellency of a Gospel Minister," he warned against not preaching good tidings to the meek, "to bind up the broken-hearted . . . to comfort all that mourn: they are to lead those that labour and are heavy-laden to their Savior."[37]

Edwards, then, did not preach in order to terrify people, assertions to the contrary by several historians notwithstanding. It has been estimated that about one-third of his extant sermons have an imprecatory element in them.[38] The remaining sermons include such topics as the love of Christ, Christian charity, the joys to be experienced with respect to the knowledge of God, and many other uplifting aspects of Christian experience. Still, it was Edwards's efforts to instill a sense of sin that lay at the heart of his revival theology.

But it is on the question of imprecatory discourse that denunciation has been handed out by some of Edwards's interpreters. The leaders of the Great Awakening and Evangelical Revival have been dealt an unkindly assessment by historians, and while it is understandable coming from secular historians, there is a common thread worth noting. Usually, one comes away suspecting an element of embarrassment in the critique, as if what

---

Yale, 4:247–48.

36. Edwards, "Distinguishing Marks," 248.

37. Edwards, "The True Excellency of a Gospel Minister," *Works,* Yale, 25:92.

38. Simonson, *Jonathan Edwards: Theologian of the Heart,* 133.

leaders of the revival movement had to say was either too coarse and vulgar or too hopelessly inconceivable to take seriously. This prejudice has been a deterrent to clarity, and instead of shedding new light on the revival period, earlier historians restricted themselves, by and large, to conveying unease or even annoyance with their subject. Not until the mid-twentieth century was this overcome. This is perhaps the primary reason why, to countless freshmen studying American literature, the sermon "Sinners in the Hands of an Angry God" is all that Edwards ever did.

Writers have presented an intemperate picture. J. P. Thompson berated Edwards for literalizing the subject of future punishment and surrounding it with various "inquisitorial devices of torture."[39] The nineteenth-century historian Sir Leslie Stephen was particularly adept at setting him up as the vengeful Puritan clergyman. According to him, Edwards sentenced infants to hell, never shrinking "in cold blood from the most appalling of his theories."[40] Anyone who supposed Edwards to have been a gentle, meditative individual, Stephen said, was willfully naive. Stephen "would rather have supposed his solids to be of bronze and his fluids of vitriol," a preacher relishing in the invective he poured on his listeners. A. V. G. Allen, while writing with some sympathy for his subject, had similar sentiments when confronted by Edwards's imprecations. Edwards ought not have been "let loose" on New England. He was "some organ of vast capacity whose strongest stops or combinations should never have been drawn."[41] Oliver Wendell Holmes Sr. is quoted as saying that Edwards's theology was "rooted in the deepest depths of hell."[42] Clarence Darrow, lawyer of Scopes Monkey Trial fame in the early 1920s, wrote, "It is not surprising that Edwards's main business in the world was to scare silly women and little children, and blaspheming the God he professed to adore. Nothing but a diseased or disturbed mind could have produced his 'Sinners in the Hands of an Angry God.'"[43]

These scholars were undoubtedly trying to foster new interest in the Great Awakening and its leading evangelical proponents but were hardly

---

39. Thompson, "Edwards: His Character, Teaching, and Influence," *Bibliotheca Sacra* 18, no. 72, 833.

40. Stephen, "Jonathan Edwards," *Littell's Living Age* 20, 228.

41. Allen, quoted in Simonson, *Jonathan Edwards*, 130.

42. Holmes quoted in Simonson, *Jonathan Edwards*, 131.

43. Darrow, quoted in Lloyd-Jones, "Jonathan Edwards and the Crucial Importance of Revival," in *The Puritan Experiment*, 107.

doing so in a way that those leaders would have subscribed to. Perhaps it is fair to say that critique of this kind reveals more about the writers than it does about their subject.

Abandoning, to a large extent, the stereotypical images handed down, more recent scholarship has penetrated deeper into the spirit of the Great Awakening and, seeking a message for today, has attempted an honest reconstruction of sermons that drove the revival forward. But many an attempt has miscarried at the outset due to an unwillingness to accept the logical implications inherent in the theology of the revival period. Writing in an age when the immense capabilities of humanity and scientific progress find so much evidence,[44] these historians have cringed when face to face with the doctrinal emphasis so explicit in the preaching of that time, especially that of Edwards. Vernon L. Parrington exemplifies this school when he claims that the theology of Calvin lay like a heavy weight upon the soul of New England, "and there could be no surer way to bring it into disrepute, than to thrust into naked relief the brutal grotesqueries of those dogmas."[45]

In a sense, Perry Miller deserves to be called the father of modern Edwardsean studies. Like many Puritans who knew of the tension between doctrinal teaching and the passion with which it was done, Miller, in his attempt to deconstruct the Puritan era, struggles to keep the balance between their ideas and their emotions. In his biography of Edwards, too, published in 1949, Miller argues that, actually, Edwards was an artist who had no relevant and convenient outlet for his gifts and therefore entered the Puritan ministry to exercise his talents in theology and preaching. In so doing Miller posits that Edwards's sermons were, for him, an art form and that to find the meaning of Edwards, one must read between the lines. In the foreword of the biography, he says, "The student of Edwards must seek to ascertain not so much the peculiar doctrines in which he expressed his meaning as the meaning itself."[46] So, according to Miller, what Edwards expressed was a foil beyond which lay his real intent. This is deconstruction at its earliest. For Miller, there was some secret code, some hidden meaning, to Edwards's preaching that was an expression of his art. Miller sees his sermons as "an

---

44. Note, e.g., that the first moon landing took place in 1969, the year Parrington was writing.

45. Parrington, "Jonathan Edwards Was an Anachronism," in *Jonathan Edwards and the Enlightenment*, ed. John Opie, 19.

46. Miller, *Jonathan Edwards*, "The Preface".

immense cryptogram. . . . There was an occult secret in them."[47] Moreover, Edwards's written discourses were "almost a hoax, not to be read but to be seen through."[48] Carl Bogue is correct in his critique: Miller's work is "grounded on the thesis that there is a discrepancy between what Edwards said and wrote, and what he really thought."[49] Miller oversteps the plain sense and, like some others, engages in unwarranted deconstruction of the text. What Edwards taught was a preoccupation of his own soul and mind since he was a young man. He struggled personally with the doctrines he preached, and these struggles are described more than adequately in his diary and *Personal Narrative*. The consistency between the youthful entries in his diary and his public discourses militates against Miller's thesis. Conrad Cherry, in a reappraisal of Edwards, speaks not only of Miller when he says, "Interpreters of Edwards still feel uncomfortable with Edwards's Calvinism. To alleviate the pain of embarrassment, features of Edwards's theology are frequently searched out which transcend his Calvinism. . . . Perhaps such a procedure would not be totally inappropriate if he had not consciously chosen Puritan Calvinism as the framework for so much of his thought." And says Cherry, "Perry Miller leads one to conclude that Edwards is to be appreciated primarily at points other than where traditional Calvinist tenets receive extensive treatment."[50] Thankfully, this school of scholarship has been surpassed.[51]

For the first few years of Edwards's tenure at Northampton, he performed his normal pastoral duties, and as far as one can tell, there was little

47. Miller, *Jonathan Edwards*, 51.
48. Miller, *Jonathan Edwards*, 51.
49. Bogue, *Jonathan Edwards and the Covenant of Grace*, 4.
50. Cherry, *The Theology of Jonathan Edwards*, 3. Perry Miller and others have characterized Edwards's philosophical position as that of an empiricist so far ahead of his time that the twentieth century was barely catching up. They credit Edwards's reading of John Locke as the decisive event in his intellectual life. Miller did a great deal toward bringing Edwardsean scholarship to a new level of respectability, from which it has not returned. However, the modern consensus among historians is that he was fundamentally wrong in laying aside Edwards's religious thought and instead highlighting his philosophical empiricism. But in what is probably an overreaction to Miller's school, scholars are unwilling to allow that Edwards had any sympathy with or made use of English empiricism at all, and they insist, instead, that he threw himself in with Continental rationalists. See, e.g., Fiering, "The Rationalist Foundations of Jonathan Edwards's Metaphysics," *Jonathan Edwards and the American Experience*, ed. Hatch and Stout, 73–101.
51. See, e.g., Cherry, *Theology of Jonathan Edwards* 3; Helm, "John Locke and Jonathan Edwards: A Reconsideration," *Journal of the History of Ideas* 29 no. 1:51; Hoopes, "Jonathan Edwards's Religious Psychology," *Journal of American History*, 69 no. 4:849.

evidence of a revival of "vital piety" until the winter of 1734 to 1735. By this time, it seemed that a good portion of his congregation had become persuaded to accept his preaching as a plain, unvarnished description of reality. Of course, by virtue of the lengthy ministry of Solomon Stoddard before Edwards's own, the level of theological awareness was high. Other shades of religious leaning were easily discerned, and these were quickly critiqued and anathematized. Especially Arminianism, which had penetrated the area, was soon noticed, and a clamor arose that Edwards referred to as "the great noise" as folks heard of disparate sorts of preaching in the area. Northampton quickly felt the threat and knew that the religious homogeneity of the neighborhood could not be taken for granted. The controversy served as a catalyst for growing spiritual concern, and friends "of vital piety trembled for the fear of the issue," said Edwards. There was widespread fear that "God was about to withdraw from the land, and that we should be given up to heterodoxy and corrupt principles. . . . Many seemed to have a kind of trembling fear lest they should be led into by-paths to their eternal undoing . . . and they seemed with much concern and engagedness of mind, to inquire what was indeed the way in which they must come to be accepted with God."[52]

Edwards determined to meet this state of mind by vigorous preaching on several doctrinal themes coming out of the controversy. Accordingly, he preached a series under the general heading "Five Discourses on Important Subjects, Nearly Concerning the Great Affair of the Soul's Eternal Salvation." This series, according to Edwards, had a great impact on the people of Northampton and its surroundings. It was in the latter part of December 1734 that "the Spirit of God began extraordinarily to set in and wonderfully to work amongst us." The whole town came under that influence, for "a great and earnest concern about the great things of religion and the eternal world, became universal in all parts of the town."[53]

---

52. Edwards, "Faithful Narrative," 1:148. The focus of the controversy was Robert Breck, a recent Harvard graduate, at Springfield, a town just downstream from Northampton on the Connecticut River. An anti-Breck faction in that congregation proceeded against his settlement there on grounds of alleged Arminianism, and a time of bitter quarrel ensued. Edwards mentions this incident in his introduction to the "Faithful Narrative." "I suppose," he wrote, "we have been the freest of any part of the land from unhappy divisions and quarrels in our ecclesiastical and religious affairs, til the late lamentable Springfield contention."

53. Edwards, "Faithful Narrative," 1:149.

Some were "seized" by the Spirit of God suddenly, while others were awakened more gradually. All who were affected, however, "set themselves seriously to meditate on those things that have the most awakening tendency." Their sense of "misery had fast hold on them," reported Edwards, and with most the cry was "What shall we do to be saved?" He saw that the method of the Spirit in his "legal strivings" was to persuade sinners of their "absolute dependence on His sovereign power and grace and a universal necessity of a mediator."[54]

Edwards was out to foster conviction, and he believed this direct method of preaching was being blessed by God. Many were broken in heart and owned their sinfulness. Within six months about three hundred had come to profess faith in Christ.[55] Curious visitors, coming to observe for themselves what they had heard, were greatly taken in. In this way the whole Connecticut River Valley became the scene of revival, a precursor to the Great Awakening of the 1740s.

Edwards found that in his attempt to foster conviction, sermons that contained a discriminating and searching element in them were the most useful. Of the "Five Discourses," the one that had the most effect on his hearers was the aforementioned "The Justice of God in the Damnation of Sinners." The sermon pitted the self-righteousness of humanity against the unmitigated justice of a holy God. Edwards attested to its effectiveness.[56]

Since it was this sermon that Edwards deemed most effectual, it is appropriate briefly to summarize its contents. The sermon encapsulates the theology that predominated before and during the awakening by the leaders of the Evangelical Revival.[57] When reading Edwards one is immediately captured by his inescapable logic. The text, from Romans 3:19, was "that every mouth may be stopped." Edwards began by providing detail with respect to the sinfulness of both Jews and gentiles and explaining why the law was sufficient to "stop the mouths of all humankind." Once he left the exegetical part of his sermon to expand on the doctrinal implications of the text, he established the evil nature of all sin, "or how much sin men are guilty of," and developed the premise that crime or guilt deserved a degree of punishment

---

54. Edwards, "Faithful Narrative," 1:163.
55. Edwards, "Faithful Narrative," 1:164.
56. Edwards, "Faithful Narrative," 1:168.
57. Broadly speaking, one must allow for some differences with the Wesleyan variety but on the basics of salvation doctrine the leaders were of one mind.

relative to the degree of evil in the crime. "A crime is more or less heinous, according as we are under greater or less obligations to the contrary."[58]

Humanity's obligation to love and obey someone must be in direct proportion to that person's loveliness, honor, and authority. God is infinitely lovely and honorable and has infinite authority over his subjects. "Hence sin . . . must be a crime infinitely heinous and so deserving infinite punishment." It was the case, then, that any sin against God must be a sin of infinite consequence. It was rational to suppose that God's wrath and hatred of sin would be as infinite as he was infinite and that he would therefore justly demand infinite and eternal punishment.[59] Moreover, God had a right to determine whether any or all, or how many, would be redeemed. "He might," Edwards argued, "if He had pleased, left all to perish, or might have redeemed all, or He may redeem some and leave others."

Thus, the justice of God in the damnation of sinners was established in very stark terms. The remainder of the sermon took the form of personal application. Here Edwards's logic was combined with an earnestness and compassion for his people. He pleaded for a turning to the Lord, who was waiting to receive them. He closed with a gospel invitation, centering on what sinners miss when they do not have Christ as Savior.

Capitalizing on the fear of being (justly) passed by was not an unreasonable approach by Edwards and other leaders such as George Whitefield. Contrary to the vast majority today, all of churchgoing New England believed in the reality of hell and heaven, just as Western humanity today believes in the laws of science. This was, of course, a great advantage for preachers of the eighteenth century hardly available to us now. Audiences sitting in the pews or listening to field preaching felt singled out by the sermons; offenders began to blush and fidget, especially persons putting faith in their moral rectitude or social successes, such as the Puritan "civil man." Churchgoers soon understood their vulnerability when the preacher arrived at the application. No one could appeal inwardly to virtue. No one could indulge themselves with shallow excuses. Sin was not only what people did or did not do. Sin was a virus that stemmed from their innate culpability inherited from the great fall of their first parents in the garden of Eden. It affected everyone. In order, therefore, to find favor in the eyes of

---

58. Edwards, "Justice of God," 1:342.

59. In Edwards's defense of the "Great Doctrine of Original Sin," he used a similar argument against the attempt by Arminians to demolish that doctrine. Edwards, "Original Sin Defended" *Works*, Yale, 3:39.

God, sinners needed to surrender all hope in personal righteousness and ask for mercy for Jesus' sake.

This sermon concluded with an argument for the superior joy of the regenerate state. Edwards asserted that the atoning blood that Christ shed on the cross was fully sufficient "to pay the debt you have contracted," and seeing that Christ "has suffered so much for poor sinners, God is willing to be at peace with them . . . so that you need not at all be discouraged." Indeed, it was only on Christ's account that God offered salvation "to any sinner of you all, not one in this congregation excepted." In a sermon that Edwards himself identified as crucial in the revival of 1734 and 1735, the great purpose was to produce conviction, conviction that sin had rendered each person accountable to a God who would be in his right to condemn them.

Imprecatory preaching was but a means to an end. Foundational to the revival theology of the Great Awakening was the idea that a sense of sin was basic to evangelical conversion. No healing would take place without wounding. "The Justice of God in the Damnation of Sinners" can be seen as typical in the revival setting. These sermons usually addressed three subtopics: human sin and guilt before God, the sovereignty of grace, and the abundant willingness of God to redeem.

There was a wonderful symmetry between the way of salvation as presented by the likes of Edwards and the subsequent pattern of conversion he and others observed during the Awakening. In his description of the revival, in which this sermon was particularly instrumental, Edwards reported a three-stage conversion process:[60] sinners were awakened to

---

60. It is, in my view, less helpful than one might think to divide Edwards's portrayal of the conversion experience as if he meant to splinter the description of it into many little steps, one after the other. Some have pinpointed what they believe are a host of identifiable stages. Samuel Logan, for example, believes he has unearthed in the "Faithful Narrative" a profusion of little stages whereby a sinner is led to Christ, eight of them in all. He does admit that others might not agree with his findings, and I believe Edwards himself would have demurred. It is difficult to find clear lines of demarcation between several of Logan's eight stages. What appear to Logan to be definite steps in the work of the Holy Spirit are often simply diverse characterizations of the same one. In all probability Edwards's purpose was not so much to impress his readers with the complexity of God's work in the soul as to simplify. And rather than seek to elucidate many steps in the conversion process, Edwards seems instead to stress the variability of the Spirit's work from one person to another as the subtitle of "Section II" suggests: "The Manner of Conversion Various, Yet Bearing a Great Analogy . . ." I do, however, find evidence pointing to three distinct stages in Edwards's account of the revival. See Logan, "Jonathan Edwards and the 1734-35 Northampton Revival," *Preaching and Revival*, 69-73.

their guilt, then they surrendered to divine sovereign grace, and then they emerged into the light of redeeming grace and assurance.

One aspect needs mention in the context of conviction. Edwards observed that "persons under great awakenings were concerned because they thought they were not awakened, but still miserable, hardhearted, senseless, sottish creatures still and sleeping upon the brink of hell." Folks under deep conviction thought they were bereft of conviction. This is the mysterious paradox in conversion as recorded in so many spiritual biographies; sinners are truly awakened to find themselves with a stony heart. They were most sensitive to their failings and misery and yet felt themselves to be spiritually dead. Edwards notes that they "seem to themselves to be very senseless, when indeed most sensible."[61]

While Edwards declared that conviction was "preparatory to grace," it was the preparation of the Holy Spirit's striving or contending with the spirit of fallen humanity. Accordingly, Edwards cannot be ranked with the preparationist school of evangelical thinking in the sense that sinners must prepare themselves in their own strength to come to God in a fit manner. He never preached that kind of preparationism.[62] Nevertheless, he believed that there was a work of conviction or quickening in a person before regeneration. It was the time of seeking. Sinners prayed to God, struggled, felt guilt and inner corruption, and experienced godly sorrow.

It was a stage rife with intense introspection. Afraid of the tiniest suggestion of self-deception, seekers would examine themselves for marks of the Spirit's work, often with depressing results, and they would often find themselves more doleful and heavyhearted than before this all began. This state could descend into a morbid sort of self-scrutiny, and a person thus afflicted would seek and benefit from pastoral counseling. When preachers of the Great Awakening discerned their level of despondency they would present the free offer of the gospel.

However, avoiding the stage of conviction could be fatal. Edwards suggested it would have promoted "self-flattery and carelessness" and would have served "utterly to undo them" had he withheld the truth that God was under no obligation to show mercy. Had he counseled troubled souls that God might take pity upon them because of their sense of sin or because of their struggle to reform themselves, he would have placed the foundation

---

61. Edwards, "Faithful Narrative," 1:167.

62. Logan makes the same point in, "Jonathan Edwards," 70; Also Murray, *Jonathan Edwards*, 127–29.

of salvation where it did not belong and would seriously have hindered them from proceeding on the way to heaven. Therefore, a period in which the sense of sin prevailed came before rest and peace and joy.

Aside from a few who succumbed in the struggle and ended up depressed and debilitated, there were many whose heart were changed for the better. They emerged from the raging battle of "legal striving" to position themselves meekly before the Lord, in frank recognition of what they had always owed him. They surrendered to the gospel of free and sovereign grace. Having a clear understanding of God's justice and their own culpability, they were simply submissive and quiet, "with great humbling in the dust before God."[63]

In this way hearts had been prepared. Edwards observed in his people a new apprehension of the truth of the gospel with "joyful surprise." The objective facts of the way of salvation, known since youth, when subjectively applied seemed like a whole new revelation to them. It was with the pleasant shock of new discovery that sinners were overwhelmed by the great love of God and the knowledge that it was actually for them. New desires filled their soul. The redeeming love of Christ showed itself in converted sinners, first of all, in their longing after God. They wished to know him and be joined in communion with him. Their desire was to know Christ and be instructed and serve him. Divine things became beautiful. Edwards spoke of "a sense of the superlative excellency of divine things, with a spiritual taste and relish of them, and an esteem of them as their highest happiness and best portion." Often persons "after their legal distresses . . . some comfortable and sweet view of a merciful God, of a sufficient Redeemer, or of some great and joyful things of the Gospel, immediately follows, or in a very little time."[64] Self-centered exertions with a view to obtaining righteousness, attempts to placate God, and other forms of "legal striving" were a thing of the past and were abhorred. It was these observable elements of change that, for Edwards, confirmed the genuineness of their conversion.

He related how he was often instrumental in bringing the newly converted to assurance of salvation. He was censured for doing so. But when a person came to him for spiritual counsel and he was satisfied as to their "good estate," he would make it known to them. "No one knows," he says, "how long they would continue without assurance, were they not helped by particular instruction."

63. Edwards, "Faithful Narrative," 1:169.
64. Edwards, "Faithful Narrative," 1:171.

Edwards's preaching and counsel had borne fruit by the blessing of the Spirit of God. Clarity of exposition and logic of presentation, permeated with the pathos of a personal acquaintance with sin and grace and keen insight into the human heart, were mighty instruments in effecting spiritual change. He wrote, "The town seemed... never so full of love, nor of joy, and yet so full of distress as it was then."[65]

The congruency between his homiletical method and what he was able to observe during the revival is indeed remarkable. Not only this, the religious experience observed during the revival is reminiscent of Edwards's history as outlined in his *Diary* and *Personal Narrative*. The two-sided quality, "sweet" and "vile," ran through the experience of Northampton in similar fashion.

Edwards's peers in the ministry were very much aware, and had seen and heard much, of the events in Northampton, and some urgency crept into the efforts and messages heard on Sunday. Itinerant evangelists similarly aimed at the conversion of sinners in the "perceivable and knowable" way as was outlined in the "Narrative..." A theology of revival began to play a role in the pastoral ministry of a considerable part of the New England clergy.

Edwards's sermons, especially the more famous ones,[66] were soon published in Boston and were then circulated on both sides of the Atlantic. Benjamin Trumbull, the Connecticut historian, spoke to eyewitnesses of the great events and reported, "There was in the minds of the people, a general fear of sin and of the wrath of God denouncing it.... At lectures there was not only great attention and seriousness in the house of God but the conversation out of it was generally on the great concerns of the soul."[67]

Samuel Blair of Pennsylvania witnessed a "visible appearance of much soul-concern" in 1744. The number of the awakened in New Londonderry was increasing "very fast." He reported that the "Sabbath assemblies soon became vastly large; many people from almost all parts around inclining very much to come."[68] William Cooper of Old South Church in Boston reported that "more came to him in one week in deep concern about their souls, than in the whole twenty-four years of his preceding ministry."[69]

---

65. Edwards, "Faithful Narrative," 1:151.
66. Such as "Sinners in the Hands of an Angry God."
67. Trumbull, *A Complete History of Connecticut*, 2:145.
68. Mode, *Sourcebook*, 127.
69. Mode, *Sourcebook*, 219.

The history of the many revivals that took place throughout the British Isles, Europe, and New England is well known. What is remarkable is that the undercurrent of conviction that provided impetus concerned innate depravity, outward decency notwithstanding. The doctrine of original sin was not merely adhered to because it was enunciated by the Westminster and Savoy Confessions or by the Heidelberg Catechism. Rather, it had become a vital element in Christian preaching during the early to mid-eighteenth century. In scholarship's search for the origins of the Great Awakening and for the forces that drove it forward for decades, it would be useful to consider this aspect.[70]

This element remained a vital part of gospel preaching throughout the eighteenth century. While the nineteenth century saw a decline in evangelical preaching, there were several who brought forward the older evangelical convictions. Charles Simeon and his circle, Charles H. Spurgeon, and J. C. Ryle are among the foremost. There were a host of others. Evangelical preachers continued to present conviction as a first phase of genuine conversion, or one indispensable strand running concurrently with others. The Scottish preacher Robert Murray McCheyne's (1813–1843) sermons reflect the same emphasis. In a letter to a young lady, McCheyne advised the girl to "seek to know your corruption." He asked the important question, "Do you think you have been convinced of sin?" And then, "Oh! Pray for deep discoveries of your real state by nature, and by practice. . . . Have you seen yourself as vile as Job saw himself; undone, as Isaiah saw himself? Have you experienced anything like Psalm 51?" McCheyne went on to confess his own sinfulness: "I seldom get more than a glance at the true state of my soul in its naked self. But when I do then I see that I am wretched, and

---

70. A scholarly consensus has not been achieved to date. There are wide-ranging views on the origins of the awakening phenomenon, stretching from a purely sociological thesis that highlights the social upheavals created by the early Industrial Revolution to an ecclesiastical viewpoint that fingers Anglicanism's spiritual and theological malaise. Each of these has merit in its own right, and perhaps the sum of them would yield a portrait comprehensive enough to satisfy. Still, it was a religious movement, and it seems in order, therefore, that one's search for origins embraces a religious explanation for it. Most importantly, one must consider the divine or supernatural. The participants and leaders of the revival ascribed the origin to the work of the Holy Spirit, and it seems rather arrogant of us all to deny the possibility. Surely the common conviction of the participants has merit. Henry Rack, in his important work on John Wesley, has provided a helpful survey of the search for sources of the Evangelical Revival: *Reasonable Enthusiast*, 171–80.

miserable, and poor and blind and naked [quoting Revelation 3:17] ... Every faculty of our mind is polluted."[71]

A Current Problem: Finney and Modern Evangelicalism

Often, well-meaning evangelical leaders today avoid making strong, penetrating statements from the pulpit. To talk about prevailing sins in an attempt to call forth a sense of need for God's saving grace is deemed too difficult to bear for congregants who are struggling with the vagaries of life. But when the gospel first came to pagans in the world of the Roman Empire, it was received and welcomed as "good news." Christianity offered relief and assurance of redemption in a time when the Greek and Roman gods evoked raw fear. During the time of the Protestant Reformation, the gospel was received with great relish after centuries of darkness, and a very large revival took place. Later, under the preaching of evangelicals discussed earlier, the same occurred. Preaching that brought the claims of God to bear upon a fallen world rang loud throughout Europe and the English-speaking world of the mid–eighteenth century.

This is still the case in many areas. In fact, a resurgence of interest in the things of God is apparent in our day, and many pastors are deeply serious about the truth of God's Word. However, it must be admitted that pastoral ministry frequently seems to lack the unction that was present in former times. Consequently, the sharper tones of an earlier, riper theology are not heard in every place.

How did this happen? J. I. Packer, in his book on Puritanism, lays the finger on one person, Charles G. Finney (1792–1875). Finney rejected the Augustinian-Reformation-Puritan belief in total inability, the belief that fallen human beings are unable to repent and believe without the renewing grace of the Holy Spirit. Finney was clear and emphatic in his Pelagian belief that everyone was naturally able to turn to the Lord once convinced that it was the needful and advantageous thing to do. The human will was entirely free to decide and was not hindered by inability. Strong persuasions by preachers, therefore, was the key. While people were always able to reject moral persuasion,[72] the stronger the appeal, the more likely it was that success would result. Therefore, every means of increasing the level of persuasion, the most "frenzied excitement, the most harrowing emotionalism, the

---

71. McCheyne, *Works of McCheyne*, 223.
72. Packer quotes Finney: "Sinners can go to Hell in spite of God."

most nerve-racking commotion in evangelistic gatherings," was entirely appropriate.[73] According to Finney—and he preached this fervently—listeners could at any time yield themselves to the Lord and become a Christian. It was the preacher's task to plead for immediate decision. Packer says, "For Finney, evangelistic preaching was a battle of wills between himself and his hearers, in which his task was to bring them to breaking-point."

But browbeating for a "decision" can actually hinder the work of the Holy Spirit. Some who responded to Finney's call were ill prepared and yet came forward, were validated as Christians, went through the motions, and went away thinking they had arrived, when in reality they had received nothing more than the affirmation of an evangelist. The result was a crop of false conversions which did nothing more than entrench moral pride in people who were not saved. Packer says, "When an evangelist takes it on himself to pick the fruit before it is ripe,"[74] the result can be a gospel hardening rather than a humbling encounter with God.

At issue was Finney's view of humanity. He denied the imputation of Adam's sin to all humankind. "We deny that the human condition is morally depraved," he said. Humans were not innately sinful. Sin was a choice. Therefore, "the sinner has all the faculties and natural abilities requisite to render perfect obedience to God. . . . All the sinner needs," Finney contended, "is to be induced to use these powers and attributes as he ought."[75] How is the sinner to be induced? Simply by creating "excitement sufficient to wake up the dormant moral powers."[76] The "New Measures" Finney defended, such as altar calls, appeared in rural camp meetings and through him became a part of mainstream evangelicalism in America.

Iain Murray, in what might be his most important book, *Revival and Revivalism*,[77] concurs. He spends a great deal of time on the revivalism of Charles Finney, and none of what he says is very flattering. Evangelicalism turned away from the old idea of conversion in the nineteenth century. Regeneration, in the minds of many, became synonymous with confession of faith or a decision to believe. By the beginning of the twentieth century,

---

73. Packer, *Quest for Godliness*, 292.
74. Packer, *Quest for Godliness*, 300.
75. Finney, *Lectures on Systematic Theology*, 391–405.
76. Finney, *Revivals of Religion*, 9.
77. Murray, *Revival and Revivalism*, 230–40, 255–74 (esp. 261), and most of chap. 14. It is an excellent treatment of the whole period and adds much to our understanding of the present day.

the transition effected by Finney's influence was accepted in most circles as the norm. A few, such as Asahel Nettleton, Lyman Beecher,[78] and Gardiner Spring, spoke in opposition. But in the main, conversion wrought by the convicting work of the Holy Spirit in the inner person was replaced by a mere decision to come forward, to raise a hand, or to say the *Sinner's Prayer*.

David Wells in his penetrating work, *Turning to God*, has said that, under Finney and others, there was a shift from the older Reformational interest in the inability of the sinner and the sovereignty of grace to newer concerns that were at least Arminian and often startlingly Pelagian about a sinner's ability to appropriate Christ. The enabling grace of the Holy Spirit was not essential. In the conversion process sinners were not expected to be acted upon by the work of God. Instead, they were expected merely to make a decision with the assurance that God would be right pleased. The phenomenon of calling sinners to come forward and make a decision in front of an audience tended to transform the doctrine of conversion into an experience bereft of any understanding of biblical truth. Where "conversion is reduced to an experience, and indeed, an experience that can almost be induced, it is disengaged from the whole corpus of belief in which it should have found a place. Truth is replaced by experience. What Christ did on the cross (objectively) becomes what Christ does in sinners (subjectively)" automatically.[79] The evangelist aims to reap decisions rather than bring humbled, penitent sinners to the only source from whom forgiveness can be had. This, says Wells, "is all a natural outgrowth of the approach pioneered by Finney and Moody, neither of whom doubted that immediate, wholehearted repentance was possible for anyone who had been sufficiently 'broken down' (Finney's phrase) by the pressure or allure of the evangelist's persuasive speech."[80] Princeton theologian B. B. Warfield remarked that "God might be eliminated from Finney's theology entirely without essentially changing its character."[81] Michael Horton says, "He is

---

78. Nettleton (1783–1844) was an American theologian and evangelist from Connecticut who was highly influential during the so-called Second Great Awakening. The number of people converted to Christianity as a result of his ministry was estimated by Bennet Tyler and Andrew Bonar at about thirty thousand. See Tyler and Bonar, *The Life and Labours of Asahel Nettleton*. He participated in the New Lebanon Conference, which was called in 1827 to settle the dispute regarding Finney's "New Measures." Both Nettleton and Beecher opposed the teachings of Finney.

79. Wells, *Turning to God: Biblical Conversion in the Modern World*, 93.

80. Wells, *Turning to God*, 94.

81. Warfield, *Perfectionism*, 2:193.

the tallest marker in the shift from Reformation orthodoxy, evident in the Great Awakening under Edwards and Whitefield to Pelagian revivalism evident from the Second Great Awakening to the present.[82]

This was something new on the American scene, an aberration that soon became the norm in spite of resistance from the likes of Asahel Nettleton, Lyman Beecher, Gardiner Spring, William Sprague, the Alexanders, the Hodges and other "old line" preachers. Finney's evangelistic methods accompanied the westward expansion of the United States. Preachers, convinced of the effectiveness of his teaching, adopted his brand of revivalism as their modus operandi. But Finney's revivalism created chaos in many churches. It was responsible for the division of congregations, not only because of his general criticism of other ministers "but because of the very nature of his teaching on revival."[83] In his opinion, any minister faithful and mature ought to be able to induce revivals, leaving only one possible conclusion about preachers who failed to do so.

---

82. Horton, "The Disturbing Legacy of Charles Finney," *Modern Reformation*, January 2, 1995.

83. Murray, *Revival and Revivalism*, 264–65.

6.

A Cloud of Witnesses
The Great Itinerants

> "I offer you salvation this day; the door of mercy is not yet shut, there does yet remain a sacrifice for sin, for all that will accept of the Lord Jesus Christ. He will embrace you in the arms of His love."
>
> GEORGE WHITEFIELD

FRELINGHUYSEN AND THE TENNENTS, WHITEFIELD, AND WESLEY

Jacobus Frelinghuysen and the Tennents

IN AMERICA, ONE OF the earliest contributors to the Great Awakening was Theodore Frelinghuysen (1691–1747), a Dutch minister who came to the new world in 1720.[1] Frelinghuysen served as minister to several of the

---

1. When Frelinghuysen, ministering in Ost Friesland (now a part of Lower Saxony, Germany adjacent to the Dutch provinces of Friesland and Groningen), received his call letter to be the pastor of a church, he assumed the church was located in the Netherlands and was ready to move there when someone told him the call had come from a church in the new world. He absorbed the shock of this discovery with grace and traveled across the ocean.

Dutch Reformed churches in the Raritan Valley area of New Jersey.[2] He is not often included in accounts of the itinerant preachers of the First Awakening even though his pastoral ministry extended to five churches and his wider influence in the region was significant. Although his theological assumptions were Calvinistic, he was influenced by the more scholastic Calvinism of Theodore Beza, and his Christian experience bore resemblance to the experiential Pietism of Francke and Spener. As a young man he read William Perkins, William Teellinck,[3] and Gisbertus Voetsius.[4]

Coming to the Raritan Valley of New Jersey, he found the churches there fairly bereft of spiritual vitality and was shocked to discover that many people in the congregations were unconverted, believing, as did many in the Dutch Reformed churches, that baptism and church membership would give them a foot into the kingdom without reference to the new birth. Frelinghuysen designed his preaching strategy to meet the need. Convinced that people could essentially be divided into two categories, converted and unconverted, he began to preach sermons sprinkled with descriptive distinctions, inviting his congregants to examine themselves for evidence of saving grace. In contrast to many Presbyterian and Dutch Reformed pastors who were content to view churchgoers to be on the way to heaven, Frelinghuysen was out to inculcate the conviction of sin, a sense of one's need for a Savior, and a desire for holiness, all of which he found woefully absent.

His Pietist convictions drove him to believe that a sense of sin was an integral part of true conversion, and he soon realized that his audiences were appalled to find that he thought so. His sermons were unsettling. Such was the sharpness of his imprecations that many were offended. Moreover, Frelinghuysen believed in the purity of the sacrament and consequently "fenced" the table, disallowing certain congregants from partaking of the Lord's Supper. It was the latter, even more than his preaching, that stirred

---

2. Raritan, New Brunswick, Six-Mile Run, Three-Mile Run, and North Branch.

3. Teellinck (1579–1629), a Dutch pastor, studied at the University of St. Andrews and then received a doctorate from the University of Poitiers. He then lived in England and rubbed shoulders with early Puritanism. Teellinck brought Puritan theology with him when he returned to the Netherlands, where he studied under Jacobus Arminius but later became a high Calvinist.

4. Voetsius (1589–1676) was a Dutch Calvinist theologian. He played an influential role at the Synod of Dordt and was a strong opponent of Arminianism. He was a protégé of Teellinck, and both of them helped infuse Dutch Pietism with English Puritan theology.

up controversy within his churches, and a sizeable group signed petitions for his removal. One parishioner stated, "We welcomed him with joy and love, in the hope that his service would be for our edification. But alas! to our great sorrow, we, soon, and increasingly found that the result was very different. His denunciations [were] uttered against all of us from the pulpit . . . and on all occasions, to the effect that we were all unconverted and therefore we were discouraged from partaking of the Lord's Supper."[5]

His *ordo salutis* was derived from the Pietism in his background. According to Maze,[6] the Pietist *ordo salutis* he worked with was conviction, conversion, and then holiness. His delivery style was direct and blunt. The reading of Beza, Perkins, and the analytical formulae of Petrus Ramus shaped Frelinghuysen's views of conversion and the Christian life. Hence, he acted aggressively with respect to empirical sanctification, stressing observable evidence of being born again. If congregants did not measure up, they were disallowed from attending the Lord's Table.

He was an eloquent preacher but struggled against the empty formalism of the churches. His preaching methods conflicted with several powerful leaders such as Henry Boel, who considered Frelinghuysen's preaching unnerving and unnecessarily offensive to the staid conservatism of the Dutch Reformed congregations. Boel, a pastor from New York, initiated a *Complaint* (*Klagte*) against Frelinghuysen the proceedings of which lasted several years and take up the last sixty pages of volume 3 of the *Ecclesiastical Records of the State of New York*.[7] Frelinghuysen stressed self-examination with respect to religious experience in an effort to instill self-awareness of lethargy and superficiality.

Frelinghuysen considered it normal for people to experience intense struggle with guilt and feelings of unworthiness prior to conversion. What he conceived of was very similar to the *Busskampf* of the German Pietists. He repeatedly attacked the presumption of godliness in his audiences, believing that false conversions would be unearthed by an emphasis on conviction as a starting point to true conversion. His preaching revealed some inconsistencies in his otherwise supralapsarian theology[8] derived from his reading of Perkins and Beza, for he often presented a choice between

---

5. *Boel's Complaint against Frelinghuysen*, translated and edited by Loux, 30.
6. Maze, *Theodorus Frelinghuysen's Evangelism*, 53–54.
7. Hastings, ed., *Ecclesiastical Records*, 3:2244–308.
8. Maze, *Theodorus Frelinghuysen's Evangelism*, 78–79.

heaven and hell and gave the invitation of the gospel.⁹ Still, his fearless insistence on conviction of sin as an essential prerequisite of the new birth remained a part of his sermon application.¹⁰ By 1726 a revival began under Frelinghuysen. His five churches were especially affected, with several people added to membership. The number of new conversions during this time totaled 180.¹¹

The practice of owning a slave was generally seen as acceptable at the time, and Frelinghuysen had purchased James Albert Ukawsaw Gronniosaw. He taught the African about the means of grace and instructed him on how to pray. Gronniosaw became greatly convicted of his sinfulness once he came to an understanding of his condition by nature. Upon hearing Frelinghuysen preach one Sunday, Gronniosaw said, "He preached the law so severely, that it made me tremble," and he wished he could die. His conversion to Christ came soon after: "I was one day in a most delightful frame of mind; my heart so overflowed with love and gratitude to the Author of all my comforts . . . so awed and filled by the Presence of God that I saw light inexpressible dart down from heaven upon me, and shone around me for the space of a minute. . . . Joy unspeakable took possession of my soul."¹² Gronniosaw's experience reveals something of the efficacy conviction has as the Holy Spirit brings a person from darkness to light.

After meeting Frelinghuysen, George Whitefield expressed his high esteem: "A Dutch Calvinistic minister, named Freeling Housen. He is a worthy old soldier of Jesus Christ, and was the beginner of the great work which I trust the Lord is carrying on in these parts. He has been strongly opposed by his carnal brethren, but God has appeared for him. . . . He has long since learnt to fear him only, who can destroy both body and soul in hell."¹³ He also came to the notice of Jonathan Edwards in Northampton, Massachusetts, in the 1730s, and Edwards recorded hearing of a "very considerable revival of religion . . . under the ministry of a very pious young gentleman, a Dutch minister whose name as I remember was Freelinghousa."¹⁴

9. Maze, *Theodorus Frelinghuysen's Evangelism*, 102.
10. For a collection of Frelinghuysen's sermons, see Beeke, ed., *Forerunner of the Great Awakening*.
11. Maze, *Theodorus Frelinghuysen's Evangelism*, 147.
12. Gronniosaw, "A Narrative of the Most Remarkable Particulars in the Life of James Albert Ukawsaw Gronniosaw," quoted in Maze, *Theodorus Frelinghuysen's Evangelism*, 60-61.
13. Whitefield, *Whitefield's Journals*, 352.
14. Edwards, "A Faithful Narrative of the Surprising Work of God in the Conversion

A Cloud of Witnesses

Providentially, the greatest influence Frelinghuysen was able to exert on a wider plane came through his contact with Gilbert Tennent (1703–1764), a son of William Tennent who had established the famous Log College on his farm, just north of Philadelphia. The Tennents were Presbyterian of Irish background. Presbyterian pastors had often been educated in the British Isles but of late had been deterred by the cost and danger inherent in an Atlantic passage. Thus, the Log College became the center where Gilbert and others received their training. He received a call from a church at New Brunswick, New Jersey, not far from Frelinghuysen. He adopted the homiletical methods that he observed in the Dutch preacher's ministry and had great success. Tennent spent several months with George Whitefield on a preaching tour and later became pastor of a Presbyterian church in Philadelphia. George Whitefield said after hearing him preach, "He convinced me more and more that we can preach the gospel of Christ no further than we have experienced the power of it in our own hearts. Being deeply convicted of sin, and being from time to time driven from his false bottom and dependencies by God's Holy Spirit at his first conversion, he has learned experimentally to dissect the heart of the natural man. Hypocrites must either soon be converted or enraged at his preaching." Whitefield called him a "'son of thunder' who does not regard the face of man."[15]

John Tennent (1707–1732), Gilbert's younger brother and the third son of William Tennent, followed in the footsteps of his father and brothers. John was educated in the Log College. When he was a young man, his own struggle was intense, almost to the point of making him despair, but his conversion was experienced with great joy. He was a gifted and powerful preacher, but sadly, his career was cut short by a "consumptive disease," and he died at twenty-five years of age. His earnestness in preaching is preserved in his recorded sermons. In a sermon titled "Regeneration Opened," he appealed to his congregation, "Has sin been discovered, and applied to your consciences with power?" And, "Have you been made to see your lost and deplorable state by nature, so as to be exceedingly distressed?" And, "Have you been made to inquire after and seek for relief with anguish of soul?" And finally, "Has the Lord Jesus been discovered by his word and Spirit to your inquiring, burdened, anxious soul in his

---

of Many Hundred Souls in Northampton," *Works* Yale, 4:156.

15. Whitefield quoted in Alexander, *The Log College*, 30. Original source not identified.

mediatorial excellency and sufficiency?"[16] Here again we find the emphasis on a sense of need in gospel preaching.

Frelinghuysen's ministry in the Raritan Valley of New Jersey was a precursor to the Great Awakening. It occurred a decade before the revival in Northampton under Jonathan Edwards in 1734 and 1735. His influence on the Tennents and other preachers in the Middle Colonies should not be underestimated.

George Whitefield

In England, George Whitefield (1714–70), an Anglican throughout his life, stepped into an era of spiritual decline. His conversion was preceded by a period of intense conviction, during which he swung from the one extreme of trying to appease God by self-improvement to the other of being pulled into all kinds of mischief. He enrolled at Oxford at seventeen years old and joined the Holy Club,[17] believing that association with serious Christians would prevent his dalliances into sin. There he met the Wesleys, John and Charles. Yet while being part of the Holy Club placed Whitefield in proximity to some very good company, it gave him little advantage in terms of spiritual peace. The books they studied together concerned topics such as self-discipline, mysticism, and good works. The club did not learn of God's free and sovereign grace and, according to Arnold Dallimore, did not read the Reformers and the Puritans.[18] Whitefield continued to be a serious follower of outward Christianity, striving to be a better person, but missed the actual surrendering to divine grace.

But at one point during Whitefield's time of conviction, Charles Wesley, a tutor at Christ Church, gave Whitefield a book by Henry Scougal, a young Scot.[19] In the book Scougal explained four essentials (faith, love, purity, and humility), characteristics of Christian spirituality, and the means

---

16. Tennent, "Regeneration Opened," in *Sermons and Essays by the Tennents*, 297.

17. The Holy Club was a small organization at Oxford that functioned from 1729 to 1738. The name was a contemporary nickname for students who came together for Bible study, devotional exercises, pious discipline, and charitable work. John and Charles Wesley were its most prominent members. Others included Whitefield, John Clayton, John Gambold, Westley Hall, James Hervey, Benjamin Ingham, Robert Kirham, and John Whitelamb. Students not belonging to the club sometimes used the nickname as a form of derision. Outler ed *John Wesley*, 8, 10.

18. Dallimore, *George Whitefield*, 1:72.

19. Scougal, *The Life of God in the Soul of Man*.

of grace. This little book contradicted all Whitefield and his fellow members believed about salvation, and the disagreement gave him cause for anxious disquiet. Later Whitefield said he never really understood what true religion was until he read Scougal's book. He discovered that regeneration was indispensable; he must be born again "or be damned! I learned that a man may go to church, say his prayers, receive the sacrament, and yet not be a Christian. . . . How did my heart shudder!"[20] Curiously, instead of heeding the instruction in Scougal's book, he acted in the opposite direction, likely in despair, plummeting himself into more legal striving and good works, all in a desperate attempt to please God. He wept, he fasted, he punished himself with physical hardship, and he confessed his sins.

The oppression he felt was satanic. Rather than finding relief, he became even more hesitant and fearful. Finally, he abandoned everything that was dear, including his friends, and locked himself in his study for days. He lost weight, to the great concern of Charles Wesley, who brought him to his brother John. The latter began to counsel Whitefield about the state he was in and gave him Thomas à Kempis to read. Whitefield needed to discover the great truth that there was no life in the law but that life was in the gospel. Bondage such as his could be broken only by the grace of a settled assurance in believing. It was a period of some confusion for Whitefield. He had found little comfort in the legalism of the Holy Club but had not yet discovered liberty in the gospel of grace.

Finally, the turning point came. Whitefield records, "God was pleased to set me free in the following manner. One day, perceiving an uncommon drought and a disagreeable clamminess in my mouth and using things to allay my thirst, but in vain, it was suggested to me, that when Jesus Christ cried out, 'I thirst!' His sufferings were near at an end. Upon which I cast myself down on the bed, crying out, 'I thirst! I thirst!'" And at that cry, God sent deliverance. Soon after this I found and felt in myself that I was delivered from the burden that had so heavily oppressed me. The spirit of mourning was taken from me . . . and my joy gradually became more settled and blessed be God, has abode and increased in my soul." This was the critical moment in his young life. After months of conviction of his sinfulness, and after a legalistic tug of war, he surrendered to the grace of God. His days of "mourning ended. . . . The Day Star arose in my heart. O! With what joy, joy unspeakable, even joy that was full of and big with glory, was my soul filled, when the weight of sin went off, and an abiding sense of the pardoning love

---

20. Quoted in Dallimore, *George Whitefield*, 1:73.

of God, and a full assurance of faith, broke in upon my disconsolate soul! Surely . . . it was a day to be had in everlasting remembrance!"[21] The discovery of the new birth in Whitefield's life now a sure thing, he arose to preach the message of conversion to a worldwide audience.

Whitefield's conversion experience had taken on a pattern similar to Francke's in Germany and the earlier Puritans' and Jonathan Edwards's in America. The general congruence of experience across different social and ethnic settings should not be missed. The Evangelical Revival was not bound by a single culture, language, or political context as it spread through Europe to North America. This congruence is indicative that a divine work was taking place.

The Wesleyan Methodist movement emerged from his ministry. Churches being too small, he began preaching in the open air, in the fields and in the streets, and quickly became a famous evangelist. While some of the clergy invited him to their pulpits at first, it soon became apparent that his ministry was, in fact, in competition with that of the established clergy, many of whom lacked the theological and spiritual depth that was obvious in his sermons. Whitefield was instrumental in originating the Welsh Calvinist Methodists but lacked the skill of administration and leadership, hallmarks of John Wesley's strengths. Whitefield was primarily a traveling evangelist, and spent much of time in the New World. In the meantime, John Wesley was asked to step in and provide leadership and take over Whitefield's itinerant ministry. Whitefield wrote to Wesley, "You must come and water what I have planted."[22] In this way, Wesley took hold of Whitefield's evangelistic ministry. Whitefield was set to travel to America.

Whitefield and America

Whitefield decided to visit America for the first time in 1738 and then again the following year. During his forays into the New World, he established orphanages and preached on an itinerant basis, first in Georgia and then in New England. Wherever he went he discovered that little awakenings were taking place here and there but were not connected, one town unaware of what was going on in another. Through his ministry of preaching in the open air as he traveled, he gave spark to a greater awakening. There

21. Whitefield, *Whitefield's Journals*, 58.
22. Dallimore, *George Whitefield*, 1:271. Also Tyerman, *The Life of the Rev. George Whitefield*, 1:193.

developed among the population a general feeling of solemnity about eternal matters.

Whitefield's sermons reveal an application of doctrine reminiscent of that offered by other leaders of the Evangelical Revival. Although steeped in biblical doctrine, his sermons were designed as much to leave an enduring impression about the great need for salvation as they were an appeal to the cognitive domain. Leaving his audiences with a felt need for redemption was his goal. Sarah Pierrepont Edwards,[23] in 1740, wrote this to her brother in New Haven about George Whitefield:

> I want to prepare you for a visit from the Rev. Mr. Whitefield, the famous preacher of England. He has been sojourning with us a week or more, and . . . is going to New Haven. . . . *He makes less of the doctrines than our American preachers generally do, and aims more at affecting the heart.* You have already heard of his deep-toned, yet clear and melodious voice. O it is perfect music to listen to that alone.[24]

To a greater or lesser extent, the direct appeal to the emotional life of the audience was generally maintained by the Awakening preachers.

Whitefield's orations can only be imagined, but by taking note of the persuasive language he used, we might receive an inkling of what Sarah Edwards meant. In a sermon on the marriage at Cana, he made a persuasive call for the listeners to come to the fountain of grace: "Do not say, you are miserable, and poor, and blind and naked, and therefore ashamed to come, for it is to such that this Invitation is now sent." By contrast, he said, "the Polite, the Rich, the Busy, Self-righteous Pharisee of this Generation have been bidden already, but they have rejected the Counsel of God."[25] Note that his method follows the pattern set by Christ and shown especially in the Gospel of Luke, where sinners and sufferers are deliberately contrasted with the self-righteous. The gospel is for all, for all are bidden, but only those with spiritual needs actually welcome it as good news.

Similarly, in a sermon entitled "The Folly and Danger of Not Being Righteous Enough," Whitefield warned his audience not to appeal to the Lord "Pharisee-like, telling God what you have done, how often you have

---

23. She was the wife of Jonathan Edwards.

24. Sarah Edwards, "A Letter to Her Brother," *Banner of Truth Magazine*, special issue no. 79, 25. Emphasis added.

25. Whitefield, *The Sermons of George Whitefield*, ed. Gatiss 2:101–2. This sermon was preached in 1739.

gone to church. Do not be rich in spirit proud and exalted for there is no blessing attends such." He then invited the sinners to come to Christ in faith as "poor, lost, undone, damned sinners. Come to Him in this manner and He will accept of you. . . . Be poor in spirit, for theirs is the kingdom of God."[26] Conviction was a key element in the conversion of a sinner under his preaching. Whitefield said in perhaps his most famous written work, *The Method of Grace*, "Before ye can speak peace to your hearts, ye must be made to see, made to feel, made to weep over, made to bewail your actual transgressions against the law of God."[27]

Whitefield and then the Wesleys developed the art of open-air preaching, following the example of the Welshman Howell Harris. In areas such as Kingswood, today on the eastern edge of Bristol, which was coal-mining country, there was no church building available to a potential congregation, and even if there had been one, a church would not have been large enough to accommodate everyone. More than this, however, the appeal of preaching in the open air was that the speaker would address the people, who may have initially felt alienated from the established church, on their own territory. Whitefield's enthusiasm for open-air preaching is clear from his journals. On one occasion he came to Kingswood at the time the coal miners left work for the day. At first only a few hundred miners stood to listen, but the word spread quickly, and the number mounted until an estimated twenty thousand folks came to listen.[28] Few of them, said James Macaulay, had ever heard the gospel or worshipped in a church. Said Whitefield, "The first discovery of their being affected was by seeing the white gutters made by their tears, which plentifully fell down their black cheeks. Several hundreds of them were soon brought under deep conviction, which the event proved, happily ended in a sound and thorough conversion."[29]

Later in New England, Whitefield received a letter from Thomas Prince, a well-known Congregational minister and historian of Boston, and a supporter of the Awakening. The letter was dated December 6, 1741, and was penned after Whitefield ministered south of Boston. "The Spirit of God came down and seiz'd them at once by Scores and Hundreds, that every one

---

26. Whitefield, *The Sermons of George Whitefield*, ed. Gatiss, 1:182–83. This sermon was preached and published in *The Christian's Companion* in 1739.

27. Whitefield, "The Method of Grace," in MacFarlan *The Revivals of the Eighteenth Century*, 22.

28. Green, "George Whitefield at Kingswood," *Building Conservation Magazine*, July 8, 2020.

29. Macaulay, *Whitefield Anecdotes*, 40–41.

A CLOUD OF WITNESSES

in the large Congregation clearly saw and own'd it was a Work of God, and in three Days time it was computed there were a Thousand in Bitterness and Anguish, 'What shall I do to be saved?' Yea, the wondrous Work even spread into the Church of England there."[30]

The famous case of Nathan Cole needs to be included here. Cole was a farmer in Farmington, Connecticut, and when he heard that Whitefield was to preach in the aera, he dropped his tools and, with his wife, raced to the location where Whitefield was speaking. The experience gave him a "heart wound." "By God's blessing my old Foundation was broken up and I saw that my righteousness would not save me.... When I was young... I intended to be saved by my own works such as prayers and good deeds." After listening to Whitefield, Cole was "loaded with the guilt of sin. I saw I was undone forever; I carried such a weight of Sin in my breast or mind, that it seemed to me as if I should sink into the ground every step.... I went month after month begging for mercy"[31] But the time came when Nathan Cole was led out of darkness to God's marvelous light, and he wept with joy.

Whitefield visited the colonies seven times, and it seemed he was attached more to the American scene than his home country. A steady pace of traveling brought him to many towns and cities from Georgia to New York, and he set a punishing pace for himself, preaching over fifteen thousand times. In Philadelphia he met Benjamin Franklin (1706-1790), the most sought-after publisher in the city, who then became Whitefield's own publisher. Their friendship grew at the personal level even though Franklin ignored the appeal of Whitefield's sermons.[32]

Anecdotes taken from Franklin's *Autobiography* indicate something of the style and effect of Whitefield's preaching as he toured the colonies. Franklin wrote of the remarkable range of Whitefield's voice,

> He had a loud and clear Voice, and articulated his Words and Sentences so perfectly that he might be heard and understood at a great Distance, especially as his Auditors [audience], however numerous, observ'd the most exact Silence. He preach'd one Evening from the Top of the Court House Steps, which are in the middle of Market Street, and on the West Side of Second Street which crosses it at right angles. Both Streets were fill'd with his Hearers

30. Prince, "Letter to Reverend George Whitefield," in Lovejoy, *Religious Enthusiasm and the Great Awakening*, 39.

31. Cole, "The Spiritual Travels of Nathan Cole," in *The Great Awakening*, Bushman, 67-71.

32. Franklin, like some other of the Founding Fathers, was a deist.

to a considerable Distance. Being among the hindmost in Market Street, I had the Curiosity to learn how far he could be heard, by retiring backwards down the Street towards the River; and I found his Voice distinct till I came near Front Street, when some Noise in that Street, obscur'd it. Imagining then a Semicircle, of which my Distance should be the Radius, and that it were fill'd with Auditors, to each of whom I allow'd two square feet, I computed that he might well be heard by more than Thirty Thousand. This reconcil'd me to the Newspaper Accounts of his having preach'd to 25,000 People in the Fields.[33]

Franklin also noted the oratorical finesse of the itinerant preacher:

By hearing him often, I came to distinguish easily between Sermons newly compos'd, and those which he had often preach'd in the Course of his Travels. His Delivery of the latter was so improv'd by frequent Repetitions that every Accent, every Emphasis, every Modulation of Voice, was so perfectly well turn'd and well plac'd, that without being interested in the Subject, one could not help being pleas'd with the Discourse, a Pleasure of much the same kind with that receiv'd from an excellent Piece of Music. This is an Advantage itinerant Preachers have over those who are stationary: as the latter cannot well improve their Delivery of a Sermon by so many Rehearsals.[34]

During his seventh visit to America, Whitefield accepted an invitation to preach at Exeter, New Hampshire. Exhausted and suffering from repeated asthma attacks, he planned to speak in the Second Parish Church on Front Street, but when the crowd swelled to nearly six thousand, he reverted to his open-air style. Some boards were laid across two barrels, and as he got up to speak, a friend commented that he should instead perhaps be in bed. "True, sir," he replied, "Lord Jesus, I am weary in thy work but not of it." He spoke for two hours and later rode to Newburyport, Massachusetts. He spoke to a small group there and wearily went to bed, dying quietly during the night.[35] There was a throng of about eight thousand at the funeral.

---

33. Franklin, *The Autobiography of Benjamin Franklin*, 131–32.

34. Franklin, "Benjamin Franklin Describes George Whitefield" in Lovejoy, *Religious Enthusiasm*, 37–38.

35. "The Last Sermon of Rev. George Whitefield of Exeter," *Portsmouth Herald*, August 21, 2009.

Ministers of all denominations came to mourn the loss. Several of them "related how his ministry had been the means of their conversion."[36]

The Controversy about Whitefield: Naturalism or Confessionalism?

Recent historians have engaged in a squabble over the approach history writers should take when writing about Whitefield and, by extension, other important Christian figures of the past. Harry Stout, currently the Jonathan Edwards Professor of American Religious History at Yale and a professed Calvinist, has written a fairly critical history of Whitefield and his times and has suffered some backlash from fellow evangelicals.[37] Admirers of Whitefield at first welcomed the new publication, which elevates him as one of the most important figures in the world of religion during the eighteenth century. But that is as far as it went.[38]

By some accounts, Luke Tyerman's monumental two-volume *The Life of the Rev. George Whitefield* (1876–1877) is still the most important study of Whitefield.[39] However, Stout referred to Tyerman and Arnold Dallimore as "filiopietistic biographers."[40] Stout proposed the thesis that Whitefield used acting techniques learned in his youth to influence crowds and that his impact was due more to technique than to the application inherent in his preaching of the word. He went as far as to say that Whitefield's life was almost exclusively for "public performance" and that Whitefield was an "actor-preacher . . . who adopted the assumptions of the actor."[41] Stout's criticism irritated many. By attributing Whitefield's success to his acting

---

36. Tyerman, *Rev. George Whitefield*, 2:601.

37. Stout, *The Divine Dramatist: George Whitefield.*

38. For a careful and detailed account of the clash over history writing, see Clary, *Reformed Evangelicalism,* 47–57. The entire book is a must-read for Christian historians and theologians interested in Christian historiography.

39. But after Tyerman's work, Whitefield had, for many decades, been ignored by historians until the publication of Arnold Dallimore's massive work, beginning with volume 1 in 1970. Dallimore's gracious and sympathetic biography was a great success and has gone through several printings, both in the UK and in the United States. I also need to mention Thomas Kidd's contribution, another sympathetic undertaking, theologically in tune with Whitefield, a thorough and even-handed treatment. Kidd attempts to help "bridge the secular academic and Christian perspectives on Whitefield that have clashed in recent decades." It might well become the standard work. Kidd, *George Whitefield,* Yale University Press, 2014.

40. Kidd, *George Whitefield,* 259.

41. Stout, *Divine Dramatist,* xv, xix.

ability, Stout alienated himself from those who maintain that Whitefield depended on the work of the Holy Spirit to convert sinners. Whitefield did have some training in theater prior to his conversion, and the skills he learned did indeed help him in his presentation of the gospel. With the use of voice and gesture, he was able to keep audiences spellbound. Victorian-era historian James Macaulay relates that Whitefield described a blind man unconsciously drawing nearer and nearer to a precipice so realistically that the audience was held in breathless suspense until Lord Chesterfield spontaneously burst forth, crying, "Good heavens! He is over!" Preaching in Philadelphia to a large crowd of sailors, he described a storm at sea and shipwreck. His illustration was so effective that the imagination of the audience was irresistibly carried along. With the ship floundering, some of the sailors shouted, "Take to the long boat!"[42]

Harry Stout is certainly correct to highlight Whitefield's ability as a speaker. At times folks actually fell down, overcome by suppressed emotion kindled by his eloquence. However, he was not functioning as an actor. He was simply an extremely gifted preacher. It is to be wondered whether Stout, an expert on the work of Jonathan Edwards, which chair he occupies at Yale, would evaluate the experience of Edwards's audiences in like fashion. At Enfield, Connecticut, when he preached his most famous sermon, the congregation erupted into moans and crying, and some people fell to the floor under the weight of Edwards's descriptions of the horrors of the damned. That was not a result of clever acting.

Arnold Dallimore, moved with indignation, has written a scathing review. He observes that Stout disparages Whitefield's conversion as a "humanly contrived" experience copied from the Puritans. According to the review, Stout's interest is not in theology, and he ignores the theological content of Whitefield's published sermons. Dallimore also claims that Stout ignores Whitefield's role in the beginnings of Methodism and attributes to Whitefield a lack of courage. Dallimore refutes the final notion by citing pieces of evidences, such as the abuse he suffered while preaching in the open air. But for Dallimore, Stout's worst offence is his deliberate act of misrepresentation in averring that Whitefield engaged in hypocrisy. Many of Stout's assumption and misstatements suffer from lack of scholarly documentation. The reviewer identified more than three hundred historical errors. Dallimore ends by saying, "The knowledge of Whitefield which has

---

42. Macaulay, *Whitefield Anecdotes*, 111.

long been degraded by Arminian writers is further dishonored by this book which portrays him as chiefly a self-promoting actor."[43]

Others have joined on Dallimore's side. Allen Guelzo says that Stout "returns to a theme first suggested by Robert Philip in 1837; he argues that Whitefield's dramatic methods and his use of the media were as awakening as his message."[44] John Piper, preacher and chancellor of Bethlehem College and Seminary in Minneapolis, writes that Stout's biography, "is the most sustained piece of historical cynicism I have ever read. In the first one-hundred pages of this book, I wrote the word *cynical* in the margin seventy times."[45] D. A. Carson accuses Stout of reductionism. Stout, he says, "belittles Whitefield's interest in theology" and leaves no place for the Spirit of God.[46] Iain Murray, then editor of *Banner of Truth Magazine*, writes that Stout's portrayal of Whitefield is "barely recognizable" and that Stout has failed to write history from "the standpoint of supernaturalism."[47] Murray invited Stout to respond, and he has done so: In his view, professional historians "agree to settle for something less than ultimate explanations," and the academic "canons of evidence and interpretation" leave no room for notions of providence and the work of the Holy Spirit.[48] For Stout, then, professionalism dictates that scholarly writing uses a secular or natural perspective exclusively. Fair enough, but to many in the evangelical community, that assertion smacks of worldly compromise.[49]

The writers of Christian biography are well aware that the reverence with which important Christians of the past are treated needs to be carefully handled if not muted. Yet it happens. One can easily find biographies of evangelical heroes in which the warts and other blemishes have been

43. Dallimore, review of "The Divine Dramatist," in *Reformation and Revival* 1, no. 4, 125–28.

44. Guelzo, "George Whitefield and His World," *Christianity Today*, para. 10.

45. Piper, "I Will Not Be a Velvet-Mouthed Preacher!" para. 11 Presentation at Desiring God 2009 Conference for Pastors.

46. Carson, *The Gagging of God*, 484–86.

47. Murray, "Editorial," *Banner of Truth Magazine*, no. 370, 8.

48. Stout, cited in Clary, *Reformed Evangelicalism*, 52–53.

49. Stout's approach, while critically understandable, suffers from a detachment between the original intent of the subject and he, the author, and therefore remains unsatisfying. Stout would do well to remember that the supernatural is a basic presupposition of Christianity. By creating an interpretation of a Christian subject from a perspective that prima facie rules out that necessary premise results in a written work that is not believable. Stout might at least try out a supernatural perspective to see whether such an approach can make better sense of the facts.

sanitized. However, that does not mean it is appropriate to bring to the fore every fault and deficiency of the subject and it can be argued that Stout has overreacted. Especially accusation of hypocrisy was galling to Whitefield admirers. Writing from a naturalist perspective, this is, in the view of many, what Stout has done.[50] Much of secular scholarship that deals with revival in America presupposes that contemporary preachers, who ascribed the success of the Great Awakening to the Spirit God were not objective observers and were thus blankly contradicted or ignored. Luke Tyerman's comment is relevant here: "Whitefield's power was not in his talents, nor even in his oratory, but in his piety."[51]

In summary, George Whitefield's life and ministry serves as a reminder of the power of the gospel to bring profound change to individual lives and thereby to impact society at large.[52] He was the most influential Anglo-American evangelist of the eighteenth century. Wesley exceeded Whitefield in leaving behind an enduring organization that lasted, and Edwards stood above him as an intellectual and as a theologian. But Whitefield, of the three, tied together the many little pockets of evangelical revival in America as he criss-crossed the colonies and preached the gospel from town to town, addressing thousands at a time. The Great Awakening became a national phenomenon to a significant degree because of his ministry. Whitefield also pioneered the premium evangelicals place on preaching and on the doctrines of the Bible, even to the present day. He was a celebrity like none before him on the American scene.[53]

John Wesley

A hard-bitten Calvinist once asked George Whitefield, "Do you think we shall see John Wesley in heaven?" Whitefield replied, "I fear not. No. He will be so near the throne and we at such a distance, that we shall hardly get a sight of him." This is indicative of the warmheartedness with which the two men related to each other.

50. See the discussion of natural versus supernatural history writing in the introduction.

51. Tyerman, *Rev. George Whitefield*, 1:vi.

52. See Wellum, "George Whitefield (1714–1770)," *Southern Baptist Journal of Theology* Vol. 18, no. 2, 8.

53. Kidd says, "With apologies to the Beatles, George Whitefield was the first 'British Sensation'" (*George Whitefield*, 260).

Most even-handed readers of succeeding generations spoke of both men similarly. Charles H. Spurgeon said in his *Autobiography*, "If there were two apostles to be added to the number of the twelve, I do not believe that there could be found two men more fit to be so added than George Whitefield and John Wesley."[54] Iain Murray, staunchly Reformed historian that he is, wrote in the same spirit. In his biography of Wesley, he cites John Newton's glowing testimony: "I know of no one to whom I owe more as an instrument of divine grace." And Murray himself offers his opinion about Wesley's doctrinal positioning: "The foundation of Wesley's theology was sound. On the objective facts of the salvation revealed in Scripture . . . Wesley was clear."[55] Anglican bishop J. C. Ryle (1816–1900) warned anti-Wesleyan readers against demonizing those with different opinions:

> Has any one been accustomed to regard Wesley with dislike on account of his Arminian opinions? Is any one in the habit of turning away from his name with prejudice, and refusing to believe that such an imperfect preacher of the gospel could do any good? I ask such a one to remould his opinion, to take a more kindly view of the old soldier of the cross, and to give him the honour he deserves. . . . Whether we like it or not, John Wesley was a mighty instrument in God's hand for good; and, next to George Whitefield, was the first and foremost evangelist of England a hundred years ago.[56]

Less irenic writers are more critical, and the bias at times reaches unreasonable levels. The antipathy is due usually to Wesley's perceived theological missteps on predestination. At other times it is due to what is seen as Wesley's character flaws, which reveal themselves especially in his relation with George Whitefield.

Arnold Dallimore's biography of Whitefield is an example.[57] Dallimore takes issue with the claim, made by Wesley's admirers, that he was the

---

54. Spurgeon, *Autobiography, The Early Years*, 1:173.

55. Murray, "Wesley and Men Who Followed," 71, cited in Sanders, "Calvinists Who Love Wesley," *Scriptorium Daily*, June 21, 2011, para. 2.

56. Ryle, *The Christian Leaders of the Last Century*, 75–89.

57. In fact, Dallimore's publisher, Banner of Truth, felt it needed to challenge Dallimore's interpretation of Wesley. In an editorial entitled "Supporting Arnold Dallimore," the magazine stated, "They were particularly concerned that, in his [Dallimore's] concern to give Whitefield his true place in the Evangelical Revival, Arnold Dallimore verged on discrediting John Wesley's importance." Cited in Clary, *Reformed Evangelism*, 93–95. Dallimore subsequently began to accept Banner's viewpoint on Wesley, says Clary.

founder of Methodism. Wesley was not. He did inherit the nascent movement from the more popular George Whitefield when Whitefield asked him to help with the open-air ministry in the surrounding area of Bristol, but he was not the original founder. Dallimore also disputes the long-held view that Wesley's conversion occurred at the Aldersgate society, though he does not definitively say when it did happen.

The famous Aldersgate experience took place on May 24, 1738, when his heart was "strangely warmed."[58] He wrote that while listening to a reading of Luther's preface to his book on Romans, "I felt I did trust in Christ alone for salvation, and an assurance was given me that he had taken away my sins, even mine, and saved me from the law of sin and death."[59] That it was a breakthrough for Wesley there is no doubt. But it is more akin to someone reaching assurance of salvation than to an initial turning to God. Wesley's religious experience began in 1725 at Oxford, when he read Jeremy Taylor's *Rule and Exercises of Holy Living and Dying*; in 1726 he read Thomas à Kempis's *Christian Pattern* and, a year or two later, William Law's *Christian Perfection* and *Serious Call to a Devout and Holy Life*. Wesley was determined then to be "all-devoted to God; to give him all my soul, my body and my substance." This can be interpreted, in evangelical parlance, as "legal striving," which sometimes occurs during the beginning stages of conversion. But Albert Outler, a Wesley expert, calls Wesley's experiences before Aldersgate "a conversion if ever there was one."[60]

Other comments by Dallimore make clear his disapproval of what he sees as Wesley's arrogance and jealous temperament. Dallimore complains that Whitefield did not get his due because "Arminian" writers favored Wesley. It is a little painful to note that some Wesley scholars consign Whitefield to a few brief comments, as if they are oblivious to his contribution. It needs to be said, however, that a reader is occasionally startled by obvious biases from both sides. These biases would have been unwelcome to the two

---

58. Peter Böhler, a Moravian Pietist, convinced him that what he needed was simple faith in Christ and his work on the cross and that trying to work his way into favor with the Lord would not save him. Wesley also discovered Luther's commentary on Galatians, which emphasized the scriptural doctrine of justification by grace alone through faith alone. On May 24, 1738, in a Bible study comprised largely of Moravian Pietists at the Moravian Fetter Lane Chapel, Aldersgate, in London, Wesley's intellectual conviction became a heart-felt experience. From this point onward—he was thirty-five—Wesley viewed his mission in life as one of proclaiming the good news.

59. Wesley, *Works* 1:103.

60. Outler, ed., *John Wesley*, 7.

evangelists. Whitefield was careful to keep their friendship intact, theological differences notwithstanding. Wesley, although at times prickly, did the same and preached Whitefield's memorial sermon.

Wesley is an incredibly influential figure in the history of the Evangelical Revival. The doctrine of sin played a major role in his theological development. From the Moravian Pietists he learned of the need for conviction as an important facet of the salvation doctrine that later would help drive the revival forward. It was under Moravian influence at the Fetter Lane Bible study in London that he received the Aldersgate breakthrough from darkness to light. Wesley very quickly decided to visit the town in Germany where these Pietists came from. He spent four months at Herrnhut[61] and found "living proofs of the power of faith; persons saved from inward as well as outward sin by the love of God shed abroad in their hearts, and from all doubt and fear by the abiding witness of the Holy Ghost given unto them."[62]

The Moravian Pietists were of Lutheran extraction and insisted on the distinction between true, saving faith and mere intellectual acceptance of biblical truth. The Christian faith, over against the dry orthodoxy of German Lutheranism of the eighteenth century, was not just a reasoned assent to the doctrines of the church. The believer must have a new sense, a heartfelt longing for God and his service. This sense could be obtained, according to classic Pietism, only by penitential struggle, as I have noted in an earlier chapter. Before people could be saved and could receive assurance, they must be convinced and convicted of their own sinfulness. To reinforce that point Augustus Francke had written, "Twist and turn as much as you like; if you wish to become the temple of God and his holy Spirit, then you must ask him first that you be convinced of your wretchedness and corruption." A broken, contrite heart was the only proper place in which Christ could be glorified. If this did not occur, "then nothing can be understood about the spirit of God and its power.[63] No *Busskampf*, no saving faith.

While Francke's insistence on conviction as a precursor to faith was strictly held as a basic principle by the Moravians at Herrnhut, Count Zinzendorf's views diverged. By mid-century the idea of its necessity was officially abandoned. But *Busskampf* piety persisted sporadically in spite

---

61. Herrnhut was in Saxony, Germany, and was the eventual destination of refugees from Moravia where Roman Catholic forces were trying to eliminate them. They fled to the estates of Count von Zinzendorf in 1722.

62. Wesley, *Works*, 1:483.

63. See Dreyer, *The Genesis of Methodism*, 38–52.

of Zinzendorf's rejection of it. Wesley's personal experience corroborated what he had learned from the Pietists, especially from the Francke perspective. During his ministry he carried with him the insistence that a sense of sin was a necessary strand of any true, biblical conversion.

For Wesley though, a wise word of caution was added to the formula. At Herrnhut he listened to the preaching of Christian David, a leader of the original migration of refugees from Moravia, a historical region in the east of the Czech Republic, historically known as Bohemia, to Herrnhut in Saxony. Wesley was deeply impressed and wrote a summary of the sermon in his journal.[64] While a sense of need is psychologically necessary, David said, the only groundwork for reconciliation to God is found in the blood of Christ, "wholly and solely." People may grieve for their sins, but this does not justify them before God: "Nay, observe that it may hinder your justification; that is, if you build anything upon it; if you think, I must be so or so contrite, I must grieve more before I can be justified." The basis for our justification lies not even in anything that the Holy Ghost places within us. It is "something without you vix. the righteousness and the blood of Christ," said Christian David. For Wesley and for the Evangelical Revival, this was a very important caveat. Arguably, in spite of what some high-Calvinistic folk wish to believe even today, there is no such thing as a saving conviction. Conviction, important as it is, is but a means to faith in the person of Christ.

Nevertheless, when Wesley returned to England, he included the *Busskampf* in his repertoire of sermons. A sense of need for the saving grace of the gospel was encouraged. Preaching a sermon called "The Way to the Kingdom," he not only delineated the conversion process but also made urgent appeals to his audience: "Awake then, thou that sleepest. Know thyself to be a sinner, and what manner of sinner thou art. Know that corruption of thy inmost nature, whereby thou art very far gone from original righteousness. . . . Know that thou art corrupt in every faculty of thy soul."[65]

However, Wesley was not one to leave his audience hanging on to their conviction. He appealed for immediate salvation through a personal turning to Christ. Examples abound. In a sermon called "Justification by Faith," Wesley closed with a passioned entreaty: "Thou ungodly one who hearest or readest these words, thou vile, helpless, miserable sinner, I charge thee before God, the judge of all, go straight unto him with all thy ungodliness. . . . Go as altogether ungodly, guilty, lost, destroyed, deserving and

---

64. Wesley, *Works* 1:118, 119.
65. Wesley, "The Way to the Kingdom," *Works* 1:33, 225.

dropping into hell, and thou shalt then find favour in his sight, and know that he justifieth the ungodly.... Thus look unto Jesus!"[66]

His brother Charles was equally convinced of the prerequisite nature of conviction. In his *Journal*, Charles noted how fruitless was the practice of encouragement until a convert had experienced penitence: "It is good for the choicest of God's children to receive, and that for a long time, the sentence of death in themselves."[67]

The Wesleys organized societies, first in London and then throughout the country, for the purpose of Bible study and mutual accountability. These small societies were begun on the Fetter Lane Moravian model. The purpose, in the first place, was so that for members "it may the more easily be discerned, whether they are indeed working out their own salvation." The minimum test for admission was a sense of sin. Wesley stated from the General Rules of the Societies, "There is only one condition previously required in those who desire admission: a desire to flee from the wrath to come, to be saved from their sins."[68] Soon these societies dotted the English landscape, independent of the state church, and from them the Methodist denominations later developed. This was, in part, the gift Wesley brought to the revival movement. He was not only a great preacher. The Methodist denominations were derived from his acumen for process. In this he excelled beyond Whitefield, who was so instrumental in preaching from town to town. Wesley was an organizational genius and left behind a structure that, in denominational terms, remains to this day.

From the Moravians, Wesley learned of *Busskampf*, the first of several stages in the conversion of sinners. It was under the direction and encouragement of the Moravian Pietists that Wesley experienced his own conversion and assurance of faith. Conviction of sin, he insisted, was an essential element in true conversion. It was also from the Moravians that the Wesleys learned of the efficacy of Bible societies. More than his roots in Anglicanism, John Wesley's spiritual nurture was predicated by what he learned from the Moravian Pietists.

Having seen the effects of the preaching of the Evangelical Revival and the revival leaders' personal acquaintance with the doctrine of sin, we will turn, in the next chapter, to some theological considerations.

---

66. Wesley, "Justification by Faith," *Works, Sermons* 1: 1–33, 198–99.
67. Wesley, *Journal of Charles Wesley*, 168.
68. Wesley, *Work* 8:269–71. See Dreyer, *Genesis of Methodism*, 50.

7.

Calling for Conviction

"Brethren, it is easier to declaim against a thousand sins of others, than to mortify one sin in ourselves."

JOHN FLAVEL (1627–1691)

SOME PRACTICAL CONSIDERATIONS

Introduction

IN UNDERLINING THE SIGNIFICANCE of the conviction of sin in conversion, it is important that we explore the practical side of the doctrine of sin itself. Sin doctrine—or, in theological parlance, *hamartiology*—cannot be placed neatly into little analytical boxes and still have practical bearing. Sin can be described from a distance as an act of offense against God involving a challenge to his authority and his law and a maliciousness toward fellow humans. Sin can and is often discussed in classroom academia without any notice being taken of its heinousness. Sin is often dealt with as theory without consideration of the wretchedness it has visited upon humankind. Sin can find connection with moral philosophy, practical ethics, biblical psychology, and other disciplines in the social sciences. Even more boxes can be filled with concepts about sin, and the observer may still remain aloof to its pernicious character. But one needs to burrow in a bit deeper for a practical understanding of sin and its consequences. What the fall has inflicted on every individual and on every organization can leave one unnerved and frightened.

Consequences

In terms of the consequences, the most fearful is the kindling of the anger of God. In Romans 3:19 the apostle says, "Now we know that whatever the law says it speaks to those who are under the law, so that every mouth may be stopped, and the whole world may be held accountable to God."[1]

The apostle assumes that the mouths of humanity are wide open in protest against restraints, against the obvious presence of the great God, and against the claims and laws he has laid down. Paul therefore declares that all of humanity, each individual, is guilty before God without any possible back talk. Mouths are stopped. In Jeremiah's time the children of Israel stood guilty before God, and the Lord declared, "I am full of the wrath of the Lord; I am weary of holding it in" (Jer 6:11). In the Epistle to the Ephesians, Paul calls Jews as well as gentiles "children of wrath" (Eph 2:3). There are illustrations enough in the Bible that reveal the kind of action God takes when he is angry. It is indeed a fearful thing to find oneself "in the hands of an angry God"!

Secondly, as sinners we are lonely and alone. The biblical doctrine of reconciliation implies a state of estrangement, loneliness, and aloneness. It also implies a state of enmity with God and the absence of loving fellowship with others. Jesus summarized the commandments with two irreducible laws: loving God and loving one's neighbor. It needed to be said. The enmity against the great Lord of the universe is clearly and openly displayed, more so today it seems than in previous generations. Every age has had its predominant sins; ours is not different. But our generation has taken further steps: a self-indulgent raising of the high fist against God's created order.

Moreover, bitterness and racial anger toward neighbors abound. Only the cross and the resurrection, with the resultant fellowship with our Lord and Savior, can heal our isolation. Sin separates. Sin drives wedges between people. And the deep-seated sense of guilt[2] we feel drives us to hide from

---

1. See the summary of Jonathan Edwards's sermon on this text in Chapter 5.
2. Lewis says, "All men alike stand condemned, not by alien codes of ethics, but by their own, and all men therefore are conscious of guilt." Lewis, *The Problem of Pain*, 10.

the God whom we dread. When the gospel of the grace of God saves someone, it saves him or her not only from sin itself but also from loneliness.

Another frightful consequence of sinnership is the lostness. In Jesus' parabolic teaching, lostness plays a leading role: there are the lost sheep, the lost coin, and the lost son of Luke 15. Bernard Ramm has said that being lost means "lost to God, lost to oneself, and to the kingdom of God and its purposes... Wilful sin produces this lostness."[3]

Finally, sin results in death. First came spiritual death, then physical. Being dead spiritually implies an inability to know God and to hear him speak. God is Spirit. He is a remote, wholly other being who is unreachable, and we still need to hear him speak. Spiritual death also implies that spiritual realities are incomprehensible: "The natural person does not accept the things of the Spirit of God, for they are folly to him, and he is not able to understand them because they are spiritually discerned" (1 Cor 2:14). God is angry with sin, sinners are lonely and alone, they are trapped in lostness, and finally, they are dying. Sin is serious business. It is in the sinner's best interest to gain some conviction about it.

Recent Revolt Against the Doctrine of Sin

We have shown several reasons for the loss of a sense of sin prior to the great revivals in the early eighteenth century. Some of these reasons still exist today. However, aside from discussions in written work and in Bible-college and seminary classrooms, the word "sin" has largely disappeared from discussion. Even some evangelical churches frown on its use simply because it is unpleasant. At least in the eighteenth-century folk believed in a God who was transcendent and understood that there was a great chasm between his majestic perfection and the depravity that characterizes human existence. Today we have, broadly speaking, lost this sense of transcendence. "Our Father who art in heaven" refers to a transcendent Being, the very idea of which tends to be denied by the rationalistic thinking of post-Enlightenment scholarship. All that exists is the world between our horizons, and for some people in the rising generations, what is at the

---

3. Ramm, *Offense to Reason*, 112. I am indebted, for some of the ideas put forward in this chapter, to Ramm's useful study of sin doctrine on pp. 38–174. Bernard Ramm (1916–1992) has received criticism from the likes of Cornelius Van Til and C. F. H. Henry because of his appreciation for Karl Barth, under whom he studied for a time.

center is just us and our digital device. Sin cannot be fully comprehended in that worldview. It can be understood only in relation to transcendence.

Once we have disposed of any consideration of a transcendent Creator, we quite naturally lose respect for the sanctity of what he has made. This is the logical next step. The self has, in many respects, replaced God. That is one reason why gender has, for the first time in history, become the focal point of identity. Given a level of discontent with that identity, people pursue change. It may not be a conscious rebellion. However, it represents the ultimate disrespect for God's image in created humanity.

What else has done damage to the traditional concept of sin? First, in psychiatry, psychology, and counseling, there is an insistence that religion is a source of neurosis in patients, and therefore, religion is denigrated as harmful to the health of the human psyche. Psychiatry and psychology in the West embrace a humanistic viewpoint regarding moral standards, and many counselors have rejected the concept of absolute truth. Vulnerable people are encouraged to rationalize away distress caused by a guilty conscience. Credibility is given to patterns of behavior that Christians would characterize as sin. The biblical-counseling movement, spearheaded by Jay Adams and others in the 1960s and 1970s was a response by believers as psychology and psychiatry gained influence during the latter part of the previous century.

The Allies who defeated Germany sent psychologists to Europe at the end of WWII by the hundreds to have them debrief captured German soldiers and to interview the Nazis. Since then, the fields of psychology and psychiatry have carved for themselves a status of indispensability. That is most likely why many pastors view counselors, in both fields, with suspicion. The impact of secular thinking, starting with Freud, is seen as having corrupted the behavioral sciences and pitted them against any biblical construct. Another contributing factor to the mistrust of mental-health professionals among church leaders is the reality that, compared to other physicians or academics, psychiatrists and psychologists are not likely to be involved with church.[4]

A second factor damaging the traditional understanding of sin is the lobbyists and influencer groups that argue for more permissiveness and fewer rules about behavior. They are further eroding the traditional

---

4. Grcevich, "The Sins of Psychiatry . . . and Psychology," iDisciple, no date, para. 7. Grcevich serves as president and founder of Key Ministry, a nonprofit organization providing free training, consultation, resources, and support to help churches serve families of children with disabilities.

concept of law and, with it, the idea of sin. The law as we knew it in the middle of the twentieth century placed a high level of importance on the sanctity of life. But increasingly, the emphasis is on property and material protection. This shift is symptomatic of the contemporary lack of a sense of sin and accountability to a transcendent God. Increasingly, governments and law enforcement agencies in the West are enamored with the ancient Code of Hammurabi, with its heavy emphasis on concerns about money, property, and business transactions. While these are addressed in the Mosaic law, a much higher level of importance is placed on moral laws, loving and honoring God and one's neighbor, and one's relation to God. It can be argued that this shift represents a paradigmatic deviation from a focus on the biblical view of sin.

Since the midpoint of the previous century, interpretations of the law have been increasingly relativistic. During previous centuries the law was interpreted through the grid of divine justice, as it had been in the early centuries and the medieval period. The great William Blackstone (1723–1780) wrote his magisterial *Commentaries on the Laws of England*, which contributed to the foundation of British and American common law. In that writing Blackstone professed his debt to biblical law.

Blindness and Self-Deception

Blaise Pascal made the comment that humanity can study itself but in seeing cannot understand. To adapt a famous line from the venerable Sherlock Holmes, "We see but do not observe."[5] Humanity has lost objective perspective. It is a spiritual matter, and being sinners by nature, we do not have the spiritual equipment to understand the essence of our existence (see 1 Cor 2:14). Humanity is therefore incomprehensible to itself. In fact, the prophet Jeremiah, in the middle of reflecting on the human condition, points this out: "The heart is deceitful above all things, and desperately sick; *who can understand it?*" (Jer 17:9). Here he suggests that the heart is far too defiled to be understood.

C. S. Lewis speaks about the intrinsic quality of self-deception that characterizes the psychology of sin:

> Now error and sin both have this property, *that the deeper they are the less their victim suspects their existence;* they are masked evil.

5. Adapted from the famous quote in Arthur Conan Doyle's *A Scandal in Bohemia*, 9: "*You see, but don't observe.*"

> Pain is unmasked. . . . Every man knows that something is wrong when he is being hurt. . . . We can rest contentedly in our sins and in our stupidities, but pain insists upon being attended to. God whispers to us in our pleasures, speaks in our conscience, but shouts in our pains. . . . It is his megaphone to rouse a dead world.[6]

The Watergate scandal of the 1970s produced many instances of self-deception. John Dean, one of the central figures in the scandal, gave testimony to the Senate Committee that was articulate and detailed. Everyone was amazed and impressed with his ability to remember precisely who said what and when, months after their occurrence. But Dean's testimony was found to be "wishful memory" once a clear picture emerged from the Nixon tapes.[7] Dean had remembered things that had never occurred, and these memories placed him in a more favorable light in the scandal than the bare truth later did.

In the same vein, consider the wives of mafiosi who work at developing a degree of self-deception, not asking why the associates look like bandits or where all the money comes from. Consider the German guard at the extermination point of Jewish people off-loaded from a train who, when a distraught lady grabbed his weapon and mortally wounds him, cried, "What have I done that I must suffer so!?"[8] Examples abound. Self-deception is one of the most injurious characteristics of sin.

We deceive ourselves when we are persuaded that God is pleased with our native uprightness. Remember the "civil man" repeatedly castigated by Puritan preaching. Even in our day, the evangelical movement is shot through with the Finneyesque deception of replacing the necessity of regeneration with a mere show of profession.

Says Anthony Hoekema, "Sin is usually masked."[9] It is always committed for some "good reason." We see sins very clearly in others but often fail to recognize our own. Moreover, we tend to cover up our sins, once recognized. David expressed it thus: "When I kept silent, my bones wasted away through my groaning all day long." The Pharisee thanked God that he was so much better than other men. It is breathtaking how effortlessly

---

6. Lewis, *Problem of Pain*, 57–58, emphasis added.
7. Plantinga., *Not the Way It's Supposed to Be*, 106.
8. This illustration was given by Cornelius Plantinga, my prayer-group leader in seminary, during a group meeting.
9. Hoekema, *Created in God's Image*, 174, 175.

we mask our sinfulness and comfort ourselves with the big lie . . . until we discover that covering up hurts. Confession is cathartic.

The Second World War and subsequent history provided many occasions for people in the Allied nations to deceive themselves that God is pleased with them, often learning the lesson the hard way. During the war the democracies felt a sense of moral goodness as they prosecuted the great struggle against Nazism and Japanese imperialism. Upon the liberation of Europe in 1945, the Allies discovered successive locations where abhorrent crimes against humanity had been performed, especially the extermination camps and slave work camps. Treblinka, Dachau, Buchenwald, Auschwitz, and others had been systematically governed as extensions of state policy. The high degree of cruelty necessary to carry out this national crime meant, for many, that there must be a strain of moral evil inherent in the German people that other nations are free from. It was also thought by some that the Holocaust, during which about six million Jews went to their death, resulted from hatred inherent in German antisemitism.

These interpretations tidied things up nicely for the victors, who could believe themselves incapable of such crimes. On the other hand, the more thoughtful of the Allies were devastated by the Holocaust, not because it rendered the Nazis blameworthy but because, says Susan Neiman, it brought a realization of a *possibility in human nature we hoped not to see*.[10] As subsequent history unfolded, the self-satisfaction of the victors evaporated to some extent with instances of mass murder such as the My Lai Massacre of 1968 during the Vietnam War. Rationalizing and the closely linked deception of self are some of the most subtle facets of human sin, and an especially subtle form of self-deception is the tendency to think that God is pleased with our moral uprightness.[11]

---

10. Nieman, *Evil in Modern Thought*, 254.

11. Some of our readers may find this disturbing. It is not my intention to shock. But we do need to be clear. Witness communist and fascist institutions of the last century, when Joseph Stalin murdered twenty-five to thirty-five million of his own people in the pogroms and the Gulag of the Soviet Union. Witness the millions brutally murdered by Pol Pot of Cambodia in the 1970s. Witness the burning of churches in Indonesia, in this present century, committed while worshippers were inside. At time of writing, Vladimir Putin, unprovoked, is bombing schools, train stations, hospitals and the homes of civilians in Ukraine.

The cruelty of terrorism knows no bounds as the terrorist organization, Hamas, has demonstrated in its harrowing raid of murder, torture and decapitation in October, 2023. Israel's IDF had recovered a phone call in which a Hamas terrorist called his parents to boast of the number of Jews he killed during the raid. "Hi dad, I am speaking to you from

Calling for Conviction

It is this attitude that Jesus rails against in the Gospels. He loves people in need, sinners and sufferers. His sympathy to them is clear for the reader of the Gospel narratives. By contrast, his harshest words are aimed at the Pharisees and other groups with similar attitudes. He condemns the Jewish leadership six times in Matthew 23 for their attachment to legal traditions handed down to them. The parable of the Pharisee and the tax collector praying in the temple illustrates Jesus' unflagging admonitions to "some who trusted in themselves that they were righteous, and treated others with contempt" (Luke 18:9). Jesus clashes with the Jewish leaders repeatedly about the issue of true righteousness. Moreover, he is concerned to warn his disciples about the same pitfalls, in one instance telling them, "Apart from me you can do nothing" (John 15:5). The apostle Paul's argument against works righteousness in Romans begins with the condemnation of the self-righteousness of the Jewish leaders (Rom 2:17–24). In Romans 10 he expresses his desire that they may be saved. They seek God's approval based on their own blamelessness, showing how ignorant of true righteousness they are. The apostle Paul says that the only righteousness of value is that which is found in Christ, who is the end of the law (Romans 2:4).

Sadly, Christians are familiar with this form of self-deception. We were originally created to perform, to achieve righteousness through the quality of our virtue and our effort. This characteristic did not leave us when Adam and Eve fell into sin. It is therefore difficult to keep the amazing grace of God front and center. The subtlety of trusting in self is startling when discovered, like the shock of detecting hidden danger. If we are not watchful, insidious self-righteousness will creep in, and we will slide into the presumptuous spirituality of the Jewish leaders. By all accounts, Jesus hates self-righteousness. It is a betrayal of the high price he paid for our

---

Mefalsim," the Hamas terrorist is heard saying. "Open your WhatsApp and look at how many [Israelis] I killed with my own hands; your son killed Jews! "Dad, I am speaking to you from a Jew's phone, I killed her and her husband, I killed ten with my own hands", the terrorist excitedly told his Gazan parents. The father can be heard crying with joy. "May God protect you, my son," his father said as the mother told the terrorist, "I wish I was there with you," as her son is heard shouting directions at fellow terrorists to "kill, kill, kill! kill them!" "Terrorist live-streamed horrors of massacre to Gazan parents" *The Jerusalem Post*, October 24, 2023.

On the individual level, witness the many disturbed, confused, and often abused killers who provide reasons for people in a highly civilized society to be afraid to walk the streets after dark. The perpetrators are human beings—no more, no less. When we penetrate our basic, natural condition as fallen and broken humans, we receive an inkling of the extremity of our common wretchedness by nature. We may say, "there, but by the grace of God. . ."

salvation, and it grieves the Holy Spirit, whose function it is to glorify the name and work of Christ. The genuine humility that conviction engenders is characteristic of a life of faith. That is why the Great Awakening preachers considered conviction of sin a necessity for sincere conversion and a blessing for the Christian.

Coming to Grips with Sin: Conviction

For us the question is, how can we come to some understanding of the horrendous nature of sin and sin's calamitous effect on the human race? The medieval theologian Anselm of Canterbury (1033–1109) famously asked that question. "Who has truly pondered the weight of sin?" His answer was this: "The one who has truly pondered the weight of the cross." The doctrine of sin can be understood best through the cross of Christ. Apart from the redemption accomplished at the cross, the enormity of sin cannot be fathomed. *It was the Son of God* who was tortured and killed. References to sin, therefore, in both the Old and the New Testaments must be seen Christologically. So, we are given some light about sin from the standpoint of the gospel, the good news. We cannot measure how sinful or how confused humans are by nature, nor can we plumb the depths of our depravity, apart from the divine remedy located at the cross of Calvary and in the empty tomb.

The Psalms provide clarity on this. Within the category of lament psalms there are six or seven penitential psalms. These are the most pointed. David's experience with Bathsheba and her husband Uriah is not only sin at the human level. First and foremost, David sinned against the holiness of God (Ps 51:4):

> Against you, you only, have I sinned
>   and done what is evil in your sight,
> so that you may be justified in your words
>   and blameless in your judgment.

We may infer from this passage that when we sin against our fellow humans or our community, it is first and foremost a sin against the ineffable perfection of God. That is what sin does. It violates the majesty of our Lord and wilfully seeks to expunge the image in which he created us. The prodigal son in the parable became aware of this fact: "Father, I have sinned *against heaven* and before you" (Luke 15:21).

Calling for Conviction

In the Bible sin is always defined in relation to God. The Epistle of James observes that if a person breaks just one law, he or she is guilty of breaking all of them, since the same God spoke all of the Ten Commandments. The inference is that to sin at all is to sin against the very Being of God in his holiness, his truth, his love, and his righteousness (Jas 2:8–11).

Some have claimed that sin can be defined only as a negative.[12] But sin is more than not holy or not perfection or not the good; sin is positively brutal and violent, the willful initiative of ruthlessness in human behavior, restrained only by God's common grace. Moreover, there are the seeming demonic elements of sin—namely, the cold and heartless calculations that precede acts of sin and that reveal what brutish behavior humanity is capable of. Accounting for sin as a negative will not do. It is positively an aggressive virus of spiteful meanness, containing the most far-reaching and most shameful possibilities.

As we have seen, the conversion process involves a new self-awareness or self-understanding, the sense that the leaders of the Great Awakening described as the sense of the heart. Prior to that we do not have a right or true understanding of ourselves. We do not have the perspective or categories that allow for self-assessment. But when the sinless perfection that is Christ the Son of Man is preached and taught, we, by mirror reflection, develop some degree of conviction of the enormity of sin. With Jesus Christ held before us as the ideal human in sinless perfection, however that is communicated, we begin to see, by comparison, what raging brutes we can become as fallen and broken human beings capable of the most nefarious crime.

Benefits of Conviction

The Christian doctrine of sin provides a necessary aid to human self-awareness. Without the former, we do not get the latter. Holy Spirit conviction helps explain why a young woman's life is shattered by men who are without much of a moral center, or why a young man thinks his way forward is made up of a parade of good times and ends up bankrupt like the prodigal son, or why the cheapskate who scrapes together every last penny and gets away without tipping finds himself isolated from any positive fellowship with other human beings, or why a man or woman traveling alone begins to seek out lustful dalliances with a stranger while the faithful spouse remains

---

12. For example, Hendrikus Berkhof, *The Christian Faith*, 208. Berkhof denies the historicity of the fall and of a garden called Eden.

at home. Without the knowledge that everyone is a sinner, we lack a fundamental understanding of self, and we remain in a doleful state, so blind that the excuses we manufacture seem legitimate.

When the apostle Paul was a young man, he had remarkable achievements, but his self-understanding was characterized by self-deception. He was completely unaware of his vulnerability and his actual standing before God. When he was converted, he discovered immediately that he was a blasphemer and a murderer and therefore made repeated postconversion confessions: "I am the foremost of sinners." Paul's case makes it clear that one can be very religious and not have any self-understanding that comes from a sense of sin (Phil 3:2–6; 1 Tim 1:13, 15).

An awareness of our status as sinners reveals something of the struggle we face on a daily basis. In the core of our being is the very source of our decision making. It is where our appetites and propensities come into play, where our decisions for action are formed. We make sinful decisions: we lie; we steal; we swear and curse; we abuse others, often those very close to us; we become jealous and angry; we have murderous thoughts. Sometimes our sinful decisions produce action, and sometimes they do not. Without a sense of sin, we simply cannot grasp this.

Awareness of our status as sinners also helps us understand the temptations we face daily. A non-Christian might go through a violent experience of temptation and be puzzled as to why they so easily veer off course. Without a sense of sin, there is no basis for clarifying the experience. But Christians get it: since we have a deep understanding of the doctrine of sin, we can explain temptation. Even though temptation may be relentless and difficult, at least we are helped in overcoming it by a knowledge of where it comes from and why it happens.[13]

Sin can seem innocuous and be subtle in its presence, like a serpent deep in the grass. It need not be crass and brutal, as in the gross sin of murder. It can be refined and cultivated. One emits a calculating word or tone in close conversation, or adopts a barely screened attitude in personal relations, or carries out a shrewd manipulation of another person, or leaves a promise or need unfulfilled. These barely visible sins might inflict damage that is as far reaching as the damage caused by sins that are starkly transparent.

Sin can be discovered in the way rationalizing takes place. A person cheats in a business deal and, by giving more than usual to the church,

---

13. The point is Ramm's *Offense to Reason*, 148.

rationalizes that on the scale of good versus bad, it lands in the positive. Many a Christian counselor has to deal with people trying to rationalize, to make bad seem good even though it is plainly sin. C. S. Lewis, in *The Great Divorce*, deals with rationalizing in terms of making evil acts, words, or practices into good ones. Lewis says that the human race is always trying to bring together "heaven and hell." But while evil can, at times, be undone through a process of redemption and forgiveness, it cannot be rationalized into a seeming good.

All of this is to say that sin is more than a neutral theological construct, an academic subject for detached analysis. It is never that. If one does not have a sense of sin, one cannot understand its consequences, its effects, temptation, and how and why we rationalize, nor can such a person understand his or her troubled existence in this world. Rather than something to be avoided at all costs, as many counselors would have it, a clear conviction of sin is a giant step toward reconciliation, healing, and forgiveness.[14]

However, there is a word of caution in the Bible. The presence of conviction can also result in utter bafflement and resulting angst. Believers should take seriously Paul's expression of misery and torment at the internal struggle he is having, as outlined in Romans 7. Possessing self-awareness does not mean that a believer is able to sail smoothly through the vagaries of life's experiences. Paul, while expressing confusion and dismay at the struggle between flesh and spirit, shows great wisdom and maturity: "I do not understand my own actions. For I do not do what I want, but I do the very thing I hate." This confusion can leave a believer drained of spiritual energy and crying out with Paul, "For I delight in the law of God, in my inner being, but I see in my members another law waging war against the law of my mind and making me captive to the law of sin that dwells in my members. Wretched man that I am! Who will deliver me from this body of death?"[15] Charles H. Spurgeon says it is "the cry of one who is

---

14. Lewis, *The Great Divorce*, 7.

15. I realize that this interpretation of Paul's words is the subject of debate. I favor the position that Paul is speaking of himself as a mature Christian. There are other interpretations that can be considered, and the debate over this issue seems to be at a stalemate, with commentators agreeing to disagree. The position that Paul is writing as a mature believer is held by Charles H. Spurgeon, Martin Luther, John Calvin, F. F. Bruce, C. E. B. Cranfield, Leon Morris, John Murray, J. I. Packer, and John Stott among others. The position that Paul is writing about his experience prior to conversion is the opinion of Martyn Lloyd-Jones, William Sanday, Craig Keener, F. Godet, James Denney, Herman Ridderbos, Robert Gundry, and Douglas Moo, among others. Thomas Schreiner, in his masterful commentary on Romans in the Baker Exegetical series, suggests that both

fainting."[16] John Calvin writes, "Paul teaches us, that the most perfect, as long as they dwell in the flesh, are exposed to misery, for they are subject to death; nay, when they thoroughly examine themselves, they find in their own nature nothing but misery."[17] In fact, Paul seems overwhelmed by the antagonist within. That "other law" wins the struggle every time. It is the "law" of indwelling sin. The verbs in verse 23 are in the present tense, sharply delineating the never-ending battle that always seems to end in failure. Therefore, an important caveat is appropriate here: for the believer, even one with acute self-awareness about indwelling sin, there is not, in every instance nor for all time, happiness and clear sailing.

I conclude this chapter with a pastoral consideration. Seekers under conviction sometimes want pastoral advice on how deep a sense of sin is needed before a breakthrough can be expected. This is understandable, but it is the wrong question. It implies a legal desire to achieve self-improvement before coming to the throne of grace, and related to the legal striving is the often-morbid inward focus. At this point there is a great conflict going on, for it is excruciatingly difficult for a person to come to him- or herself as the prodigal son did. Seekers need to come to the place where they are bereft of resources, to end up in Hosea's wilderness (Hosea 2:14). Faith then stops looking inward for betterment. Faith needs to look for help outside of the self.

Even though the question is not the right one, it does indeed have an answer, and this answer is obvious to Christian pastors and counselors. The sense of sin needs to be deep enough that the person can no longer remain in that condition. Sometimes a degree of self-loathing accompanies conviction, the purpose of which is to drive the seeker to look away from self to the great remedy that Jesus provides at the cross. Looking to Jesus crucified is integral to the breakaway from introspection. The early German Pietists called it *Durchbruch* ("breakthrough") and believed it came after a period of the necessary *Busskampf* ("penitential struggle"). It was coaching by the Pietists that encouraged John Wesley in his struggle for assurance.

Jesus stands at the door, knocking (Rev 3:20). He wants to enter through the door of our hearts, to come in and dine with us.[18] He is aware

---

positions need careful study. G. K. Beale and N. T. Wright interpret Paul's comments as representative of the nation of Israel.

16. Spurgeon, "The Fainting Warrior," *Spurgeon.org*. Section 3, para. 1.

17. Calvin, "Commentary on Romans 7:24," para. 3.

18. A literal example is the account of Jesus inviting himself to dinner at the house of Zacchaeus (Luke 19:5).

of our seeking and our conviction and would come near to have a talk with us about our sin and the remedy he offers freely and without price. All that is required of us is that we express our need and look to him for help. None has ever been turned away. He will "abundantly pardon" (Isa 55:7).

8.

Preaching Today, Part A

"Christianity now has to preach the diagnosis."

C. S. Lewis, 1940

PARABLES AND METHODS

The question that remains is, can preachers take the lessons proffered by the preaching of the Great Awakening and the Evangelical Revival and transfer them to today's world?[1] These final two chapters will be an attempt at offering some suggestions.

The gospel is offered to everyone, and the free offer of grace is unfettered; it has no conditions. Many who hear it, however, are satisfied to go forward without its benefits, because they do not see themselves as sinners or they have not come to a place of suffering in their lives. The gospel is good news only to people who sense their need. That is why the principle that faith is born of need is a universal principle. As C. S. Lewis says, "Before we can be cured, we must want to be cured."[2] That is also why one of

---

1. As an aside, the late Tim Keller had a nice bit of encouragement for young preachers: "Your first 200 sermons, no matter what you do, are going to be terrible." *Eucatastrophe* 101.

2. Lewis, *Mere Christianity*, 92.

the basic elements of the doctrine of salvation is conviction. How, then, can preachers arouse in a person acknowledgment and an awareness of a sinful condition, given the climate of egocentricity and material self-indulgence in our culture? The Laodicean church of the Book of Revelation was accused of a similar fault: "For you say, I am rich, I have prospered, and I need nothing, not realizing that you are wretched, pitiable, poor, blind, and naked" (Rev 3:17).

Can preachers in our time employ homiletical methods similar to that of the Great Awakening? About 150 years ago, the evangelical Anglican bishop J. C. Ryle suggested the answer was a resounding affirmative. He wrote, "I am obliged to say plainly that, in my judgment, we have among us neither the men nor the doctrines of the days gone by. Once let the evangelical ministry return to the ways of the 18th century, and I firmly believe we should have as much success as before. We are where we are, because we have come short of our fathers."[3] We should say the same thing today. While the content should be, in essence, the same, each generation needs to hear the gospel in its own language and through the lenses of its own culture. From Augustine to Luther there is continuity in much of the substance of the teaching but radical change in how that content is presented. Helmut Thielicke similarly says, "The Gospel must constantly be forwarded to a new address, because the recipient is repeatedly changing his place of residence."[4] That is not to say that the methods of bringing the word today should be couched in all manner of gimmickry and fancy. Preaching the Gospel remains the divinely sanctioned means of grace. But the church

---

3. Ryle, *The Christian Leaders of the Last Century* 26–30. This reference is also available in a small booklet: *The Agency That Transformed a Nation* (Banner of Truth, 2011). In *Christian Leaders*, Ryle summarizes the content of preaching during the Evangelical Revival, and it seems helpful to provide a partial summary here: The preachers of the Evangelical Revival taught their hearers plainly that they were spiritually dead by nature and must be made alive again and that they were guilty, lost, helpless, hopeless, and in imminent danger of eternal ruin. Strange and paradoxical as it may seem to some, their first step towards making men good was to show them that they were utterly bad, and their primary argument in persuading men to do something for their souls was to convince them that they could do nothing at all. They also taught constantly that Christ's death upon the cross was the only satisfaction for man's sin and that when Christ died, he died as their substitute, "the just for the unjust" (1 Pet 3:18 KJV). The same preachers insisted on the universal necessity of heart conversion and a new creation by the Holy Spirit. They proclaimed everywhere to the crowds whom they addressed, "Ye must be born again" (John 3:7 KJV). And they taught, as doctrines equally true, God's eternal hatred against sin and God's love towards sinners.

4. Thielicke, *A Little Exercise*, translated by Taylor, 31.

today needs to send the gospel message to a location that in many cases is radically different from what Augustine or the Reformers were dealing with.

People still need to be "allure[d]" to the wilderness, where God "will speak tenderly to them" (Hosea 2:14). They need to be led gently to the place where the prodigal son "came to himself" (Luke 15:17). It is appropriate for sinners to stand beside the tax collector in the temple and, without daring to look up, pray his prayer: "God, be merciful to me, a sinner!" or more accurately, "*the* sinner" (Luke 18:13). It is likewise appropriate for sufferers to "implore him that they might only touch the fringe of his garment" (Matt 14:36). The degree or the intensity of conviction is not the issue. The issue is, Do I need forgiveness? Do I need healing and transformation, either for the first time or many a time throughout the Christian life? By way of healthy self-examination, both seekers and those walking the Christian walk should ask themselves whether they have ever truly answered these questions in the affirmative.

This was a key element, homiletically, for the evangelists of the Evangelical Revival and the Great Awakening, and it became integral to their theology of revival. I venture to say that a smattering of this would be healthy within our congregations and that it is too important to ignore. C. S Lewis, in his typical exacting manner, says this: "A recovery of the old sense of sin is essential to Christianity. Christ takes it for granted that men are bad. Until we really feel this assumption of His to be true, though we are part of the world He came to save, we are not part of the audience to whom His words are addressed. We lack the first condition for understanding what He is talking about."[5] We now, therefore, turn to explore the biblical requisite methods and conditions for the recovery of the "old sense of sin."

Instruction from the Soils

There are various kinds of people who make up the audience during Sunday services. They are represented in much of the teaching of Jesus. For example, in the parable of the soils (Matt 13:1–23), we are given a picture of what might be typical in a congregation. The congregation in the parable is the population of Palestine, where Jesus ministers. It is where "he came to his own" (John 1:11). The Sower of seed represents the preacher of the Word. The seed is the Word preached. The soils are the various types of listeners. The main idea of the parable is that the hearing of the gospel always

---

5. Lewis, *Problem of Pain*, 45.

depends on the condition of the hearer, on the heart of the listener. Jesus explains that there are four kinds of soils, or four kinds of listeners: the one that is shut up to the message, the one that is thoughtless and fickle, the one that is distracted, and the one that is open to the message.

The first soil makes up the hard, packed-down, well-trodden paths around the edges of farmers' fields. Jesus explains to his disciples that the Word is heard by hardhearted people who have not built fences or boundaries around their lives. Their hearts have become expressways of countless temptations and sins every day. They are left open to them, without protection. Their hearts are tough, impervious to the power of the gospel and the great love of God, never having enjoyed the benefit of conviction. This person might be outwardly religious and appear praise-worthy and upright but is smugly resistant to transforming grace. It is the soil of the Pharisee. Jesus said such people are like anonymous whitewashed tombs; they are dead on the inside, while to an observer they are paragons of virtue. They are harsh in judging outward sins in others and often are able to express with clarity the biblical gospel to all and sundry and couch it in an impressive demeanor. Of them C. S. Lewis has said,

> The sins of the flesh are bad, but they are the least bad of all sins. All the worst pleasures are purely spiritual: the pleasure of putting other people in the wrong, of bossing and patronizing and spoiling sport and back-biting; the pleasures of power, of hatred. For there are two things inside me, competing with the human self which I must try to become. They are the Animal self, and the Diabolical self. The Diabolical self is the worse of the two. That is why a cold, self-righteous prig who goes regularly to church may be far nearer to hell than a prostitute. But, of course, it is better to be neither.[6]

No cultivation has yet taken place. The person's so-called holiness is outward and involves pride. This ground needs plowing and harrowing. The seed is good seed, but it cannot penetrate the soil. Finally, the birds come to pick it all away until there is none left. John says, "[Jesus] came to his own, but his own people did not receive him" (John 1:11). Satan has won the day as he picks the seeds up before there is any possibility of taking root. It is a frightful picture. The sad thing that needs to be said is that there is something of the hypocrite in all of us.

---

6. Lewis, *Mere Christianity*, 94–95. See also Reeves, *Evangelical Pharisees*, for a sharply stated analysis of the modern Pharisee.

The second soil is representative of hearers who are fickle and impulsive (Matt 13:20–21). The seed falls on rocky soil. Jesus explains, "As for what was sown on rocky ground, this is the one who hears the word and immediately receives it with joy, yet he has no root in himself, but endures for a while, and when tribulation or persecution arises on account of the word, immediately he falls away." This hearer listens to the sermon and leaps for joy, saying, "Wow! This is great!" He or she believes they have found substance to remedy the hollowness of life, maybe some relief from the drudgery of the everyday. So, the person declares, "See you next week!" Next week they are back displaying the same ardor and a few more Sundays, but then the congregation sees this person only on occasion and finally no more. It was just a flash. The root of the matter was not there. The soil was rocky. There was no abiding conviction. Note that this person professed to believe, yet might have turned completely away from the Lord to the point of rank unbelief. We have more than a few say, "I tried, but I really don't need it." Pastors deal with this type of soil often, and it takes hours of their time. There is great excitement at first, but then come the nuts and bolts of the Christian life, with the daily battle against the world, the flesh, and the devil, and the hill is just too big to climb. Realization dawns that the cost is too high. This hearer lacks a sense of need.

"As for what was sown among thorns," says Jesus, "this is the one who hears the word, but the cares of the world and the deceitfulness of riches choke the word, and it proves unfruitful" (Matt 13:22). This is the third type of soil. It is infested with weeds and thorns. The seed that is sown has great difficulty, and for a time it is scrambling on the very edge of survival. Jesus expounds the meaning: This person is receptive to the Word, but the cares of the world get in the way. Like so many in today's world, this person is self-absorbed and career conscious to the point of recurrent distraction. The lure of material possessions, or just the idea of money, draws him or her away from taking heed. The message of the gospel does not bear positive fruit. Weeds, difficult to control and native to the heart, overwhelm the good seed. There may have been a sense of need, but it is long forgotten.

The fourth and last type of hearer provides hope. This person binds the congregation together and moves it forward under the blessing of God. They represent the core of the church. For such a person the Word is food for the soul, and it must be carried into the coming week for nourishment and growth. There is conviction. There is a sense of need. This person is serious. This is good soil. The seed is sown in the same way as it is in all the other soils. Everyone hears the same word. But only these receive it savingly. The Markan version says they "hear the word and accept it and bear fruit" (Mark 4:20). Luke's Gospel amplifies the description: they "hold it fast in an honest and good heart" (Luke 8:15). The Holy Spirit has cultivated the soil. There are weeds present no doubt but they are under control. The harvest is ripening in abundant fruit. Sin is taken seriously. There is repentance, faith, and perseverance.

Note that there is no explanation on the part of Jesus about the sower and none about the seed. It is the same sower in each case and the same seed. The only area where there are lines of demarcation is the soil. The great question is, how do we respond to the faithful preaching of the gospel?

No one really knows which kind of soil a person in a congregation is. But we know that sometimes the Word falls on hardhearted hearers who are content to present themselves as religious, sometimes it falls on the impulsive and shallow of character and cannot take root, and sometimes it penetrates but in the end fails being overwhelmed by the "cares of the world." But there is also good soil, folk with a Spirit-wrought sense of alienation who have returned to the Father.

The itinerant preachers of the Great Awakening concentrated on two types of hearers, the unregenerate and the regenerate. Their preaching was intended as a means of conversion as they passed from one town to another. From that perspective, the homiletical focus of the itinerant preachers was simpler. However, for the pastors of local congregations it is more complicated. Their audience is much more varied. It is therefore relatively more arduous to be a pastor of a local congregation. The pastor needs to be aware of the four types of hearers that Jesus refers to in his parable. They all need biblical preaching and faithful pastoral care, and the pastor needs careful discernment in carrying out the tasks of ministry.

In Jesus' parable and other teaching there is development beyond the two targeted audience of the Evangelical Revival. Still, it can be argued that the basic needs of everyone in the congregation remain similar, for even mature believers are given illumination by reminders of the most elemental truths. A fundamental and decisive component in the sermon schedule should be the fostering of a sense of need, which is a necessity for the unsaved and a blessing for those who are good soil.

Preaching Strategies

Over the centuries, preachers have tried various strategies of inculcating conviction in their hearers. Some of the older strategies are still in vogue, at least remnants of them. The Puritans developed a model of preaching that was very successful in their time. An exemplar can be found in the sermon of Jonathan Edwards outlined in Chapter 5, since he arguably represents the last of the Puritan tradition. The sermon began with biblical exposition. Next came the doctrinal lesson, and finally the practical application.

Another strategy includes the law-and-gospel motif, which has been very successful as a homiletical tactic. However, it assumes that the audience is educated to some degree in the basic tenets of the faith and understands the law of God. In other words, it is designed for hearers who are in the Christian tradition. This method is consistent with the apostle Paul's comment that the law is a "tutor" to bring sinners to Christ (Gal 3:24).[7] This was a strategy used by some of the itinerant preachers of the Great Awakening. They would visit a town for a five- to six-day period, preaching at least once per day, usually two or even three times, and began the visit by preaching on sinners' transgression of the divine law and the claims of God for obedience. Only after convincing the audience of their guilt and corrupt nature would they bring an inviting appeal of the Gospel.

This kind of preaching on sin is not to be confused with gloomy and pessimistic preaching. Centering on daily failings, struggles, weaknesses, and mistakes is depressive and has yielded minimal results. Bible thumping about sin is not winsome to the gospel. None of the revival preachers had a habit of repeated imprecations, and those who periodically gave such accusatory messages, such as Jonathan Edwards, also brought a free and unconditional gospel call. Equally unhelpful is a focus on cataclysmic events such as impending war, blackmail by terrorists, the coming hurricane season, and other disasters, the idea of which is to scare the audience out of a sense of security. One wonders whether the results this tactic brings are what the New Testament means by a sense of sin.

Another method comes out of Continental Reformed churches that have as their basis the Heidelberg Catechism, with its fifty-two Lord's Days. The catechism is divided into three main sections—guilt, grace, and gratitude—and in some communions preachers are quite strictly mandated to

---

7. Galatians 3:24 says, "So that the law is become our *tutor* to bring us unto Christ, that we might be justified by faith" (ASV). Some translations have "guardian." The KJV has "schoolmaster."

base sermons on one of the Lord's Days instead of a biblical text.[8] The question-and-answer format of the Heidelberg Catechism is centered on salvation doctrine and a postconversion life of gratitude. It is a way of keeping the congregation focused on the basics of biblical truth on a weekly basis. In churches that have two services, this focus is usually found during the morning service, when people are fresh and open to a more lecture-based presentation. Congregations that are acquainted with this method do benefit. However, the sermon is based on a creed, not on the exegesis of a biblical text. Some find this an inherent weakness in the method. The Heidelberg Catechism, while adhering to the meaning of the Bible, remains a document written by humans. It is not Scripture.

Moreover, there are several seminary locations, both in the United States and in Europe, where students are taught to preach using the guilt-grace-gratitude prescription for any given text of Scripture. The result is a narrow, almost exclusively soteriologically driven ministry that might unintentionally avoid the wider claims of the Word of God. While this kind of preaching can be rich and edifying, there is a danger of handling the Word of God eisegetically[9] rather than exegetically. What is more, it assumes a level of knowledge found only in a stable, mature congregation where everyone is on the same page.[10]

A more reflective, contemplative, and reasoned approach in preaching is used by many preachers. Helmut Thielicke (1908–1986), a pastor, a seminary professor, and a member of the Confessing Lutherans under the Nazi regime who was interrogated by the Gestapo, preached in this fashion. His vast experience of life under an oppressive regime and the devastation the people of Germany endured in the Second World War gave him

---

8. The Heidelberg Catechism is a human construct of great value, along with the Belgic Confession of Guido deBres (1522–1567), a student of Calvin and Beza at Geneva, and the Canons of Dordt. These three documents are together known as the "three forms of unity," binding all Continental Reformed churches together in a loose federation, regardless of specific denominational affiliation. The catechism, first completed in 1563, adheres to the doctrines of the Protestant Reformation of the sixteenth century and, it is opined, was surpassed by the more mature Westminster Confession, with its Shorter and Larger Catechisms (1647). Still, the Heidelberg Catechism is a wonderfully personal document that is still useful for the edification of the church.

9. Whereas exegesis begins with a study of the original text, eisegesis begins with a pre-held supposition such as, in this case, the theology of a given Lord's Day in the catechism.

10. See Bruggink, ed., *Guilt, Grace, and Gratitude,* and Bethune, *Guilt, Grace and Gratitude.*

keen insight into the human condition. His sermons usually were based on accounts of characters in the Gospels whose conviction was a result of a distressing and disordered life. Thielicke often depended on biographical accounts and encounters with Jesus in the Gospels to show how a person's failure in life can be explained best from the point of view of someone's life experience.[11] In the opinion of Bernard Ramm, "this comes closer to the core of the problem than some of the other methods."

Finally, Karl Barth believed that to foster a biblical sense of sin, one needs to preach Christ. If Christ is the ideal human, the model of human nature, then the true sense of a person's sinfulness will arise if one preaches Christ.[12] While certain aspects of Barth's theology can be disputed, his view of how and what to preach for the purpose of promoting a sense of need seems to be close to the mark.

Expository Preaching: Detractors and Apologists

There is an abundance of biblical precedents and directives for an expositional style of preaching. For our purposes the term "expositional" will be held to be synonymous with "expository." This method takes seriously the original language of the passage and brings the exegesis to a faithful exposition of the Word of God with application that arises directly from, and is consistent with, the text.

It must be said at the outset that not everyone agrees. The staunchly Reformed and highly respected evangelical historian Iain Murray demurs. One of his principal criticisms is as follows:

> Too many tyros have tried to preach verse-by-verse through major books of Scripture with near-disastrous results. It is arguable that this is one of the reasons why 'reformed' preaching has, in more than one place, been criticised as 'heavy' or plain 'dull'. The less ambitious, who also adopt the 'expository' mode, make no attempt to use single verses for their texts and that is the danger that too easily turns preaching into a running commentary.[13]

---

11. Thielicke wrote many books of sermons that reveal his method. They have been translated into multiple languages and are still valuable as resources for preaching material.

12. Ramm, *Offense to Reason*, 108.

13. Murray, "Expository Preaching: A Time for Caution," *Banner of Truth Magazine*, June 18, 2010.

Preaching Today, Part A

I agree that a running commentary on the biblical text is not acceptable. Neither is it tolerable to be "dull" or "heavy." Yet it is unfortunate that Murray sees these dangers as necessarily elemental to expositional preaching. It need not be the case. An expository method ought to be lively, captivating, and engaging but requires skill and maturity.

Admittedly, it is, of all preaching methods, the most difficult and commands the most energy in preparation. To open up the text of Scripture takes prayer, submission to the text, and hard work. Whether one preaches on one verse or on one complete pericope, the steps from language analysis to exposition to application can be arduous. A preacher may grow into this style, not being able to handle the biblical text in every case from the beginning. Therefore, church leaders may not be making the wisest choice in demanding that their young pastor consistently preach in this fashion. The student preacher needs time to grow and accumulate experience. Still, as a method of bringing the Word of God to bear on the hearts and lives of the congregation week by week, it is the most effective. A steady diet of biblical exposition with relevant and pointed application, whether moving consecutively through a book or a single verse or touching on various biblical themes, tends to provide steady, consistent growth.

There are reasons for this. First, the Bible stands in support of this method. The apostle Paul's *Epistles to Timothy* are replete with instruction. In his second Epistle, Paul admonishes him to "preach the Word" (2 Tim 4:1–2).[14] Another passage contains the well-known Pauline principle regarding the Scriptures (2 Tim 3:16–17).[15] Other references include Hebrews 4:12, where the Word of God is sharper than any two-edged sword, and Ephesians 6:17, where the sword of the Spirit is the Word of God. All of these and many more lend credence to expository preaching as a biblically sanctioned method whereby the sermon stays within the trajectory of the biblical text, both in exposition and in relevant application. A preacher ought to be able to say for every sermon, "This is the word of the Lord."

---

14. The words Paul uses are Κηρυξον τον λογον, meaning "to proclaim the word" or "to herald." Timothy is to speak like the Old Testament prophets. The Old Testament prophets acted as ambassadors, speaking for their master. Their message was not of their own making, not reflective of a favored hobby-horse, and not an expression of the preacher's personal agenda. The content of the proclamation was simply τον λογον, "the Word."

15. The Scriptures are θεόπνευστος, "God-breathed," revealing the intimacy of the inspiration of the Holy Spirit upon the inscripturated speech of God. The bible stands alone in this regard. No other author or book can make this claim. And it is this book, this Word, that must be proclaimed, and preachers must be the herald of its message.

Conversely, congregants ought to be able to say, "We heard the Word of the Lord," not report that they heard another rendition of the preacher's vision for the church or a homily filled with anecdotes and the like.

Second, two implications of the Holy Spirit's inspiration of the Scriptures are that preaching should be exegetical and that eventual applicatory comments should arise naturally in the process of sermon making. God can use any medium or method to convict and to edify, but it appears natural that he would honor his own word and, through that medium, speak to human hearts. Donald A. Carson has suggested several benefits of expository preaching that are worth mentioning.[16]

One thing is certain: preachers need to be disturbers. Our prosperity in an age of material and consumer advantage is not enough to become a blessing that lasts. Even our modest wealth and the portions we can leave to our children are, in the end, meager, and if we have not learned to know God in Christ, we will be quite wretchedly alone and lonely. That is why preachers need to be disturbers. Congregants need to be troubled at times. They need to be warned of their insufficiency, which one day will come to haunt them. The good life they live, materially speaking, and their self-righteousness stand in the way between them and the recognition of their need. God seeks to make that "good" life less attractive. The people need to heed the Puritan response to the "civil man." It is a horrible prospect to realize too late that one's own resources just will not cut it.

How, then, does a preacher lead a person to Hosea's wilderness or to the prayer of the tax collector in the temple, in order that the good news may be received? The next chapter will make some suggestions.

---

16. Carson says, "It is the method least likely to stray from Scripture; it teaches people how to read their Bibles; it gives confidence to the preacher and authorizes the sermon; it meets the need for relevance without letting the clamor for relevance dictate the message; it forces the preacher to handle the tough questions; and finally, it enables the preacher to expound systematically the whole counsel of God." Carson then uses John Calvin as an example of expository preaching: "In the last 15 years of his life, John Calvin expounded Genesis, Deuteronomy, Judges, Job, some psalms, 1 and 2 Samuel, 1 Kings, the major and minor prophets, the Gospels in a harmony, Acts, 1 and 2 Corinthians, Galatians, Ephesians, 1 and 2 Thessalonians, and the pastoral epistles. I'm not suggesting we organize ourselves exactly the same way. But if we are to preach the whole counsel of God, we must teach the whole Bible. Other sermonic structures have their merits, but none offers our congregations more, week after week, than careful, faithful exposition of the Word of God." See Carson, "6 Reasons Not to Abandon Expository Preaching," The Gospel Coalition, November 5, 2013.

9.

Preaching Today, Part B

> "For the Christian church . . . . to ignore, euphemize, or otherwise mute the lethal reality of sin is to cut the nerve of the gospel. For the sober truth is that without full disclosure on sin, the gospel of grace becomes impertinent, unnecessary, and finally uninteresting."
>
> CORNELIUS PLANTINGA (2000)

SOME SUGGESTED APPROACHES

BILLY GRAHAM ENTITLED HIS autobiography *Just as I Am*.[1] The title comes from the 1835 hymn by Charlotte Elliot:

> Just as I Am, without One Plea
> But that Thy blood was shed for me
> And that Thou bid'st me come to Thee
> Oh, Lamb of God, I come, I come

The complete lyrics have been put to music and performed by several artists, recently by Carrie Underwood and a little earlier by Johnny Cash, himself no stranger to the grief and despair that life can bring.[2] It reminds

---

1. Graham, *Just as I Am*.
2. Underwood, "Just as I Am" March 26, video, 3:19; Cash, *My Mother's Hymnbook*

one of the oft-repeated invitational refrain, "Come just as you are!" The invitation to come to the Christ of the Scriptures assumes that the invitees have an understanding of what the cross signifies, especially in relation to people's propensity by nature to try to achieve salvation through their own performance. Such an invitation can be very confusing for folk who have never been taught *just what they are*. Hence, "Come just as you are" makes little sense to them and might lead to self-indulgent, emotional sentiment instead of conversion.

C. S. Lewis says, "Everyone has noticed how hard it is to turn our thoughts to God when everything is going well with us. We 'have all we want' is a terrible saying when 'all' does not include God. We find God an interruption. As St. Augustine says somewhere 'God wants to give us something, but cannot, because our hands are full—there's nowhere for Him to put it.'"[3] A quotation from Lewis already given in the introduction is apropos here: "Christianity now has to preach the diagnosis—in itself very bad news—*before it can win a hearing for the cure.*"[4] Without a sense of need, the Christ of the Scriptures can hardly be embraced. Saving faith unites us to the One who is needed.

In the previous chapter, I came down on the side of expository preaching as the most difficult but the most biblical and most effective of all methods. Bryan Chapell, has written what is, in my view, a brilliant and helpful study of this topic in his *Christ-Centered Preaching*. One of his main theses has to do with finding the "fallen condition" of the original recipient of the text. Through the study of the text, this condition will emerge. The apprehension of this truth will be helpful in determining not only the meaning of the words of the text but also, as importantly, why it was written. This is the point where application begins to take shape. The fallen condition of the original audience can find transference to present-day people and circumstances. In this way the preacher is handed a powerful homiletical tool.[5] The "fallenness" of the original recipients should not be taken in the general sense of humanity's sinfulness and impermanence. Rather, the

---

Sony Music Entertainment, April 6, 2004.

3. Lewis, *Problem of Pain*, 59.

4. Lewis, *Problem of Pain*, 43, emphasis added.

5. Chapell has unlocked for us an effective approach to textual preaching and, as R. C. Sproul remarked, an outstanding homiletical tool. J. I. Packer said, "I like the applicatory concern that shines through it all." The theology undergirding the book is of the riper, biblical sort. See Chapell, *Christ-Centered Preaching*.

specific aspect and shape of the sin or the suffering that are reflected in the biblical text should be determined and linked to the present day.

This method of textual approach falls nicely into what is known as the redemptive-historical hermeneutic, especially when it used with preaching on the Old Testament. Instead of using the Old Testament as a catalogue of moral examples for present-day congregations to emulate (e.g., "Go and be like Joshua"), this method seeks to portray Old Testament history, principles, and people as types that find fulfilment in New Testament history, principles, and people. For example, preaching on the life and achievements of Solomon would not merely find application in the moral lives of listeners but would function as a path to the redemptive person and work of Christ. In this instance the Bible makes explicit use of this approach: "Something greater than Solomon is here!" (Luke 11:31). With this method creating a window into a chosen text, we can approach Scripture with some idea of what we are looking for without imposing a human construct onto the text, since the Bible itself makes use of this method. This is not to denigrate the moral-example approach. Often a certain text will fit that category as easily.

An important question is how preachers today can foster a sense of need. The right way is arguably not the fire and brimstone preaching of the old camp meetings of the so-called Second Great Awakening and of Charles Finney. And it is doubtful that Jonathan Edwards's descriptions of a spider hanging over the fire of hell would appeal in our rationalistic culture.[6]

Also undesirable are sermons that have conviction as its subject. The evangelists of the Evangelical Revival and the Great Awakening did not, by and large, preach such messages. *Rather than describe what conviction of sin was, they preached in order to have sinners convicted.* They did not preach *about* the experience. They preached to *foster* the experience. Conviction came about as a result of their preaching on the biblical text, usually in expository fashion, following the example of the Puritans. C. S. Lewis has this to say to fellow writers: "Instead of telling us a thing is terrible, describe it so that we'll be terrified. Don't say it was a delight, make us say 'delightful' when we read the description. You see, all those words (horrifying, wonderful, hideous, exquisite) are only saying to your readers, 'Please, will you do my job for me.'"[7]

---

6. See Edwards's famous sermon "Sinners in the Hands of an Angry God," *Works* Yale 22: 404.

7. Lewis, *Letters of C. S. Lewis,* edited by W. H. Lewis, cited in Capill, *The Heart is the Target,* 152–53. Having been convinced for many years that application that arises naturally from the text of Scripture is crucial to the sort of preaching that transforms, I

Application is the Goal

That the main thrust or goal of exposition is application should be accepted by all. One could ask, why else preach? Without application as the main purpose of the sermon, what the congregation is left with is a certain amount of information about the doctrines of the Bible or some enlightenment about biblical history. Not only might the hearers be bored stiff, but this kind of experience is sometimes spiritually deadening.

The record of preaching in the Bible reveals a consistent pattern of thrusting the Word into direct application. Although we do not have a sermon of Noah, the circumstances of his life and calling give warrant to believe that his preaching of righteousness (2 Pet 2:5) contains specific application. Solomon is referred to as "the Preacher" (Eccl 1:1, 12), and the book of Ecclesiastes is rife with application for life. Moses is reluctant to begin preaching the Word of God (Exod 4:10–11) but becomes God's mouthpiece to Pharaoh and later to the people of Israel. Deuteronomy 1–30 contains three of Moses' sermons, all of which have direct application to the future conduct of the Israelites. He is a passionate preacher, fearless in speaking the Word of God. Prophetic preaching after Moses is characterized by powerful application of truth. Nowhere do we find bland classroom lectures being delivered. The prophets of the Old Testament are inspired to preach applicatory messages that are relevant to the life situation of God's people.

In the New Testament, John the Baptist pointedly preaches repentance (Matt 3:2; Mark 1:4; Luke 3:3). After the temptation in the wilderness, Jesus from that time on began to preach hortatory messages, "Repent, for the kingdom of heaven has come near" (Matt. 4:17). Jesus is a preacher par excellence. His preaching is consistent with the focus and theology of preachers who preceded him, but he excels in the application, for he knows the hearts of his hearers. The apostle Peter's preaching contains convicting application (Acts 2:37), as does the sermon delivered by Stephen to the Sanhedrin (Acts 7). Direct application concerning the messiahship of Christ is the apostle Paul's burden (Acts 17:1–4). The Bible not only provides repeated examples of preaching that is edifying, comforting, convicting, imprecatory and even condemnatory; it disparages any other form by implication.

Narratives in the Bible provide a ready opportunity for finding Bryan Chapell's "fallen condition," the gracious redemption that follows, and the

---

am indebted to Capill for his insistence on application in every sermon and his development of the theme.

application that emerges naturally from the exposition. In fact, narrative occupies more space in the Bible than any other literary genre, with an estimated 75 percent of the Old Testament being narrative.

It is argued that there is far too little preaching on the Old Testament in our evangelical churches. And when an Old Testament text is chosen for a Sunday service, the sermon is sometimes just moralizing. Typology is usually ignored, promise-and-fulfilment themes remain unlooked for, doctrinal substance is lacking, and sadly, time and again the gospel itself is missing. What is left in the application is moral teaching. In many instances moral teaching is centered on humanity, and the application is rooted in human action, action that is to occur somehow without the Holy Spirit's enabling grace. Moral teaching is good and sound, but it needs to be done with a redemptive and Christological focus.

Jesus has told us how to treat the Old Testament: He says, "Was it not necessary that the Christ should suffer these things and enter into his glory?" (Luke 24:26). Why was it necessary? The answer lies in his words later in the chapter: "These are my words that I spoke to you while I was still with you, that everything written about me in the Law of Moses and the Prophets and the Psalms must be fulfilled" (Luke 24:44). Jesus teaches the two disciples on the Emmaus Road: "And beginning with Moses and all the Prophets, he interpreted to them in all the Scriptures *the things concerning himself*" (Luke 24:27). In the Gospel of John he says, "You search the Scriptures because you think that in them you have eternal life; and *it is they that bear witness about me*" (John 5:39). The Scripture Jesus is talking about is the Old Testament. Since the Old Testament is written about Christ, the Messiah, it behooves preachers to spend time studying and searching for linkages to Christ. Even texts that appear, at first reading, to be simple examples for moral teaching contain a Christological dimension that needs to be brought forward. In summary, preaching needs to find connections to the fallen condition that everyone labors under, and it must include tie-ins to the good news.

The Natural Perspicuity of the Application: Some Examples

Usually, when it comes to narratives in the Old Testament, the application begins to reveal itself as the exposition advances. The following are two examples of exposition from the Old Testament where a convicting application is implicit in the narrative and becomes explicit as the exposition progresses.

Old Testament

Lot's Choice: Genesis 13

"Lot settled among the cities of the valley and moved his tent as far as Sodom" (Gen 13:12).

Here, in the story of Lot's selfish choice of a place to settle, the exposition will begin to reveal applicatory content almost immediately. Application will rise directly from the text, as is the case with most narratives. This example lends itself to a redemptive-historical approach. However, it fits as easily into the moral-example method. The apostle Paul gives sanction to this approach: "Now these things took place as examples for us, that we might not desire evil as they did" (1 Cor 10:6; see also 1 Cor 10:11).

That Lot is a man of God there can be no doubt. Peter tells us expressly in 2 Pet 2:7 that he was "righteous and greatly distressed by the sensual conduct of the wicked." But this history shows something else: that people who genuinely fear the Lord still have their besetting sins. Lot's is worldliness, and it costs him dearly. He took advantage of Abram's generosity and chooses the better land (2 Pet 2:8–11), pitching his tent as far as Sodom. Abram is left with a barren plain and wilderness where today the strife-torn Gaza Strip is located. Lot's choice falls to the lovely green plain of Sodom, well-watered by the Jordan River and what is now the Dead Sea. When Lot sees the beauty of the place, he is reminded of how the garden of the Lord looked before the Fall or the way the rich and fertile Nile Valley in Egypt looks (2 Pet 2:10). The Jordan meanders through the green valley before him, giving life to the region. Here, Lot believes, he will find wealth and a good life.

To make outward advantage the main priority in our choice of life's path is certainly not a principle one can find in the Bible. Wealth is not the "one thing needful" (Luke 10:42). The rush to gain material stuff permeates our society. It seems to be one of the only things people think of in choosing a career. Yet the Bible discourages the seeking of earthly gain.

Lot disregards these principles. He moves his tent as far as Sodom. The very next verse says, "The men of Sodom were wicked, great sinners against the Lord." This is said in close connection with Lot's choice. Lot's neighbors enjoy the prosperity that their location gives them. In that context they have become wicked beyond what the world has seen. Ezekiel lists the three sources of Sodom's sins: "She and her daughters had pride, excess of food, and prosperous ease" (Ezek 16:49).

Lot rubs shoulders with the gross wickedness of the population. It is a dangerous place to live. When, finally, the fury of the Lord comes down from the sky, not one is saved except for Lot and his family.

The application is very apropos to our generation. We make alliances, partnerships, and friends with people and institutions that will benefit us materially. We, too, will leave our godly uncle Abram and mix with those who worship another god, or the dollar, or other forms of riches. And our families will become naturalized citizens of Sodom. All of this can happen simply by choosing a path that leads to influence by the spirit of the age in which we live. How awful it is; what jaw-dropping level of responsibility family leaders, church leaders are burdened with!

What are some of the results of Lot's choice? There can be little doubt that Lot's conscience suffers and that what spirituality he does have suffers too because of his long sojourn near that city. But the result is just as bad for Lot's family. It brings to mind Jesus words "Remember Lot's wife" (Luke 17:32). Remember *Lot's wife*! She caught the infection of the place and fell deeply in love with it. When the family did finally leave, Lot could not take her with him. She was too engrossed, too enamored with fashion, fun, and the party lifestyle. She needed one more look at her beloved city, and we know what happened to her. If there is a life given to us as a warning, it is the life of Lot.

When an audience finds itself imaginatively in Lot's position, conviction of sin can take place under the tutelage of the Holy Spirit. Here the Spirit of Christ comes seeking and contending where the proverbial shoe fits. The application rises directly from the exposition. With confidence and authority, the preacher has the liberty to say, "Thus says the Lord."

The apostle Paul has given us ample advice about trusting in the wealth that this world can provide:

> Those who desire to be rich fall into temptation, into a snare, into many senseless and harmful desires that plunge people into ruin and destruction. For the love of money is a root of all kinds of evils. . . . As for the rich in this present age, charge them not to be haughty, nor to set their hopes on the uncertainty of riches, but on God, who richly provides us with everything to enjoy. (1 Tim 6:9, 17)

The linkage to Christ is clear. Jesus himself says, "Do not lay up for yourselves treasures on earth, where moth and rust destroy and where thieves break in and steal" (Matt 6:19). Our greatest satisfaction is in Christ. He is the "bread of life" (John 6:35). To know him is to have eternal contentment.

The predominant tendency in the broader Western society is individual self-centeredness. The word "narcissism" has become a byword for our culture. It is a part of our fallen nature to be selfish. The Puritans and the evangelicals of the Great Awakening railed against this common affliction. Even though generosity and kindheartedness are attractive attributes to strive for, we are still spring loaded toward a "me first" mindset. Lot takes advantage of his uncle's generosity and chooses the lush green plain near Sodom. Doing so gets him into trouble. Christians likewise are not immune to their surroundings. We do not live in isolation from the influence of the milieu. There is real danger of a deadening effect that comes from taking material advantage. The eventual costs of a selfish choice can be high. The wonder in Lot's life is that God comes to rescue him and he enjoys the redemption that is offered. But in the meantime, it costs him plenty.

Hosea's Marriage: Hosea 1:1—2:15

Hosea is a prophet of the Lord and belongs to the group of eighth century BC prophets, along with Isaiah, Amos, and Joel. He ministers just prior to the great deportation and enslavement of the ten northern tribes in 722 BC. Hosea is called to preach to the northern tribes and he does. But a large part of Hosea's life and ministry is way out of the ordinary. It is to be a demonstration of God's pain and of Israel's treachery. The Lord commands Hosea to take a "wife of whoredom and have children of whoredom, for the land commits great whoredom by forsaking the Lord" (Hosea 1:2). This is the situation that shapes the ministry of the prophet Hosea.

Gomer is an unfaithful wife to the prophet. She has three children during the time they are together, but she becomes tired and perhaps bored with this kind of life, and she begins running after other men. She is known publicly for being sexually indiscriminate. Hosea is shattered, and he grieves. He does his level best to remain faithful to the Lord, but he is terribly ashamed. He still loves Gomer and misses her. God then asks Hosea to buy her back. In so doing the prophet acts out not only God's pain and Israel's departure from the Lord but also the restoration and forgiveness that is described in chapters 3 and 14. Who would want to be in ministry of any kind if it included the home life of Hosea? Yet that is exactly the point in this prophecy. Who would want to be God if it included the pain that he feels when his people are unfaithful and prostitute themselves with other gods?

Hosea's life is the sermon. It is the earthly analogy of what is going on between Israel and God. God loves His people. He is ever faithful. Israel, for the most part, could care less. The great majority of the population is well-off, at ease and comfortable. Most of the country is following Baal, a god who is permissive, even to the point of fulfilling their lusts, their greed and their oppression of the poor.

Still, Israel keeps her Hebrew feast-days. She continues to go through the motions of being faithful believers on an official level. The level of hypocrisy is breath-taking. Israelites prefer spending their daily lives in the service of Baal. It reminds us of religious society prior to the Great Awakening, outlined earlier.

The analogy that Hosea must act out even extends to the names of the children. The first son is named Jezreel (Hosea 1:3-4). His name predicts the place of God's judgment on the Northern Kingdom of Israel carried out through a massacre during the reign of King Jehu in the Valley of Jezreel (Hosea 1:4-5). In chapter 2 the children are tagged as "children of adultery" (Hosea 2:4). Gomer will be dishonored publicly and put to shame, just as Israel will be dishonored. The next child, a daughter, is called Lo-Ruhamah ("No Mercy"). This name also announces God's judgment on the Northern Kingdom. The third child is called Lo-Ammi ("Not My People"), and by this name God announces the official dissolution of his covenant with Israel: "You are not my people, and I am not your God" (Hosea 1:9).

And then a strange thing happens: following such an announcement is an affirmation about Israel's future, given in very strong language: "Yet the number of the children of Israel shall be like the sand of the sea, which cannot be measured or numbered. And in the place where it was said to them, 'You are not my people,' it shall be said to them, 'Children of the living God'" (Hosea 1:10-11). This is the restoration that Hosea acts out in chapter 3 by buying back his wife from the man she is now living with. He does this, and it is an act of sheer grace.

The rest of the book is a long running catalog of the sins of Israel (chaps. 4-13). In chapter 14 Israel must return to the Lord and fully acknowledge its sins. It is then that the relationship can be fully restored: "I will heal their apostasy; I will love them freely, for my anger has turned from them." This completes the picture: Israel has drifted, turned her back on the Lord. She is living according to the sensual whims of Baal. The Lord has not wavered in his faithfulness to her, but Israel's rebellion has come to the point that she is ripe for severe discipline, for some corrective punishment.

We see that a life estranged from the Lord is an endangered life. The Israelites live comfortably in their prosperity and do not really need the Lord and the Father of all mercies, who is a jealous God and is deeply hurt by this blatant treachery. Here too we see the dictum, faith is born of need. Unless we have need, we tend to take comfort in our own strength and prosperity. This principle can be applied to ourselves. Our greatest danger as Christians might well be a time of great worldly success and material comfort. Israel kept up the tradition handed down to her but rejected the heart of it.

It is time for God to act. In chapter 2 we read about his response (Hosea 2:9–13). God will prevent the grain from ripening and the vineyards from yielding fruit. As a result of all this deprivation, the festivals and feast days that have been shot through with lustful Baalism can no longer be celebrated. Why? Because there will be no animals to sacrifice and no produce to offer (Hosea 2:11). In fact, God is saying that the entire Hebrew holy calendar will be canceled. Israel's worship has been prostituted to the pagan Baals. The nation's whorish sin is summarized in the last line of verse 13: "went after her lovers and forgot me, declares the Lord." To forget the Lord is the opposite of knowing him.

God's people, the Israelites, no longer participate in that intimate relationship of love that our Lord desires to have with them and with us. That relationship requires a personal acquaintance. It also includes an active memory of all the blessings and gifts that God has given us. The Psalmist says,

> Praise the Lord, oh my soul; all my inmost being,
> praise His holy name.
> Praise the Lord oh my soul,
> and forget not all His benefits (103:1–2)

But to know the Lord is also to live *in such inner, daily, heartfelt fellowship* that we take delight in God and in his presence, see everything in life in the context of God's love and his will, and rejoice in obeying the divine direction of our lives on a daily basis. We feel the nudges of his Spirit. We lean toward a posture of loving surrender. If we rejoice in his presence, obedience becomes an automatic reflex. We want to please him. Nothing could be worse than to hurt him or leave his love for us in the lurch. At bottom it is exactly that inner life, that inner relationship of love, delight, and obedience, that Israel in the day of Hosea has dumped for the sensual and materialistic excess of the Baal gods. The biblical text asks of us all whether we know God and whether we delight in knowing him. Is he our highest satisfaction?

Israel might no longer know God. But God knows Israel, and he will not let them go. God will chastise them, but he promises to restore them and forgive them. How will the Lord do this? "Therefore, behold, I will allure her, and bring her into the wilderness, and speak tenderly to her" (Hosea 2:14). Then he will provide a "door of hope" (Hosea 2:15). In effect, the Lord will "reboot" the sacred relation with his people. He will lead her into the wilderness, just as he did at the very beginning of their history together. There, in the desert, where there is no Baal and no Baalism to come between them, the Lord will allure them, will entice them to come back to him. Literally, in the Hebrew, verse 14 says, "I will speak to her heart," for it is Israel's heart that he wants to win. He will provide for them physically, too (Hosea 2:16–23). There will be new life in the land. Israel will respond to her divine Husband in true commitment and in true faith, heart to heart, love for love. Such is the future that God purposes through the prophet Hosea.

The application is clear and rises out of the exposition. So is the linkage to Jesus. It is more than coincidental that the wilderness is a significant place for Jesus of Nazareth. He begins his ministry in the wilderness, when he is baptized by John in the river Jordan. It is in the wilderness that he faces and overcomes the temptations of the devil.

Hosea's ministry is to demonstrate all of this by acting out God's grief at the flagrant disloyalty of his people. The problem begins with a lack of need for God, and it is sensuality and materialism that leads them astray. Subsequently, the mighty hand of God chastises them, and God's incredible grace restores them. He still does that today. Let us take note that he is a jealous God and he will not be mocked (Gal 6:7). Let us strive to remain near him, within his good will for us, seeking his presence and his direction. And let us adore and worship him for the gift of his dear Son, Jesus, through whom, even today, we may find forgiveness, restoration, and genuine happiness.

Some New Testament Examples

Jesus speaks to people about their sin and sinful condition. He is very convicting, and in his omniscient awareness of a person's life situation, he reiterates the point that radical transformation is necessary. But nowhere in the Gospels does he react as the Pharisees do, by browbeating folk for being sinners; nor does he accuse suffering people of the generational sins that might have caused the suffering. The exception to this practice is his dealings with the self-righteous, for whom he has neither patience nor sympathy. His sharpest imprecations are reserved for people who believe they are models of righteousness. Jesus loves sinners and has the greatest sympathy for sufferers. In his unparalleled wisdom he inserts the Word into the weak point of a person's life and lays bare the false presumption of virtue, the guilty passion, the gross immorality, or the self-focused mindset. How does he do this? The following are three examples of his preaching that will engender conviction.

The Rich Young Man

In Matthew 19:16–22, Jesus encounters a young man who is very rich. Here, too, conviction comes about with no harangue. It appears that this young man's personal pride and identity is linked closely to his wealth. Moreover, he is a person of some virtue. He says to Jesus that he has obeyed all of the Ten Commandments, principles that he no doubt learned from his parental nurturing and from his teachers. He is a morally upright young man, an unparalleled example of personal rectitude. He is a believer by education and training and professes loyalty to the claims of God.

And yet he is not content. Something has disturbed his composure. He feels an emptiness, something missing from his materialistic lifestyle. This well-to-do young man, in all likelihood, has heard of the counterintuitive nature of Jesus' preaching, and he has begun to experience an anxious disquiet. Perhaps he has heard of the Beatitudes: "Blessed are the poor in spirit, for theirs is the kingdom of heaven.... Blessed are those who mourn, for they shall be comforted" (Matt 5:3–4). If he follows these tenets, his whole life will be turned upside down. His unease collides with the high view others have of him and his own self-respect. So, he comes to Jesus and asks, "What good deeds must I do to have eternal life"? (Matt 19:16)

How does Jesus react to his high estimation of himself? Jesus does not contradict his self-assessment, but neither does he congratulate him on his upright character. Instead, Jesus lays a finger on the one thing in the young man's life that stands between him and a realization of need: "If you would be perfect, go, sell what you possess and give to the poor, and you will have treasure in heaven; and come, follow me" (Matt 19:21). Jesus drives a wedge into the exact center of the young man's weakness. He loves his riches. Moreover, his self-worth and sense of identity are dependent on his wealth and on his high view of his character. But the choice is made clear. He can either continue living in material wealth or lose it all to follow Jesus and become a disciple. At bottom, he loves himself and his riches more. He "went away sorrowful, for he had great possessions" (Matt 19:22). We cannot have it both ways.

In this example Jesus does not give him a tongue lashing about his sin or his need for a new birth. Instead, he focuses on the lost condition of the rich young man and uses it to bring him to conviction. That he is convicted is clear in that he goes away sorrowful. His conviction does not, at this time, result in repentance and faith, and Jesus lets him go. We should notice that Jesus refrains from calling him back to provide consolation, even though he loves him (Mark 10: 21). There is no show of sentimentality or empathy for the young man and no attempt to provide solace. Jesus simply lets the Word do its work. The young man is allowed to leave, having made his choice.

Notice that the narrative itself and the exposition contain the application. Little more needs saying. In not too many words, using language that is compelling and fresh, the account of this young man can become a very convicting sermon. The fallen condition of the man is clear in Jesus' response. The link to the fallen condition of the listeners in the congregation, too, is obvious, especially in view of the materialism that is so seductive in the young man's life. Finally, the redemptive solution of becoming a Jesus follower is clear: "Go and do likewise."

The Samaritan Woman

Another opportunity to locate the fallen condition is found in Jesus' conversation with the Samaritan woman at Jacob's well in John 4. He has learned that the Pharisees have heard talk of him baptizing more disciples than John the Baptist (see John 3:23, 3:26). To avoid a fruitless clash with the Pharisees, Jesus leaves Judea to travel north toward Galilee. The route he takes is not the normal route. Jews traveling from the south to the north avoid the hostility of the Samaritans and go east, crossing the Jordan and traveling up through Perea, making for a much longer journey.

However, Jesus has a divine appointment to keep[8] and therefore travels through Samaria, coming to the town of Sychar and to Jacob's well. Jesus is always intent on fulfilling the ministry he has been given by his Father. The woman of Sychar arrives alone, in the heat of noonday. The usual time for drawing water is very early or much later on, when it is cooler. Women draw water in groups at these times. Yet this woman comes to draw water when no one else is around. The reason for this surprising decision is made clear in the text. She lives a scandalous life, having had five husbands in quick succession and now living in a common-law relationship with a man in Sychar. She is ostracized by others. But unbeknownst to her, she, too, has a divine appointment to keep.

Jesus is wearied from the long journey on foot and sits beside the well. His disciples have gone into Sychar to buy food, and in the meantime he is thirsty and asks the Samaritan woman for a drink. She is very aware of the strained relations between Samaritans and Jews and replies, "How is it that you a Jew, ask for a drink from me, a woman of Samaria?" (John 4:8–9). His reply centers on "living water" that he will give to those who ask him for it. Quietly, politely, Jesus seeks to open her heart that she might begin to ask questions about the living water. Instead, she resists and belittles the idea. She resists six times in the ensuing exchange, using sarcasm and denial, sidestepping the subject, raising an issue that is controversial, and, finally, trying to delay decision (John 4:9–25).

The narrative, at this point, has obvious applications for conviction, and they emerge effortlessly from the exposition. First, Jesus comes to seek and to save the lost. This biblical principle originates in the divine will and comes into full view in the ministry of Jesus.[9] She is a known sinner and suffers social alienation, but Jesus, in mercy, seeks out the needy. Second, with respect to sinners who suffer the consequences of their lifestyle, the exposition can encourage them to open their hearts to him who is the great forgiver of sins. Third, this woman resists the searchlight of the Word of God until finally she is stirred inwardly and begins to respond to Jesus'

---

8. In John 4:4 the Greek δει ("must needs" in the KJV, conveying emphasis) is a strong word, usually used to denote an action of divine necessity. Cf. John 9:4; 10:16; 12:34; 20:9, where there is reference to divine purpose. The word δει is used in each case.

9. See Luke 19:10: "For the Son of Man came to seek and to save the lost."

convicting words. This is nothing less than normal. Countless autobiographical accounts suggest that when the Word comes with Holy Spirit power, people spend wasted hours resisting.

The woman seems argumentative and unmoved by the quiet approach of Jesus. She is not yet convicted of her sins. He does not berate her, but his heart-searching words "Go, call your husband, and come here" (John 4:16) is a bolt of light into her conscience. At that point everything changes. She becomes earnest. Her moral failings have been discovered. Jesus has led her into a state of conviction.[10] "You are right in saying, 'I have no husband' for you have had five husbands, and the one you now have is not your husband. What you have said is true" (John 4:17-18). She now is at her most vulnerable. The Word of Christ cuts deeply. She realized that Jesus, the "prophet" (John 4:19), can penetrate her heart. A. T. Robertson says, "We may not have all the conversation preserved, but clearly Jesus by this sudden sharp turn gives the woman a conviction of sin and guilt without which she cannot understand his use of water as a metaphor for eternal life."[11] The uncovering ministry of Jesus tears at her argumentative responses and results in her salvation.

Note that she leaves her water pail in her excitement to tell others and runs into town to report to all she encounters, "Come, see a man who told me all that I ever did. Can this be the Christ?" (John 4:29). She becomes an evangelist! Forgotten is her alienation from society. She is overwhelmed by the new principle of eternal life, the living water that Jesus has referred to, and is moved with relief and love for others, hallmarks of saving grace. The woman says, "Come see a man . . ." Jesus stays two days, and many Samaritans believe in him because of the woman's testimony. In terms of application, when the grace of God is applied in the way of conversion and darkness is dispelled, the new life is evidenced by a desire to share with others. Forgiven sinners cannot help but express gratitude and with great wonder show others the way to Jesus.

One remarkable aspect of the account needs mentioning, and that is Jesus' declaration of messiahship. The woman has a general knowledge of a Messiah who is to come and understands that he will be a revealer. Jesus

---

10. Ryle says of this passage, "This should be the principle aim of all ministers of the Gospel. They should carefully copy their Master's example. . . . Until men and women are brought to feel their sinfulness and need, no real good is ever done to their souls. Till a sinner sees himself as God sees him, he will continue careless, trifling, and unmoved." Ryle, *John*, 1:205-6.

11. Robertson, *Word Pictures*, 5:64.

says, "I who speak to you am he" (John 4:26). To paraphrase, he is saying, "I am the Messiah. I am the revealer." This is the only place in the Gospel narratives where such clarity occurs. No Pharisee or scribe has heard him speak like this. But a Samaritan sinner is presented with the gift of this special revelation!

Sinners are Jesus' friends. There is no Bible thumping when they come for help. He forgives them and often affirms their faith. Jesus is expert in the psychology of conversion and is more than willing to use his penetrating skills to peel away the layers of self-deception and the defenses we build to protect our vulnerability. His love for the needy surpasses understanding, and his great joy is to provide living water. Conviction? Application? The best there is.

Jesus and the Leper

Note first the biblical-theological principle that all of Jesus' miracles are actually exhibits of a deeper reality. In Mark 1:40–45 the fallen condition is clear from the beginning. The parables show us in real terms, apart from the obvious physical wonder, the spiritual effects of his Spirit's work in our broken world. For example, giving sight to the blind reveals his projecting light into the darkness of our hearts. His stilling of wind and waves speaks of his power to bring peace to our troubled lives. His raising of the dead shows his life-giving gospel of free grace, which brings salvation to the spiritually dead. His feeding of the five thousand is a vivid display of Jesus as the Bread of Life. R. Kent Hughes says that Jesus' miracles are parables. In saying so he follows the influential Anglican bishop R. C. Trench, biblical scholar of the Victorian era who said the miracle of healing the leper was a parable of sin, an "outward visible sign of innermost spiritual corruption."[12]

Because Christ's miracles are parables of our condition, it is urgently important for preachers today to include them in plans for preaching and conveying the biblical diagnosis. As repeated in several ways in this book, without this diagnosis the gospel is not received as good news. Martyn Lloyd-Jones says it is a spiritual necessity to have the benefit of the diagnosis from the Word of God: "Unless you realise that your whole nature is wrong, until you realise that, you will never have felt the need of a Saviour. . . . You may have been inside the church all your life and actively engaged in its work, but still I say, unless you have at some time felt that your very nature

12. Hughes, *Mark: Jesus, Servant and Savior*, 53.

itself is sinful, you are in the words of St. Paul 'dead in sin' and have never known Jesus Christ as a Saviour." Hughes asks, "Can you see your leprosy? Can you say, 'unlean, unclean' and really mean it? . . . If you have you are on the threshold of the kingdom."[13]

In Mark 1:40–45 the leper expresses some uncertainty: "If you will, you can make me clean" (Mark 1:40). He believes in Jesus' power to heal but does not know whether Jesus will. He perhaps thinks, "Maybe I am too ugly and putrid for Jesus." William Barclay has described a leper:

> The whole appearance of the face is changed, till the man loses his human appearance and looks, as the ancients said, "like a lion or a satyr." The nodules grow larger and larger. They ulcerate. From them there comes a foul discharge. The eyebrows fall out, the eyes become staring. The voice becomes hoarse, and the breath wheezes because of the ulceration of the vocal cords. The hands and the feet always ulcerate. Slowly the sufferer becomes a mass of ulcerated growths. The average course of the disease is nine years, and it ends in mental decay, coma, and ultimately death. The sufferer becomes utterly repulsive—both to himself and to others.[14]

In this passage the leper is not familiar with the generous sympathy of Christ yet. He has fallen on his face before Jesus (Luke 5:12), fully aware of the Old Testament protocol and the resultant hopelessness of his condition (see Lev 13–14). Jesus is moved with pity, stretches out his hand, and touches him: "I will, be clean" (Mark 1:41).

Luke says, "he was full of leprosy" (Luke 5:12). Jesus stretches out his hand and touches him. This is his habit. Mark takes note of this aspect of Jesus' healing ministry throughout his Gospel. He touches the sufferers. There is no necessity of so doing in order to provide a cure for the leper. He simply takes delight in touching those whom he heals, knowing that a touch from another human has not been in the leper's experience for years. Jesus' touch conveys the message "I will, be clean." The incarnate Son of God, who has taken on human form, touching the leprous flesh of a sufferer is indicative of why he has come. He wants the leper to sense his love and sympathy. A great transfer takes place: the touch of Jesus symbolizes the purity of his humanity passing into the rotting flesh of the leper. The reverse is also true: Jesus takes upon himself the infirmities of this man and bears

---

13. Lloyd-Jones cited in Hughes, *Mark*, 55–56.
14. Barclay, *The Gospel of Mark*, 42–46.

them to the cross of Calvary. Isaiah says, "With his wounds we are healed" (Isa 53:5). We repeat a snippet from Psalm 103:

> Bless the Lord, O my soul ...
> Who heals all your *diseases*. (Ps 103:2–3)

Hughes's description of the healing is graphic: "The healing was sudden and complete. His feet—toeless, ulcerated stubs—were suddenly whole, bursting his shrunken sandals. The knobs on his hands grew fingers before his very eyes. Back came his hair, eyebrows, eyelashes. Under his hair were ears and before him a nose! His skin was supple and soft. Can you hear the thundering roar from the multitude? Can you hear the man crying, '*I'm clean! I'm clean!*'"[15]

What is true of biblical narratives generally is true here. The application to present-day people arises from the text itself. As the story is faithfully expounded, there is a growing awareness of the lesson inherent in the miracle. As a flower is beautifully transformed from bud to full bloom, so the application grows with the exposition. The fallen condition becomes clear, and once it is understood that the miracle is also a parable, illustrating the mercy of Christ in forgiving sinners, the application is complete. The leprosy of sin has contaminated each one of us. If that is embraced as true, there is no reason to hesitate to do what the leper did. In the next chapter of Mark, Jesus encounters the self-righteous, and a clash ensues. His response to them is "Those who are well have no need of a physician, but those who are sick. I came not to call the righteous, but sinners" (Mark 2:17). Jesus' great delight is to minister to sinners and sufferers, to touch them with his forgiving and healing power. When we come to him with our sin, he says, "I will, be clean."

Jesus and Zacchaeus

Finally, only Luke relates the episode with Zacchaeus to us (Luke 19:1–10). Here, too, conviction of sin is one of the primary motifs of the account. Application is implicit. It is ripe with convicting material. Zacchaeus is the head of a group of tax collectors hired by the Roman occupying force.[16] He

---

15. Hughes, *Mark*, 59.

16. Neale *None but the Sinners*, 190 states that Luke's sinner theme disappears from Scripture after the Zacchaeus encounter in Luke 19, "never to reappear in Luke's writings." The above mention of Paul's experience, as well as a host of other instances in the book of Acts, suggests that that is an overstatement.

is therefore very rich and has opportunity to retain some of the earnings for himself. He can extort. He can skim off the top. He can threaten. The citizens of his area usually experience fear when they appear before him, because he can call on the Roman authorities to add military muscle to his demands.

In the account, Zacchaeus is sitting in a sycamore tree so as not to miss the opportunity of seeing who Jesus is (Luke 19:3). He is likely to miss that chance on the ground because he is challenged in stature and because the crowd is thick. This is a wonderful irony that Luke conveys to the reader first. This man, feared by many, has come to the place in his life where appearances no longer matter. He looks ridiculous sitting in the tree. The sight must give the crowd below a bit of mischievous delight. But Zacchaeus is too preoccupied with his own struggles to care about how ludicrous he must appear. His one concern is to "see who Jesus was". This is the heart of the matter. He has heard of the man from Nazareth who cares for the blind and the lame and who welcomes little children, the man who, it is said, likes to spend time with sinners and tax collectors and who seems to radiate a power and a love that is unheard of among the religious leaders. *Maybe he can help my poor conscience and give me peace!* This little scoundrel is convicted of his sin. When Jesus calls him down from the tree, the dam breaks. He cried out his confession: "Believe me, I'm turning over half of everything I have to the poor, and if I have squeezed anyone out of his money, I will replace it four times over" (Luke 19:8).

Zacchaeus has come to himself, like the prodigal son. He is finished with trying to appease his conscience. No more rationalizing! And no one in the crowd, in fact in all of Jericho, knows what he has been going through. He is alone and lonely. But, surprise! He finds that Jesus already knows all about him. What a shock! Zacchaeus is a genuine seeker, but incredibly, Jesus is on his way to find him and calls him by name to come down from the tree. In fact, Jesus wants to be his guest. The seeker is really the one being sought. Jesus, as Zacchaeus discovers, seeks out the lost (Luke 19:10).

For Zacchaeus, this is an incredible discovery. Jesus knows him. He has purposed to walk down the road to where Zacchaeus sits in his ludicrous perch in the sycamore tree, because Zacchaeus needs to be rescued from his misery. Zacchaeus is drawn to the Lord. What is so amazing is that the Lord is drawn to him in sovereign grace. Jesus wants to be his guest. The Scriptures affirm that he enjoys the company of needy sinners and they enjoy being around him. The heart of Christ is so full of love for the lost that the bulk of his ministry is taken up being the "friend of tax collectors and sinners" (Matt 11:19 and Luke 7:34). His accusers, in this sense, are right. What they see in him they have not seen in any religious leader. This is the reason why people come in droves to hear him and ask for healing. Zacchaeus, by his own actions and by his own admission, is a social pariah. No one likes him. The actions of Jesus run counter to popular expectations. He loves Zacchaeus, seeks him out, spends time with him, forgives him.

There is more to say about Zacchaeus's transformation. He is no longer identified by his sins. By virtue of Jesus' forgiving friendship and assuring companionship, he is united to him. Jesus comes to be his guest! He and Jesus break bread together! The implications are enormous. His identity is now in Christ. Here, too, a great transaction takes place. Jesus comes to "seek and to save the lost" (Luke 19:10). Jesus, as Son of God with infinite knowledge and with infinite love, knows Zacchaeus to be a needy, seeking sinner. It is to those that Jesus ministers. He spends time with the broken, since "those who are well have no need of a physician, but those who are sick" (Mark 2:17).[17] Jesus' greatest delight is to welcome sinners and sufferers into the glories of the kingdom. He understands thoroughly what sin and suffering are, that they are alien invaders counter to the way life was supposed to be. For that reason, his great heart bleeds (literally) for us. We have a sorely inadequate understanding of sin and suffering, and we are in desperate need of visiting or revisiting these concepts in biblical fashion.

The reader will have taken note that all of these examples are taken from the narrative or historical genre of the Bible. Doctrinal concepts emerge from a plot and from real people. Narratives are therefore easier to handle for preachers who wish to do biblical exposition. These few examples reveal rich and deeply moving application imbedded in the text itself. A skilful preacher, finding the fallen condition and the link to the redemptive work of Christ, can, with the Spirit's guidance, doubtlessly develop a convicting message.

---

17. A recent publication is highly recommended for seekers of Jesus and for Christians who are struggling with assurance: Ortlund, *Gentle and Lowly*.

Conclusion

THE HISTORY OF THE many local revivals that took place throughout the American colonies and in the British Isles has been well documented. The work of the great itinerant preachers such as George Whitefield, the Wesleys, the Tennents, and Frelinghuysen as well as pastors such as Edwards and Davies is widely known among evangelicals. One of the chief ingredients that gave these revivals momentum was the preaching of the gospel for poor sinners. Bible-based messages with purposeful homiletics produced awareness of innate depravity, outward decency notwithstanding, and fostered a sense of need. For many, the gospel was welcome news. Conviction, through the applicatory work of the Spirit of God, gave rise to faith and to repentance.

The doctrine of original sin, says Shelton Smith, was not merely adhered to because it was "enunciated by the Westminster and Savoy Confessions. Rather, it had become a vital element in Christian preaching" during this period.[1] To quote the Connecticut observer Benjamin Trumbull again, "There was in the minds of the people a general fear of sin, and of the wrath of God denouncing it. There seemed to be a general conviction that all the ways of man were before the eyes of the Lord. Theft, wantonness, intemperance, profaneness and other gross sins, appeared to be put away.... At lectures there was not only great attention and seriousness, in the house of God, but the conversation out of it was generally on the great concerns of the soul."[2]

It has been my contention that this period of widespread revival needs serious revisiting by evangelicals today. The facts of that history speak for themselves. There are lessons to be learned, and although they might be

1. Smith, *Changing Conceptions of Original Sin*, 10.
2. Trumbull, *A Complete History of Connecticut* 1:144.

simple reminders of already-held beliefs for some pastors, they might be, for others, an entirely new discovery.

The preaching of the Great Awakening was suited for that generation. Someone has said that the people of the mid-eighteenth century believed so vividly in the afterlife that they could find heaven and hell in the atlas. This is not everywhere the case today. Preaching therefore needs to take a more appropriate turn. The truth of God's Word must be brought to every generation without variance, but the methods and ways of communicating the good news need to suit the audience. Hence, I have tried to show some of the biblical examples of convicting preaching, from both Old and New Testaments, focusing especially on the way our Lord approaches sinners and sufferers in his capacity as the Way, the Truth, and the Life.

One aspect of the success in the revivals concerned the experience of the preachers themselves. Each of the leaders could attest to personal acquaintance with the convicting work of the Holy Spirit as a means to their conversion. They all had a deep sense of their innate unrighteousness. Some, like Edwards, were able to articulate this with astounding clarity. Yet all preached with a burden for the conversion of their hearers. The earlier Puritan Richard Baxter said he preached as a "dying man to dying men."

The large geographical compass, Europe to North America, suggests there was a widespread movement afoot, and the itinerant leaders were raised up for this work. The success of the revivals was not a result of properly tuned voice modulation, or exactness of hand gestures, or any other theatrical device. Rather, the King of the church made use of people's giftedness, provided enabling grace, and, as the results revealed, placed his blessing on the great work of preaching the gospel.

Broadly speaking, the church today is using methods and techniques that, at times, render the preaching of the Word almost superfluous in a given church service. We need to admit that while the use of technology can be and is blessed of God, preaching from a biblical text is still the biblically sanctioned norm for the dissemination of God's truth. The proper handling of the text in dependence upon the illumination of the Spirit will always be effective. After all, it is his own word.

What is said about God and his Christ will be an attraction to many. People will be drawn toward convicting preaching. Slick and silly measures leave people cold. Those in whom the Lord is working and those whose circumstances in life cause them to suffer will come to hear. Most have hurts and pains, and some have a very disordered life. Most sense a level of anxiety and bewilderment that is leaving them in bondage. There is a hunger for forgiveness and direction from God, for the embrace of safe haven, and for the relief and contentment the Gospel brings. The kind of people who were drawn to him in the eighteenth century will be drawn to him now, and he to them. The obdurate self-righteous will remain what they were then, irritable and rankled, but the Lord still saves sinners and heals sufferers. Those who are drawn to Jesus have learned that there are no lasting resources, that we all "strive after wind" while in this life (Eccl 1:17 etc.). Moreover, we all have the elusive sense of the eternal and the incorruptible in our hearts. We ache for that which lasts.

Let us, then, be encouraged to preach an unfettered Gospel. Let us awaken, by God's grace, the sinners and provide comfort to the sufferers. Let us lead our flocks to Hosea's wilderness, where God is pleased to speak tenderly; to Jacob's well, where Jesus is ready with divine purpose; to the sycamore tree, where he gets personal. Let us bring Jesus and his grace to bear on the lives of all who listen.

Bibliography

Ahlstrom, Sidney. *A Religious History of the American People*. New Haven: Yale University Press, 1972.
Ahlstrom, Sidney and J. S. Carey, eds. *An American Reformation: A Documentary History of Unitarianism in America*. Middletown: Wesleyan University Press, 1985.
Aldridge, A. O. *Jonathan Edwards*. New York: Washington Square, 1966.
Alexander, Archibald. *The Log College: Biographical Sketches of William Tennent and His Students together with an Account of the Revivals under Their Ministries*. Edinburgh: The Banner of Truth, 1968.
Allen, A. V. G. *Jonathan Edwards*. Boston: Houghton Mifflin, 1899.
Augustine, Aurelius. Albert C. Outler (ed., translator). *The Confessions*. Public Domain, 1955.
Barclay, William. *The Gospel of Mark. The New Daily Bible Study Series Revised*. Louisville: Westminster John Knox, 2001.
Baxter, Richard. *Reiquiae Baxterianae, or, Mr. Richard Baxter's Narrative of the Most Memorable Passages of his Life and Times*. Vol. 1, "Introduction and Part 1: 217"; edited by N. H. Keeble, John Coffey, Tim Cooper, and Tom Charlton, 2020.
Beeke, Joel R. ed. *Forerunner of the Great Awakening: Sermons by Theodorus Jacobus Frelinghuysen*. Grand Rapids: Eerdmans, 2000.
Beougher, Timothy. *Richard Baxter and Conversion: A Study of the Puritan Concept of Becoming a Christian*. Scotland, UK: Christian Focus, 2007.
Berkhof, Hendrikus. *The Christian Faith*. Grand Rapids: Eerdmans, 1979.
Berkhof, Louis. *Reformed Dogmatics: Historical*. Grand Rapids: Eerdmans, 1937.
Bethune, George W. *Guilt, Grace and Gratitude: Lectures on the Heidelberg Catechism*. Edinburgh: Banner of Truth, 2001.
Boardman, George N. *A History of New England Theology*. New York: A. D. F. Randolph, 1899.
Bogue, Carl. *Jonathan Edwards and the Covenant of Grace*. Cherry Hill: Mack, 1975.
Bradford, John. *Writings Volume 1*. Edinburgh: Banner of Truth, 1979. Reprint of the 1848 edition.
Bremer, Francis J. *The Puritan Experiment: New England Society from Bradford to Edwards*. New York: St. Martin's, 1976.
Brown, Dale W. *Understanding Pietism, Revised*. Nappanee, IN: Evangel, 1996.

Bibliography

Bruce, F. F. *The Epistle to the Romans. Tyndale New Testament Commentaries Series.* Intervarsity Academic, 1963.

Bruggink, Donald J. ed. *Guilt, Grace, and Gratitude: A Commentary on the Heidelberg Catechism.* Grand Rapids: Reformed Church, 1963.

Bushman, Richard L. "Jonathan Edwards and Puritan Consciousness" in Alden T. Vaughan and Francis J. Bremer *Puritan New England: Essays on Religion, Society and Culture.* New York: St. Martin's, 1967.

Bushman, Richard L, edi. *The Great Awakening: Documents on the Revival of Religion, 1740–1745.* Durham: University of North Carolina Press, 1989.

Calvin, John. "Commentary on Romans 7". *Calvin's Commentary on the Bible.* https://archive.sacred-texts.com/chr/calvin/cc38/cc38010.htm

———. *Institutes of the Christian Religion in Two Volumes,* translated by Ford Lewis Battles: John T. McNeill ed. Philadelphia: Westminster, 1960.

Capill, Murray. *The Heart is the Target: Preaching Practical Application from Every Text.* Phillipsburg, NJ: Presbyterian and Reformed, 2014.

Carse, James P. *Jonathan Edwards and the Visibility of God.* New York: Charles Scribner's Sons, 1967.

Carrick, John. *The Preaching of Jonathan Edwards.* Edinburgh: Banner of Truth, 2008.

Cash, Johnny. *My Mother's Hymnbook.* Sony Music Entertainment, April 6, 2004.

Carson, Donald. "6 Reasons Not to Abandon Expository Preaching: Benefits of Exposition" in *The Gospel Coalition Website, November 5, 2013.*

———. *The Gagging of God: Christianity Confronts Pluralism.* Zondervan, 2001.

Chapell, Bryan. *Christ-Centered Preaching: Redeeming the Expository Sermon.* Grand Rapids: Baker Academic, 1994.

Cherry, Conrad. *The Theology of Jonathan Edwards: A Reappraisal.* New York: Anchor, 1966.

Clary, Ian Hugh. *Reformed Evangelicalism and the Search for a Usable Past: The Historiography of Arnold Dallimore, Pastor-Historian.* Gottingen, Germany: Vandenhoek & Ruprecht Verlage, 2020.

Cole, Nathan. "The Spiritual Travels of Nathan Cole" in Richard L. Bushman, ed. *The Great Awakening: Documents on the Revival of Religion, 1740–1745.* Chapel Hill, NC: University of North Carolina Press, 1989.

Cragg, Gerald R. *The Church in the Age of Reason 1648–1789.* Harmondsworth, UK: Penguin Books, 1970.

Cranfield, C. E. B. *Romans: A Shorter Commentary.* Grand Rapids, MI: Eerdmans, 2001.

Dallimore, Arnold. *George Whitefield: The Life and Times of the Great Evangelist of the 18th Century Revival in Two Volumes.* Edinburgh: Banner of Truth, 1970, 1980.

———. "Review of Harry Stout's The Divine Dramatist. . ." in *Reformation & Revival: A Quarterly Journal for Church Leadership.* Volume 1, #4 (1992) 125–28.

Davies, Samuel. "The Nature and Universality of Spiritual Death" in *Sermons on Important Subjects Volume 1.* New York: Dayton and Saxton (1841) 90–91.

Davison, Edward H. *Jonathan Edwards: The Narrative of a Puritan Mind.* Boston: Houghton Mifflin, 1966.

DeJong, Peter Y. *The Covenant Idea in New England Theology: 1620–1847.* Grand Rapids: Eerdmans, 1945.

Doyle, Sir Arthur Conan. *A Scandal in Bohemia.* London: Longmans, 1996

Dreyer, Frederick. *The Genesis of Methodism.* Bethlehem, PA: Lehigh University Press, 1999.

Bibliography

Drew, Donald. England Before and After Wesley 3. https://disciplenations.org/
Dwight, Sereno E. "Memoirs of Jonathan Edwards" in *The Works of Jonathan Edwards Vol. 1*. Edinburgh: The Banner of Truth Trust, 1974.
Dwight, Timothy. *Theology Explained and Defended in a Series of Sermons Vol. 3*. London: Thomas Allen, (circa 1880) 384-94.
Edwards, Jonathan. "Ideas, Sense of the Heart, Spiritual Knowledge or Conviction, Faith" ed by Perry Miller *Harvard Theological Review April*, (1948). 135.

———. *Jonathan Edwards: Representative Selections* edited by Clarence H. Faust and Thomas H. Johnson. New York: Hill & Wang (1962) 3-27.

———. *Works of Jonathan Edwards*, Volumes 2, 3, 4, 17, 19, 21, 25. New Haven: Yale University Press.

———. *The Works of Jonathan Edwards in Two Volumes*, The *Edward Hickman Edition*. Edinburgh: The Banner of Truth, 1974. Reprint of the 1834 edition.

Edwards, Sarah Pierrepont. "A Letter to Her Brother in New Haven, October 14, 1740" in Edinburgh: *The Banner of Truth Magazine Special Issue* (#79) 25.
Erskine, Ebenezer. *The Whole Works of the Late Ebenezer Erskine consisting of Sermons and Discourses Volume 2*. Edinburgh: Ogle & Murray, Wm. Oliphant & Company, Oliver & Boyd, 1871.
Ferguson, Sinclair. *The Holy Spirit*. Downers Grove, IL: IVP Academic, 1997.
Ferm, Robert L. *Jonathan Edwards the Younger: 1745-1801*. Grand Rapids: Eerdmans, 1976.
Fiering, Norman. *Jonathan Edwards's Moral Thought and Its British Context*. Chapel Hill: The University of North Carolina Press, 1981.
Fletcher, John. *The Works of the Reverend John Fletcher, Late Vicar of Madeley Volume IV*. Salem, OH: Schmul, 1974. Reprint of the 1833 edition.
Foster, Frank H. *A Genetic History of the New England Theology*. Chicago: University of Chicago Press, 1907.
Franklin, Benjamin. *The Autobiography of Benjamin Franklin*. Yale University Press, 1964.
Gatiss, Lee. "George Whitefield: The Anglican Evangelist" in *The Southern Baptist Journal of Theology*, (#18 Summer, 2014) 2.
Gaustad, Edwin S. *A Documentary History of Religion in America*. Grand Rapids: Eerdmans,1984.

———. *The Great Awakening in New England*. Gloucester UK: Peter Smith, 1965.

Gerstner, John H. *Jonathan Edwards on Heaven and Hell*. Grand Rapids: Baker, 1980.

———. *Jonathan Edwards the Preacher*. Grand Rapids: Baker, 1958.

———. *Steps to Salvation: The Evangelistic Message of Jonathan Edwards*. Philadelphia: Westminster, 1960.

Gillies, John. *Memoirs of George Whitefield*. New Ipswich, NH: Pietan, 1993.
Goen, C. C. *Revivalism and Separatism in New England: 1740-1800*. New Haven: Yale University Press, 1962.
Grcevich, Stephen. "The Sins of Psychiatry…and Psychology" in *Church4EveryChild July 28*, https://www.idisciple.org/post/the-sins-of-psychiatry-and-psychology.
Green, Edward. "George Whitefield at Kingswood" in *The Building Conservation Magazine, July 8, 2020*
Guelzo, Allen. "George Whitefield & His World: Recommended Resources" in *Christianity Today*, 2023. https://www.christianitytoday.com/history/issues/issue-38/george-whitefield-his-world-recommended-resources.html.

Bibliography

Harlan, David. *The Clergy and the Great Awakening in New England*. Ann Arbor: UMI Research Press, 1980.

Haroutunian, Joseph. "Jonathan Edwards: A Study in Godliness" in *Journal of Religion, July, 1981*.

———. *Piety Versus Moralism: The Passing of the New England Theology*. Hamden: Archon, 1964.

Hastings, Hugh ed. *Ecclesiastical Records of the State of New York Volume III*. Albany: J. B. Lyon Company, State Printers, (1902) 2244–308.

Hatch, Nathan O. and Harry S. Stout, eds. *Jonathan Edwards and the American Experience*. Oxford and New York: Oxford University Press, 1988.

Haykin, Michael. "The Christian Life in the Thought of George Whitefield" in *The Southern Baptist Journal of Theology*, (Summer 2014) 18. 2, 8.

Heimert, Alan and Perry Miller, eds. *The Great Awakening: Documents Illustrating the Crisis and Its Consequences*. Indianapolis: Bobbs-Merrill, 1967.

Helm, Paul. *Beginnings: Word & Spirit in Conversion*. Edinburgh: Banner of Truth, 1988.

———. "John Locke and Jonathan Edwards: A Reconsideration," *Journal of the History of Ideas* 29 #1 51.

Hervey, James. *The Whole Works of the Rev. James Hervey, A. M. Volume 3*. Edinburgh: T. & J. Turnbull, 1802.

Hoekema, Anthony. *Created in God's Image*. Grand Rapids: Eerdmans, 2008.

Hollifield, E. Brooks. "The Intellectual Sources of Stoddardeanism," *New England Quarterly* 45. 3, 373–93.

Hoopes, James. "Jonathan Edwards's Religious Psychology" *The Journal of American History* March 69 #4 849.

Horton, Michael. *Christless Christianity: The Alternative Gospel of the American Church*. Grand Rapids: Baker, 2012.

Howe John. "Of Reconciliation between God and Man" in *Works of English Puritans: Howe*. London: Thomas Nelson, 1846.

Hughes, R. Kent. *Mark: Jesus, Servant and Savior*. Wheaton, IL:Crossway, 2015.

Hudson, Winthrop. *Religion in America*. New York: Charles Scribner's Sons, 1973.

Jackson, Thomas. *The Centenary of Wesleyan Methodism: A Brief Sketch of the Rise, Progress and Present State of the Wesleyan Methodist Societies Throughout the World*. New York: T. Mason & G. Lane, 1839.

Jerusalem Post. "Terrorist live-streamed horrors of massacre to Gazan parents" October 24, 2023.

Keener, Craig S. *Romans. New Covenant Commentary Series*. Eugene, OR: Wipf & Stock, 2009.

Keller, Tim. "Tim Keller's Preaching Equation and Your First 200 Sermons," *Eucatastrophe 101*, December 5, 2008. https://eucatastrophe101.wordpress.com/2008/12/05/tim-kellers-preaching-equation-and-your-first-200-sermons/

Kidd, Thomas S. *George Whitefield: America's Spiritual Founding Father*. New Haven, CT: Yale University Press, 2014.

———. *The Great Awakening: The Roots of Evangelical Christianity in Colonial America*. New Haven, CT: Yale University Press, 2007.

Lewis, C. S. *The Great Divorce* London: MacMillan, 1946.

———. *Mere Christianity*. London: MacMillan, 1952.

———. *The Problem of Pain London*: London: Geoffrey Bles, 1940.

Lindberg, Carter ed.*The Pietist Theologians*. Malden, MA: Blackwell, 2005.

BIBLIOGRAPHY

Lloyd-Jones, D. M. "Jonathan Edwards and the Crucial Importance of Revival" in *Westminster Conference Publication: The Puritan Experiment in the New World*. Rippin: Evangelical,1976.

———. *Romans. Exposition of Chapter 7: 1 to 8: 4. The Law, its Functions and Limits*. Banner of Truth, 1973.

Locke, John. *An Essay Concerning Human Understanding, Book Two, Chapter One, Section Two and Section Four*. Oxford University Press, 1975.

Lockridge, Kenneth. "The History of a Puritan Church" in Alden T. Vaughan and Francis J. Bremer *Puritan New England: Essays on Religion, Society and Culture*. New York: St. Martin's, 1977 97–98.

Logan, Samuel T. "Jonathan Edwards and the 1734–1735 Northampton Revival" *Westminster Conference, Preaching and Revival*. Colchester: Christian Design & Print, (1984) 69–73.

Loux, Joseph A ed. *Boel's Complaint against Frelinghuysen*, Rensselaer, NY: Hamilton, 1979.

Lovejoy, David. *Religious Enthusiasm and the Great Awakening*. Hoboken, NJ: Prentice-Hall, 1970.

Luther, Martin. *Works of Martin Luther Volume II*. St. Louis, MO: Concordia, 2015.

Macaulay, James. *Whitefield Anecdotes: Illustrating the Life, Character, and Work of the Great Evangelist*. London: Religious Tract Society, 1886

MacFarlan, D. *The Revivals of the Eighteenth Century, Particularly of Cambuslang*. London and Edinburgh: John Johnstone, circa 1860s.

Ma'Culloch, Rev. Mr. *The Life and Times of Howell Harris*. Edinburgh: The Banner of Truth, 1998. Reprint of the 1852 edition.

Maddox, Randy L. *Aldersgate Reconsidered*. Nashville: Kingswood, 1990.

Marsden, George M. *Jonathan Edwards, A Life*. New Haven, CT: Yale University Press, 2003.

Maze, Scott. *Theodorus Frelinghuysen's Evangelism: Catalyst to the First Great Awakening*. Grand Rapids: Reformation Heritage, 2011.

McCheyne, Robert Murray. *The Works of Rev. Robert Murray McCheyne Complete in One Volume*. New York: Robert Carter & Brothers, 1873.

McClymond, Michael J. and Gerald R. McDermot. *The Theology of Jonathan Edwards*. New York: Oxford University Press, 2011.

McGever, Sean. *Born Again: The Evangelical Theology of Conversion in John Wesley and George Whitefield*. Bellingham: Lexham, 2020.

McNeill, John T. *The History and Character of Calvinism*. New York: Oxford University Press, 1954.

Miller, Perry. *The American Puritans*. New York: Doubleday, 1956.

———. "Introduction" to Jonathan Edwards "Ideas, Sense of the Heart, Spiritual Knowledge and Conviction. Faith" in *The Harvard Theological Review* 41 135.

———. *Jonathan Edwards*. New York: Meridian, 1959.

———. *The New England Mind: From Colony to Province*. Cambridge: Harvard University Press, 1953.

Mode, Peter G. ed. *Source Book and Bibliographical Guide for American Church History*. Boston: Baily, 1964.

Moo, Douglas J. *The Letter to the Romans. New International Commentary on the New Testament Series*, Grand Rapids: Eerdmans, 2018.

Bibliography

Morgan, Edmund S. *The Puritan Family: Religion and Domestic Relations in Seventeenth Century, New England* New York: Harper & Row, 1966.
Morris, Leon. *The Epistle to the Romans. The Pillar New Testament Commentary Series.* Grand Rapids: Eerdmans, 1988.
Murray, Gordon J. "The Preaching of the English Reformers" in *Preaching and Revival.* London: The Westminster Conference 1984.
Murray, Iain H. "Expository Preaching—A Time for Caution" in *The Banner of Truth Magazine June 18,* 2010.
———. "Editorial" *Banner of Truth Magazine,* no. 370: 8, 1994.
———. *Jonathan Edwards: A New Biography.* Edinburgh: The Banner of Truth, 1987.
———. *Revival & Revivalism: The Making and Marring of American Evangelicalism 1750-1858.* Edinburgh: Banner of Truth, 1994.
———. *Wesley and Men Who Followed.* Edinburgh: The Banner of Truth, 2003.
Murray, John. *Romans. New International Commentary on the New Testament Series,* Grand Rapids: Eerdmans, 1980.
Neale, David A. *None but the Sinners: Religious Categories in the Gospel of Luke.* Sheffield, UK: Sheffield Academic, 1997.
Nieman, Susan. *Evil in Modern Thought: An Alternative History of Philosophy.* Princeton NJ: Princeton University Press, 2004.
Olson, Roger E. and Christian T. Collins Winn *Reclaiming Pietism: Retrieving an Evangelical Tradition.* Grand Rapids: Eerdmans, 2015.
Ortlund, Dane. *Gentle and Lowly: The Heart of Christ for Sinners and Sufferers.* Weaton, IL: Crossway Books, 2020.
Outler, Albert C. ed. *John Wesley.* New York: Oxford University Press, 1980
Overton, Charles J. and John H. Abbey. *The English Church in the Eighteenth Century.* London: Longmans, 1887.
Packer, James I. "The Puritan View of Preaching the Gospel" in *Monergism* iii: #2.
———. *Quest for Godliness: The Puritan Vision of the Christian Life.* Wheaton: Crossway, 1990.
Parkes, H. B. *Jonathan Edwards.* New York: Minton, Balch, 1930.
———. "New England in the Seventeen Thirties" in *The New England Quarterly* (July 1930) #3.
Parrington, Vernon L. "Jonathan Edwards was an Anachronism" in John Opie, ed. *Jonathan Edwards and the Enlightenment* Lexington: Heath, 1969.
Pemberton, Ebenezer. *Ebenezer Pemberton 1704-1777.* Don Kistler, compiler, Orlando, FL: Soli Deo Gloria, 2006.
Philip, Robert. *The Life and Times of George Whitefield.* Edinburgh: Banner of Truth, 2009. Reprint of the 1837 edition.
Piper, John. "I Will Not Be a Velvet-Mouthed Preacher! The Life and Ministry of George Whitefield; Living and Preaching as Though God Were Real (Because He Is)," Presentation at *Desiring God Conference for Pastors,* 2009.
Plantinga Jr., Cornelius. *Not the Way It's Supposed to Be: A Breviary of Sin.* Grand Rapids: Eerdmans, 1996.
Porter, Roy. *English Society in the Eighteenth-Century.* London: Penguin,1982.
Prince, Thomas. "Letter to Reverend George Whitefield" in David Lovejoy *Religious Enthusiasm and the Great Awakening.* Hoboken, NJ: Prentice-Hall, 1970.
Rack, Henry. *Reasonable Enthusiast: John Wesley and the Rise of Methodism.* London: Epworth, 1992.

BIBLIOGRAPHY

Ramm, Bernard. *Offense to Reason: A Theology of Sin*. New York: Harper & Row, 1985.

Reeves, Michael. *Evangelical Pharisees: The Gospel as Cure for the Church's Hypocrisy*. Crossway, 2023.

———. *What Role Did Expositional Preaching Play in the Reformation?* IX Marks Preaching and Theology, (September 2017).

Robertson, A. T. *A Grammar of the Greek New Testament in Light of Historical Research*, Broadman & Holman, 1947.

———. *Word Pictures in the New Testament Volume 5*. Grand Rapids: Baker. Reprint of the 1932 edition.

Rosenthal, Bernard. "Puritan Conscience and New England Slavery" in *The New England Quarterly* (March, 1973) 62–81.

Rutman, Darrett B ed. *The Great Awakening: Event and Exegesis*. Huntington, NY: Robert E Krieger, 1975.

Ryle, John Charles. *Expository Thoughts on the Gospels. John, Volume 1*. Cambridge: James Clarke, 1977 reprint of the 1865 edition.

———. *Expository Thoughts on the Gospels. Luke Volume 1*. Cambridge: James Clarke, 1977 reprint of the 1865 edition.

———. *The Christian Leaders of the Last Century or England a Hundred Years Ago*. London: T. Nelson & Sons, 1868.

Ryne, Alex. *Being Protestant in Reformation Britain*. Oxford, UK: Oxford University Press, 2013.

Sanders, Fred. "Calvinists Who Love Wesley" in *The Scriptorium Daily June 21, 2011*. https://scriptoriumdaily.com/calvinists-who-love-wesley/.

Schafer, Thomas A. "Jonathan Edwards and Justification by Faith" in *Church History Volume XX*, 1951.

Scheick, William J. ed. *Critical Essays on Jonathan Edwards*. Boston: G. K. Hall, 1980.

Schneider, Herbert W. *The Puritan Mind*. Ann Arbor: University of Michigan Press, 1958.

Schreiner, Thomas *Romans: Baker Exegetical Commentary on the New Testament Series*. Grand Rapids, MI: Baker Academic, 2005.

Schuit, John. "Jonathan Edwards and Conviction of Sin: An Aspect of Eighteenth-Century Revivalism" Unpublished Thesis, Western University, London, Ontario, 1993.

Scougal, Henry. *The Life of God in the Soul of Man*. Ross-shire, Scotland: Christian Focus, a 2012 reprint with an Introduction by J. I. Packer.

Severance, Diane. "Evangelical Revival in England" www.christianity.com May 2010.

Shepard, Thomas. "The Sincere Convert" in *The Works of Thomas Shepard Volume 1*. New York: AMS Press. Reprint of Boston: Doctrinal Tract & Book, 1853.

Sibbes, Richard. "The Bruised Reed and Smoking Flax" in *The Works of Richard Sibbes Volume 1. Edinburgh*: The Banner of Truth, 1973; reprint of the 1862 edition.

Simonson, Harold P. *Jonathan Edwards: Theologian of the Heart*. Grand Rapids: Eerdmans, 1974.

Smedes, Lewis B. *Shame & Grace: Healing the Shame We Don't Deserve*. San Fransisco, CA: HarperOne, 2018.

Smith, H. Sheldon. *Changing Conceptions of Original Sin*. New York: Charles Scribner's Sons, 1955.

Smith, H. Sheldon, Robert T. Handy, and Lefferts Loetcher, eds. *American Christianity: An Historical Interpretation with Representative Documents Volume 1*. New York: Charles Scribner's Sons, 1960.

Bibliography

Spurgeon, Charles H. *Autobiography Volume 1: The Early Years*, Edinburgh: The Banner of Truth, 1962.

———. "The Fainting Warrior" *Spurgeon.org*. https://www.spurgeon.org/resource-library/sermons/the-fainting-warrior/#flipbook

Stephen, Leslie. "Jonathan Edwards" in *Littel's Living Age Volume XX January, 1874*.

Stott, John R. W. *The Message of Romans: God's Good News for the World*. Downer's Grove, IL: Intervarsity, 2005

Stout, Harry. *The Divine Dramatist: George Whitefield and the Rise of Modern Evangelicalism*. Grand Rapids: Eerdmans, 1991.

Strom, Jonathan. *German Pietism and the Problem of Conversion*. Pennsylvania State University Press, 2018.

Tennent, John. "Regeneration Opened" in *Sermons and Essays by the Tennents and Their Contemporaries*. Philadelphia: Presbyterian Board of Publication, 1855.

Thielicke, Helmut. *A Little Exercise for Young Theologians*, Grand Rapids: Eerdmans, 1962.

Thompson, J. P. "Jonathan Edwards: His Character, Teaching and Influence" in *Bibliotheca Sacra Volume XVIII, 1861*.

Tracy, Joseph. *The Great Awakening*. London: The Banner of Truth Trust, 1976. Reprint of the 1842 edition.

Trumbull, Benjamin. *A Complete History of Connecticut Volume 2*. New York: Arno Press, 1972. Reprint of the 1818 Maltby, Goldsmith & Company edition.

Turnbull, Ralph G. *Jonathan Edwards the Preacher*. Grand Rapids: Baker, 1958.

Tyerman, Luke. *The Life of the Rev. George Whitefield in Two Volumes*. London: Hodder & Stoughton, 1890.

Tyler, Bennet and Andrew Bonar. *The Life and Labours of Asahel Nettleton*. Edinburgh: Banner of Truth, 1996.

Underwood, Carrie *Just as I Am (Official Audio Video)* 3: 19. https://www.youtube.com/watch?v=qRbrK6Pydgs.

Walker, Williston. *A History of the Christian Church*. New York: Charles Scribner's Sons, 1985.

Warfield, B. B. *Perfectionism Volume 2*. New York: Oxford, 1931

Wellum, Stephen J. "The Life and Legacy of George Whitefield (1714–1770)" in *The Southern Baptist Journal of Theology, Summer 2014*. Volume 18: #2: 8.

Wells, David F. *Turning to God: Biblical Conversion in the Modern World*. Grand Rapids: Baker, 1989.

Wesley, John. *The Works of John Wesley Volumes 1, 2 and 8: Journals*, Grand Rapids: Baker, 2007. Reprint of the 1872 edition.

———. *The Works of John Wesley Volume 1: Sermons 1–33*. edited by Albert C. Outler, Nashville: Abingdon: 1984.

Wesley, Charles. *The Journal of Charles Wesley Volume 1*. Grand Rapids: Baker, 1980. Reprint of the 1849 edition.

Westminster Conference. *Preaching and Revival*. Colchester: Christian Design & Print, 1984.

———. *The Puritan Experiment in the New World*. Rippon UK, Evangelical Press, 1976.

Whitefield, George. *George Whitefield's Journals*. Edinburgh: The Banner of Truth, 1960.

———. "The Last Sermon of Rev. George Whitefield of Exeter" in *The Portsmouth Herald*, Aug. 21, 2009.

———. *Letters of George Whitefield for the Period 1734–1742*. Introduction by S. M. Houghton. Edinburgh: Banner of Truth, 1976. Reprint of the 1771 edition.

Bibliography

———. "The Method of Grace" in John Gillies ed. *Memoirs of Rev. George Whitefield*. Middletown: Hunt & Noyes, 1837.

———. *The Sermons of George Whitefield in Two Volumes*. Wheaton, IL: Crossway, 2012. Lee Gatiss ed.

Wilson-Kastner, Patricia. *Coherence in a Fragmented World: Jonathan Edwards's Theology of the Holy Spirit*. Washington: University Press of America, 1978.

Winslow, Ola Elizabeth. *Jonathan Edwards*. New York: MacMillan, 1940.

Wright, Conrad. *The Beginnings of Unitarianism in America*. Boston: Starr King, 1955.

Wright, N. T. *Romans for Everyone*. Lisle, IL: Intervarsity, 2009.

Subject Index

Arminianism
    in New England, 54, 55
    in the Church of England, 44, 46
    at Yale,
Assyrians and Israel, 5, 6

Baal gods, 4
Bekehrung (conversion) in Pietism, 70
Believers' struggle
    against spiritual dullness, 18
    concern of being unawakened while deeply awakened, 83
    intense introspection, 83
Blindness of sinners, 21–23
Busskampf (penitential struggle) in Pietism
    nature and necessity of, 70, 124
    faith a result of, 124

Children of Israel
    stiff-necked, stubborn, 3–6
    and God's clear revelation to, 3, 4
the *Civil Man* in Puritan preaching, 15,
Common grace and Special grace
    and conviction of sin, 25, 26

Declension in Britain
    preaching in the C of E, 43–46
    Arminian and Deistic encroachments, 46
    England a "vast casino", 47
    the slave trade, 47

Declension in New England
    Edwards's pessimism, 47
    decay of vital piety, 49
    clergy response, 56, 57, 60
    passing of the New England "way", 55
    Arminianism, Deism, Unitarianism, 55–57
    Religious legalism, 57, 58
Detractors
    of Wesley, 107–109
    of expository preaching, 134–136
Drunkenness
    in England, 47
    in Boston, 58
    in Northampton, 59
Durchbruch (breakthrough) in Pietism, 70, 124

Genesis account of the fall, 1, 2

Empiricism
    and John Locke, 24–25
    and Edwards, 25
Expository preaching
    detractors, 134
    Biblical sanction for, 135
    in support of, 135, 136

Free Offer of the Gospel, 6–7, 11, 27, 99, 152, 156

Half-way Covenant, 51–52

Subject Index

Judgment, 6, 7,
  inattention of, 13
  and Jesus, 13, 14

Lament Psalms, 4
Legalism
  of scribes and Pharisees,
  and the *Holy Club*, 96, 97
  in New England churches
  of Nathan Cole

materialism, effects of, xx
Mother Promise, 2
Murder
  extreme consequence of the fall, 2
  by Cain, 2
  and Lamech, 2

Naturalism and Confessionalism
  in writing history, xx
  and controversy about Whitefield, 103–106
New Birth doctrine
  as central in evangelical theology, 68, 72

Ordo Salutis
  and William Perkins
  and Sinclair Ferguson
  and Frelinghuysen, 93

parable of the Soils, 128–131
Pharisees
  browbeating sinners, xv
  self-righteousness of, 7–9
  opposition to John the Baptist, 8
  legalism of, 10
  opposition to Jesus, 8–13
  reference to by Whitefield, 99
  and self-deception, 119
Pietism, Moravian
  and the necessity of conviction, 69–71
  and Philipp Spener, 69
  and August Francke, 70
  and *Busskampf*, 70
  and *Durchbruch*, 70
  and Frelinghuysen, 92

Preaching for conviction
  of prophets and preachers, 5
  and the *civil man*, 15–18
  on the law, 66
  the Reformers, 67, 68
  and the New Birth, 68
  and German Pietism, 69–71
  and Frelinghuysen, 92–94
  and *busskampf*, 70, 110, 111
  and *bekehrung*, 70
  and *durchbruch*, 70
  tension in Herrnhut, 70, 71
  imprecatory preaching, 74, 75, 82
  in Northampton, 73–85
Preaching motifs
  in Puritanism, 132
  in the open air, 99–102
  on the Creeds, 132–133
  law and gospel, 132
  doom and gloom, 132
  and eisegesis, 133
  and Helmut Thielicke, 133
  and Karl Barth, 134
  finding the *fallen condition* of the text, 138
  and application, 140, 141
  redemptive-historical, 142
  on the Old Testament, 141
  of John the Baptist, 140
  conviction the goal of Jesus, 151, 155
Preaching from the narratives, 141
  on Lot's choice, 142–144
  on Hosea and Gomer, 144–147
  on the Rich Young Man, 148–149
  on the woman at Sychar, 149–152
  on Jesus and the Leper, 152–154
  on Jesus and Zacchaeus, 154–156
Preaching successes
  during the Reformation, 63–67
  during the Evangelical Revivals, 67, 68
Puritanism
  the "civil man", 15–16
  preaching on conviction, 16–19
  on the natural condition of humanity, 16–19
  early zeal in New England, 50
  the Cambridge Platform of 1648, 50

Subject Index

reductionist Christianity, xxi
   and Charles Finney, 87–90

Self-deception
   of the *wise and understanding*, 11
   and Watergate, 117
   and rationalizing, 118
   integral to the experience of sinning, 117
   and Mafiosi, 117
   and the Nazis, 118
   and the Pharisees, 11
self-disclosure of God
   to the Israelites, 3, 4
   to *little children*, 11
self-righteousness, 8–14
   of Nathan Cole, 101
Sin
   consequences of, 2–14, 113–114
   its propensity to hide itself, 16
   conviction of, 120–125
   practical understanding of, 113
   and loneliness, 113, 114
   and psychology, psychiatry, 114
   and permissiveness, 114
   and Code of Hammurabi, 116
   and self-deception, 116, 117, 118
   and natural works orientation, 119
   in relation to God, 120
   and self-awareness, 117–120
   and Romans 7, 122, 123
   its subtle nature, 122
   and understanding temptation, 122
   and rationalization, 121
   original, 157
Sinners, sufferers contra self-righteous, 6–11
Social conditions during the 18th Century, 47–58
Stoddardian solution, 52–55
Substitutionary sacrifice, 2,

Index of Names

a'Kempis, Thomas
    influence of upon Whitefield, 97
Aldersgate Society
    and Wesley's conversion, 108
Allen, A. V. G.
    critic of Edwards, 76
Ames, William
    and Perkins, 65
Andrews, Lancelot, 67
Anselm of Canterbury, 120
Augustine, xxi
    on lack of conviction, 138

Barclay, William
    on leprosy, 153
Barth, Karl
    on preaching, 134
Baxter, Richard, xxi, 17–18,
    on conviction, 18
    on hardness of heart, 18
    read by Spener, 69
Beecher, Lyman
    opposed to Finney, 90
Berkeley, George, 44
Beza, Theodor
    successor of Calvin, 64
    supralapsarianism of, 64
    influence on Frelinghuysen, 92
Blackstone, Sir William, 43
    expert on British common law, 116
Blair, Samuel
    on the awakening in Pennsylvania, 85

Bogue, Carl
    on Perry Miller, 78
Bohler, Peter
    influence on Wesley, 108
Bradford, John, 66
Brattle Street Church, Boston
    and hypocrisy within, 59
    and lack of religious experience, 61
Butler, Bishop, 44

Calvin, John
    and expository preaching, 63, 64
    and the Genevan Academy, 64
    and the Marian exiles, 64
    on Romans 7, 123
Cambridge Platform of 1648, 50
Carlyle, Thomas, 43
Carse, James, i
Carson, D. A.
    on Harry Stout's treatment of Whitefield, 105
    on expository preaching, 136
Chapell, Bryan
    on expository preaching, 138
    on the fallen condition in the text, 138–140
Charles, King II, 19
    and the "Great Ejection", 56
Charnock, Stephen, 67
Cherry, Conrad
    on Perry Miller, 78
Code of Hammurabi, 116

Index of Names

Cole, Nathan
    experience of Whitefield's preaching, 104
Constantine, Roman Emperor
    and the Edict of Milan, 62
Cooper, William of Old South Church
    on the awakening, 85
Cranmer, Thomas, 66

Dallimore, Arnold
    on the state of the C of E, 47
    critique of Harry Stout, 104, 105
    and Arminian writers on Whitefield, 105, 108
Daniel the Prophet, 5
Darrow, Clarence
    criticism of Edwards, 76
David, Christian
    and important corrective for Wesley, 110
David, king of Israel, 4, 120
Davies, Samuel
    Preaching on conviction, 20, 72
Dean, John
    and Watergate deception, 117
de Klagte (Complaint) against Frelinghuysen, 93
Dickinson, Jonathan, 20
Doddridge, Philip
    influenced by Pietism, 71
Donne, John, 67
Dwight, Timothy
    on Edwards's self-awareness, 36
    conviction antecedent to regeneration, 72

Edict of Milan, AD312, xix, 62
Edwards, Jonathan
    and the New England clergy, 33, 34
    biography, 31–35
    on hypocrisy, 20
    on spiritual blindness, 21–23
    on the will, 22, 23
    on the urgency of conviction,
    on the "sense of the heart", 23, 24
    and John Locke, 24, 25
    on a sense of sin, 26–30
    on the Gospel, 27, 28
    on hatred for sin in the believer, 29
    personal piety, 35–39
    on the state of morals in New England, 48, 49
    and his lecture at Boston's First Church, 33
    experiences of God's presence, 36–39
    experience as "sweet" and "vile", 39–42
    on imprecatory preaching, 75
    and "the Great Noise", 56, 79
    and his sermon on God's justice, 74–82
    and the duty of preaching the gospel, 75
    and the effect of his preaching, 80–82
Edwards, Sarah Pierrepont, 33
    opinion of George Whitefield, 99
Elijah, 5
Erskine, Ebenezer, 69

Ferguson, Sinclair
    on Perkins's *ordo salutis*, 65
Fetter Lane Bible Study, Aldersgate
    scene of Wesley receiving assurance, 109
    precursor to Wesley's Methodist societies, 111
Finney, Charles
    rejection of the Reformation, 87
    and Pelagianism, 87
    and revival methods, 88
    denial of imputation doctrine, 88
Fletcher, John
    on the necessity of conviction, 73
Francke, August
    and Philip Spener, 70
    on the necessity of conviction, 70, 71
    influence on Frelinghuysen, 92
Franklin, Benjamin, publisher
    and George Whitefield, 101, 102
Frelinghuysen, Jakob
    and Perkins, Beza, 93
    indebtedness to Francke and Spener, 92
    call to New Jersey, 91
    experiential divinity of, 92

Index of Names

on the purity of the sacrament, 93
and his pulpit manner, 93
attempt to foster conviction, 92–94
and empirical sanctification, 93
his *ordo salutis*, 93
and revival, 94
and his servant (slave), 94
and the Tennents, 95, 96
opinion of George Whitefield, 94
known of by Edwards, 94
Fuller, Thomas
and Perkins's preaching, 65

Gouge, William, 18, 19
Graham, Billy, 137
Gronniosaw, James Albert Ukawsaw
conversion of under Frelinghuysen, 94
Guelzo, Allen
on Harry Stout's treatment of Whitefield, 105

Half-Way Covenant, 50–52
and baptism, 51
Harris, Howell
itinerant preaching, 45
originator of open-air preaching, 100
Heidelberg Catechism, 132, 133
Helm, Paul
on the work of the Holy Spirit, 65
on Perry Miller, 78
Herrnhut in Bavaria
and the Moravians, 70, 109
and von Zinzendorf, 70, 71
and John Wesley, 109–111
Hervey, James
on penitence, 20
Hoekema, Anthony
on sin's deceptive quality, 117
Hogarth, William, 47
Hollifield, E. Brooks, 53
Holmes, Oliver Wendell on Edwards, 76
Holy Club
legalism of, 96
and the Wesley's and Whitefield, 96
Horton, Michael
on Finney, 90
Howe, John
and conviction, 17, 67

Hughes, R. Kent
description of leprosy, 154
Hutchinson, Timothy
and "Old Groan", 58

Jackson, Thomas
on the state of the C of E, 46
Jesus
ministry to sinners and sufferers, 7–10
aversion to the self-righteous, 7–12
kingdom of, 10–13
and judgment, 13
Johnson, Samuel, 56

Knox, John
and the Genevan Academy, 64
Knight, Rev. Titus, 45

Latimer, Hugh, 66
Laud, Archbishop William, 56
Lecky, William
on drunkenness in Britain, 47
Lewis, C. S.
on the psychology of sin, 113, 116–117
on the necessity of conviction, xx, 126
on the lack of conviction, 128, 138
on hypocrisy, 129
on descriptive preaching, 139
Lloyd-Jones, Martyn
on Romans 7, 123
on conviction, 152
Locke, John
Essay on Human Understanding, 24
on experience, 24
on the senses, 24
influence on Edwards, 25
and Perry Miller, 24
Log College, 95
Logan, Samuel
on steps in Edwards's *ordo salutis*, 82
Luther, Martin, 63, 123

Macaulay, Thomas Babington
on the state of the C of E, 100
on Whitefield's preaching skill, 104
Ma'Culloch, Rev., 45

Index of Names

Mary the First
    and the English martyrs, 64, 66
Mather, Increase
    on the state of the church in New England, 49
Mather, Cotton
    and Arminianism, 56
    influenced by Moravian Pietism, 71
Mayhew, Experience
    and Arminianism, 56
McCheyne, Robert Murray
    on conviction, 86
Melancthon, Philip
    and Luther, 63
Mendon, congregation of, 57, 58
Miller, Perry
    on Stoddardeanism, 54
    originator of modern Edwardsian studies, 77
    on Edward's empiricism, 77–79
    on sense of the heart, 24
Montague, Lady Mary Wortley, 47
Morgan, Edmund
    on the Puritans' "civil man", 15
Murray, Iain
    and Charles Finney, 88
    on Harry Stout's work, 105
    opinion of Wesley and Whitefield, 107
    critique of expository preaching, 134

Neiman, Susan
    on self-deception, 118
Nettleton, Asahel
    opposition to Finney, 89
Newton, John
    testimony regarding Wesley's influence, 107
Northampton, town of
    and the 1734 awakening, 77–80

Oglethorpe, John
    on social conditions in Britain, 47
Oliver, Robert W. xxiii
Overton, Charles, 43
Outler, Albert
    on Wesley's conversion, 108

Owen, John, 67

Packer, J. I.
    on Puritanism19
    on Charles Finney, 87, 88
    on Romans 7, 123
Parkes, H. P.
    on New England in the 1730s, 57–59
Parrington, Vernon L.
    critic of Edwards, 77
Pascal, Blaise on sin, 116
Paul the Apostle
    on the Damascus Road, 10
    chief of sinners, 122
    condemns self-righteousness, 122
    and self-deception, 122
    on trusting in wealth, 143
Pemberton, Ebenezer
    and George Whitefield, 72, 73
Perkins, William
    and Beza, 64
    on hardness of heart19
    on a Christian's doubting, 19
    and academics, 64
    on conviction, 65
Pharisees or Doctors of the Law, scribes, 7, 8, 9, 10
Piper, John
    on Harry Stout's treatment of Whitefield, 105
Preston, John, 65
Prince, Thomas of Boston
    and George Whitefield, 100, 101

Ramm, Bernard
    on the effects of sin, 114, 122
Raritan Valley region of New Jersey
    scene of Frelinghuysen's ministry, 92
Reformation, the
    preaching during, 62–67
Ridley, Nicholas, 66, 67
Ryle, J. C., 86
    on the free offer of the Gospel, 11
    in defense of Wesley, 107
    and the Evangelical Revival, 127
    on the need for convicting preaching, 151

Index of Names

Savoy Declaration, 86
Scougal, Henry of Scotland
    influence of on the Wesley's and Whitefield, 96, 97
Shepard, Thomas, 17
Sibbes, Richard, 16, 17, 65
Simeon, Charles, 86
Simonson, Harold
    On Edwards's concerns, 41
Smith, H. Shelton
    on the history of preaching, 157
Society for Promoting Christian Knowledge, 48
Society for the Reformation of Manners, 48
Spener, Philipp Jakob
    originator of Pietism, 69
    and Luther, 69
    and Martin Bucer, 69
Sprague, William
    opposed to Finney, 90
Spring, Gardiner
    opposed to Finney, 90
Spurgeon, Charles H., 86
    opinion of Wesley and Whitefield, 107
    on Romans 7, 123
Stephen, Leslie on Edwards, 76
Stoddard, Solomon, 33
    on the Lord's Supper, 52–53
    lengthy ministry at Northampton, 79
    and Arminian preaching, 53
Stout, Harry, xxii
    and his opinion of Whitefield, 103, 104
    perspective in historical writing, 104, 105
    opinion of Tyerman and Dallimore, 103, 104
    criticism of by evangelicals, 104, 105

Taylor, Jeremy
    influence on Wesley, 108
Teellinck, William
    influence of Puritanism on, 65
Tennent, Gilbert
    and Frelinghuysen, 95

Tennent, John
    and the Log College, 95
    on conviction, 95
Tennent, Gilbert, 95
Thielicke, Helmut
    on preaching methods, 127
Thompson, J. P.
    critic of Edwards, 76
Thompson, J. P.
    criticism of Edwards, 76
Toplady, Augustus, 45
Tracy, Joseph, 55
Trench, R. C.
    on miracles as parables, 152
Trumbull, Benjamin
    on preaching after Stoddardeanism, 53–55
    on Arminianism, 57
    on the Awakening in Connecticut, 85
    results of the Awakening, 157
Tyerman, Luke
    state of C of E, 46
Tyndale, William, 65, 66

Voetsius, Gisbertus
    influence of Puritanism, 65

Warfield, B. B.
    and Charles Finney, 89
Watts, Isaac
    Influenced by Pietism, 71
Welsh Calvinist Methodists, 98
Wells, David
    and Charles Finney, 89
Wesley, Charles
    preaching on conviction, 111
    relation with Whitefield, 97
Wesley, John
    and the Moravian Pietists, 73
    and Herrnhut, 109
    preaching, 110
    relations with Whitefield, 96, 98, 106
    legacy of bible study societies, 111
    and conviction, 109–111
Westminster Creeds, 86

Index of Names

White, John
    on the encroachment of Arminianism, 57

Whitefield, George,
    Harry Stout's treatment of, xxii
    opposition to Arminianism and Deism, 45, 46
    and Frelinghuysen, 94
    and Gilbert Tennent, 95
    and the *Holy Club* at Oxford, 96
    early "legal" attempts to appease God, 96
    conversion of, 97
    originator of the Methodist movement, 98
    and open-air preaching, 98–100
    homiletic skills, 101, 102, 104
    stress on conviction, 100
    early training in theatrical technique, 104
    and the Wesley's, 97–99

Willard, Samuel
    on the state of Boston's churches, 49

Zinzendorf, Count von Nicolaus
    critique of Francke's emphasis, 70, 71

Zwingli, Ulrich
    and expository preaching, 63, 64

Scripture Index

Genesis
3:15	2
4	2
12:2–3	4
13:12	142

Exodus
3:6	3
3:14	3
4:10, 11	140
32–33	3

Leviticus
13–14	153
26:28	6

Deuteronomy
1–30	130

2 Samuel
9:12–13	5

Psalms
19:1–2	4
32	5
38:13–18	5
38:21–22	5
51	5
51:4	120
81:11	3
95:8–11	3
103:1–2	146
103:2, 3	154

Proverbs
1:24–30	3
19:1–2	4
29:1	3

Ecclesiastes
1:1, 12	140
1:17	159

Isaiah
1:4–6	6
6:5	41
40:25	3
42:20	3
53:5	154
55:7	125

Jeremiah
6:11	113
17:9	116

Lamentations

1:18–20	6
6:11	113

Ezekiel

2:4–5	6
11:19	18
16 4	143
36:21	18
36:26	3

Daniel

9:5–6	5

Hosea

1–2: 15	144–147
1:2	144
1:3–4	145
1:9	145
1:10–11	145
2:4	145
2:11	146
2:9–13	146
2:16–23	147
2:14	6, 128, 147
2:14	4–13
14	145

Habakkuk

3:2	xxiii

Matthew

3:2	140
3:7	8
4:17	140
5:3–4	148
6:19	144
11:19	156
11:23	6
11:25–30	11
13:1–23	128
13	13
13:20,21	130
13:22	130
13:24–30	13
13:47–52	13
14:36	128
19:16–22	148
23	119
23:27	13
25:1–13	13
25:14–30	13
25:31–46	13

Mark

1:4	140
1:5	7
1:40–45	152
1:41	153
2:17	154, 156
3:2	140
3:5	7
4	13
4:20	131
5	7
10:21	149
10:31	12

Luke

1:47	12
3:3	140
3:12	8
4:12	10
4:18–19	12
5:12	153
5:17–26	8
5:24	8
6:7	9
6:11	8
7:29	9
7:34	156
7:36–50	9
8	13
8:15	131
10:21	12
10:21–24	11
10:22	11
10:42	142
11:31	139

13:30	12	2:4	119
15	114	3:19	42, 80, 113
15:11–32	9	5:12–21	3
15:17	9, 128	7	123
15:21	120	10:4	119
16:19–31	4		
17:32	143	**1 Corinthians**	
18:9	119	1:26–29	11
18:9–14	10	2:14	114
18:13	128	10:6, 11	142
19:8	155	15:21, 22	2
19:1–10	154		
19:10	150, 155, 156	**Galatians**	
24:26	141	3:24	132
24:27	141		
24:44	141	**Ephesians**	
		2:3	113
John		6:17	135
1:11	128, 129		
3:23	149	**Philippians**	
3:26	149	3:2–6	122
4	149	3:5–6	10
4:4	150		
4:8–9	150	**1 Timothy**	
4:9–25	150		1:13, 15
4:16	151	1:15	10, 42
4:17–18	151	6:9, 17	143
4:19	151		
4:29	151	**2 Timothy**	
5:39	141	3:16,17	135
6:35	144	4:1,2	135
7:48	11		
15:5	119	**Hebrews**	
16: 8	xi	4:12	135
Acts		**James**	
2:37	140	2:8–11	121
7	140		
9:5	10	**1 Peter**	
17:1–4	140	3:18	127
17:6	64		
Romans			
2:1–24	119		

Scripture Index

2 Peter
2:5   140
2:7   142
2:8–11   142

Revelation
1:16   10
2:12   10
3:17   87, 127
3:20   124

www.ingramcontent.com/pod-product-compliance
Lightning Source LLC
Chambersburg PA
CBHW070742160426
43192CB00009B/1536